GREAT CAMPAIGNS

# THE WILDERNESS CAMPAIGN

*Lieutenant General Ulysses S. Grant. On 4
May 1864, Grant and the Army of the Potomac advanced into the Wilderness. The battle
fought over the next few days was the first of
many bloody encounters of Grant's campaign
against Lee's army for Richmond.*

# GREAT CAMPAIGNS SERIES

*The Atlanta Campaign*
*The Chancellorsville Campaign*
*The Gettysburg Campaign*
*The Little Bighorn Campaign*
*The Philadelphia Campaign*
*The Peninsula Campaign*
*The Wilderness Campaign*

GREAT CAMPAIGNS

# THE WILDERNESS CAMPAIGN

## *May 1864*

### John Cannan

COMBINED
BOOKS

# PUBLISHER'S NOTE

Combined Books, Inc., is dedicated to publishing books of distinction in history and military history. We are proud of the quality of writing and the quantity of information found in our books. Our books are manufactured with style and durability and are printed on acid-free paper. We like to think of our books as soldiers: not infantry grunts, but well dressed and well equipped avant garde. Our logo reflects our commitment to the modern and yet historic art of bookmaking.

We call ourselves Combined Books because we view the publishing enterprise as a "combined" effort of authors, publishers and readers. And we promise to bridge the gap between us–a gap which is all too seldom closed in contemporary publishing.

We would like to hear from our readers and invite you to write to us at our offices in Pennsylvania with your reactions, queries, comments, even complaints. All of your correspondence will be answered directly by a member of the Editorial Board or by the author.

We encourage all of our readers to purchase our books from their local booksellers, and we hope that you let us know of booksellers in your area that might be interested in carrying our books. If you are unable to find a book in your area, please write to us.

For information, address:
COMBINED BOOKS, INC.
151 East 10th Avenue
Conshohocken, PA 19428

*Library of Congress Cataloging-in-Publication Data*
Cannan, John
The wilderness campaign : May 1864 / John Cannan. — 1st ed.
p. cm. — (Great Campaigns)
    Includes bibliographical references and index.
    ISBN 0-938289-16-0 : $19.95
    1. Wilderness, Battle of the, Va., 1864                    I. Title.  II. Series.
[E476.52.C36  1993]
973.7'36—dc20                                                  92-41515

First Edition  1 2 3 4 5
Printed in Hong Kong.
Maps by Robert L. Pigeon III

*To Robert L. Pigeon,*
*the man with the plan*

# Acknowledgements

Many thanks to the people of the Library of Congress, Philadelphia Free Library and Civil War Library and Museum for their help and informative sources. Special thanks go to David Chen and Art Yao for their generosity and kind use of their facilities during my period of research in Washington D.C. Susan Miller was of great help in finding a rare book invaluable to my research. Also the most esteemed appreciation must be extended to the people of Combined Books: Toni Bauer, Lizbeth Nauta, Amy Gillet and the vivacious Elaine Clarke Saad. Thanks as well to Steve Rothsching, Sam Zimmerman and my many family members (including Travis, Leo and Shane Moore) without whose support and fine conversation this project would not have been possible. Above all, I would like to thank Leigh Schofield, who probably suffered through the writing of this book as much as the author.

# Stylistic Note

To simplify matters several ahistorical conventions have been adopted in this work:

1. The identities of Union units are in *italics*.

2. Union Army corps have been designated with Roman numerals.

3. Times have been rendered on a 24-hour basis.

4. Confederate corps have been spelled out or have their commanders names (First Corps and Longstreet's Corps). Divisions and brigades also have their commanders' names (Early's Division, Gordon's Brigade).

# Contents

## Maps

# Sidebars

# Preface to the Series

*J*onathan Swift termed war "that mad game the world so loves to play." He had a point. Universally condemned, it has nevertheless been almost as universally practiced. For good or ill, war has played a significant role in the shaping of history. Indeed, there is hardly a human institution which has not in some fashion been influenced and molded by war, even as it helped shaped and mold war in turn. Yet the study of war has been as remarkably neglected as its practice commonplace. With a few outstanding exceptions, the history of wars and of military operations has until quite recently been largely the province of the inspired patriot or the regimental polemicist. Only in our times have serious, detailed and objective accounts come to be considered the norm in the treatment of military history and related matters.

Yet there still remains a gap in the literature, for there are two types of military history. One type is written from a very serious, highly technical, professional perspective and presupposes that the reader is deeply familiar with the background, technology and general situation. The other is perhaps less dry, but merely lightly reviews the events with the intention of informing and entertaining the layman. The qualitative gap between the last two is vast. Moreover, there are professionals in both the military and academia whose credentials are limited to particular moments in the long, sad history of war, and there are laymen who have more than a passing understanding of the field; and then there is the concerned citizen, interested in understanding the phenomena in an age of unusual violence and unprecedented armaments. It is to bridge the gap between the two types of military history, and to reach the professional and the serious amateur and the concerned citizen alike, that this series, GREAT CAMPAIGNS, is designed. Each volume in GREAT CAMPAIGNS is thus not merely an account of a particular military operation, but it is a unique reference to the theory and practice of war in the period in question.

The GREAT CAMPAIGNS series is a distinctive contribution to the study of war and of military history, which will remain of value for many years to come.

# Introduction

In July of 1861, Irvin McDowell led the first major offensive in the East against a Rebel army at Bull Run. He was defeated in a humiliating rout which cost the Union almost 3,000 casualties. The following spring and summer, Union hopes rested on the abilities of the handsome, dashing and sometimes arrogant Major General George Brinton McClellan, also known as the "Young Napoleon." McClellan failed to live up to the sobriquet. His timidity and extreme caution allowed victory to elude his grasp during his famed Peninsula campaign against the Confederate capital at Richmond. During the operation, McClellan's fighting force, the *Army of the Potomac*, lost over 2,000 men at Williamsburg, 5,000 men at Seven Pines and 16,000 men in the defeats of the Seven Days Battles. John Pope took command of an army in the East only to come close to losing it at the Second Battle of Bull Run where his force suffered 16,000 casualties on 29-30 August 1862. McClellan took to the field at the helm of the *Army of the Potomac* once again to fight his nemesis Robert E. Lee at Antietam on 17 September 1862. The confrontation was the bloodiest day of the war where some 12,500 men were casualties. More bloody fights awaited the *Army of the Potomac* under different commanders: Ambrose Burnside's destructive defeat at Fredericksburg on 13 December 1862, 12,600 casualties; Hooker's disaster at Chancellorsville on 1-4 May 1863, with 17,100 casualties; and Meade's bloody victory at Gettysburg on 1-3 July, 23,000 casualties. Despite this enormous cost in lives, untold suffering and misery, the position from which the *Army of the Potomac* faced off against the Army of Northern Virginia in the winter and spring of the third year of the war was not markedly different from the one occupied the year before (or even the beginning of the war). The Union was still many miles from Richmond and months away, possibly years away, from victory.

The situation in the West was much different. The lines were much more fluid and offensives were met by counteroffensives deep into enemy territory. But there, the situation was solidly in Union hands. Talented and seasoned commanders had risen through the ranks to win spectacular victories. Such men included the highest figures in the pantheon of great generals this nation has produced: Ulysses S. Grant, William T. Sherman and Philip Sheridan. The Civil War would be irrevocably changed when the most successful of the Western generals, Grant, went to Washington in early 1864 to take command of the Federal war effort.

In May of 1864, Grant began an offensive to push the *Army of the Potomac* towards Richmond. Lee and the Army of Northern Virginia contested every step of the way. The catalog of bloody names, where the soldiers of both armies clashed, rings with awesome horror: Spotsylvania where men fought in close quarters for nearly 24 hours; Cold Harbor, the battle in which thousands of Union soldiers were cut down in less than a half an hour; the Petersburg Crater where bungling leadership lost the lives of so many men without any purpose. But perhaps worst of all was the Wilderness, a confused battle fought in a thick, forbidding woodland. There the air was putrid with the smell of bodies consumed by burning leaves set off by musketry; wounded men who could not escape the fire kept loaded muskets on hand to kill themselves rather than suffer the awful fate of being burned alive. Charge and countercharge were confused in the woodlands where officers and troops could not see the rest of their lines and flanks. The battle also had the notoriety of taking place on almost the same ground as another fight a year before, Chancellorsville and contained many disturbing similarities to the earlier confrontation. The Wilderness held the outcome of the war in the balance. So many tricks of fate might have led to total victory for one side or the other, but only resulted in a myriad of "what ifs" for historians to ponder.

Perhaps the greatest significance of the battle of the Wilderness is the irony of its result. There Lee and his lieutenants demonstrated their dazzling expertise and resiliency, managing to stymie their adversary and inflict heavy casualties. But the gains won on the field were lost since it was obvious that the fighting would go on, draining the already depleted Southern ranks. For the Union it was at worst as costly a defeat as those suffered by McClellan, Burnside and Hooker, and at best a stalemate. But when Grant refused to follow the precedent set by so many before him and advanced when others would retreat, it became an important step in a long bloody road to ultimate victory. The fuel for the drive would be thousands of lives as one Civil War soldier who witnessed the campaigns later noted: "The gist of the matter is that the war could only be ended by the hardest kind of fighting, that war means blood and death and desolation, and that when the big captain took the helm he sailed over seas of blood to victory and peace."

# CHAPTER I

# The Worst Time of Year to Take a Journey

*T*he passage of 1863 into a new year of the Civil War saw the Army of Northern Virginia weathering the winter months entrenched in positions behind the Rapidan River. Most of the soldiers who lived through that inactive period were almost unanimous in their portrayals of stoic suffering from the cold and lack of supplies, especially food. Over time the supply of provisions had become increasingly deficient, so much so, that the entire army was almost on the verge of starvation. As one Confederate wrote, "The one thing we suffered most from, the hardship hardest to bear, was hunger. The scantiness of the rations was something fierce. We never got a square meal that winter." To compound the desperate food situation was the lack of clothing available to troops; items such as new shoes and overcoats were luxuries. One Confederate's trousers were "worn to a frazzle" and, since he could not secure new ones, ignominiously endured the winter by wearing a pair of cotton drawers. By January the lack of supplies had become so serious that the commander of the Army of Northern Virginia, Robert E. Lee, told authorities at the Confederate capital at Richmond that, "I fear the army cannot be kept effective and probably cannot be kept together." Still, the troops of the Confederate army were not new to such misery and bore their lot well while waiting to take to the field when spring allowed active campaigning to begin again. Snowfalls broke the monotony of camp routine and gave the "Butternuts" the chance to forget their privations by engaging in a grand snowball fight. Such affairs were often large contests between regiments, and sometimes even brigades, complete with lines of battle with flags unfurled.

During this period of inactivity, Lee himself had reason to fear for his position at the head of his beloved army, not for lack of skill, certainly, but because his abilities were needed elsewhere. Through part of the winter of 1863-1864, the commander of the Army of Northern Virginia found himself preoccupied with the annoying task of flanking an attempt to transfer him to the command of the Army of Tennessee. Out West, in the heartland of the Confederacy, the South had suffered serious military setbacks. The primary force protecting the region from the Mississippi to the Appalachians, the Army of Tennessee, under the luckless General Braxton Bragg, had been severely defeated by troops under Ulysses S. Grant at Chattanooga on 23-25 November 1863. Bragg's force was ignominiously routed clear out of its namesake state into northwestern Georgia where it spent an uncomfortable winter in misery at Dalton. After the battles at Chattanooga, the Federals were left in a fine position to advance from the city into the heartland of Georgia whenever it suited them. Furthermore, the loss also left the command of the Army of Tennessee vacant, for condemnation of Bragg from his subordinates, political leaders and the public forced his resignation from command. Bragg's successor would have to be a man of substantial skill in order to deal with the daunting task of retrieving the disastrous situation that would confront him in the West, and the brilliant Lee seemed the best candidate to turn defeat into victory. When Jefferson Davis, the president of the Confederacy, asked Lee if he was willing to take command of the Army of Tennessee, the general politely expressed no enthusiasm for any transfer. Lee was then ordered to Richmond on 9 December. The general fully expected to be sent to Dalton over his wishes and expressed his anxiety to his cavalry commander Jeb Stuart, saying "My heart will always be with this army." The conference with the president and others lasted a week with the result that Lee remained in command of the Army of Northern Virginia while the then inactive General Joseph E. Johnston took the reins of the Army of Tennessee.

Thus once more Lee would defend his native Virginia when the Yankees decided to move south of the Rapidan. Indications from the *Army of the Potomac* encamped north of the river seemed to point to a renewed offensive as soon as the weather became more hospitable and the roads dried from winter and early spring rains. There was news that a general from the West, Major General Ulysses S. Grant, had been appointed to command the entire Union army. Since Grant elected to remain in the East to direct the movements of all the Federal forces, it seemed likely to General Lee that the Army of Northern Virginia would be subjected to another Yankee offensive before too long. The Confederate general communicated these beliefs in a letter to his niece Margaret Stuart on 29 March: "The indications at present are that we shall have a hard struggle. General Grant is with the Army of the Potomac. All officer's wives, sick etc., have been sent to Washington. No ingress into or egress from the lines is now permitted and no papers are allowed to come out—they claim to be assembling a large force...."

On 10 March, Lee was back in Richmond, but this time his intention was to recall the units transferred from the Army of Northern Virginia. In the months following the battle of Gettysburg, the strength of the Army of Northern Virginia had been siphoned away to other areas. The most important command lost was First Corps under James Longstreet, most of which had been detached to serve out West with the Army of Tennessee (Longstreet's remaining division under Major General George Edward Pickett, which had been mangled during its infamous charge at Gettysburg, was detached for duty in southeast Virginia). The move had proven somewhat successful for two divisions of Longstreet's Corps had been instrumental in winning the Confederate victory at Chickamauga, Georgia on 20 September 1863. Chickamauga was to be the only real success Longstreet's men would enjoy out west. The fall and winter of the year were the scene for a

*A picket on duty during the frigid winter of 1863-1864.*

frustrating siege of Union troops at Chattanooga and then a failed campaign in Eastern Tennessee where the embittered Longstreet then spent the winter.

Throughout much of the winter and early spring, Jefferson Davis and his newly appointed military advisor, Braxton Bragg, entertained hopes that Longstreet's command could be used in conjunction with Johnston's Army of Tennessee for an offensive into the Volunteer State. Attempts to organize this bold move came to naught due to bickering between General Johnston and Davis and Bragg over the form of the planned advance. With the failure to organize an offensive in Tennessee, Longstreet received orders to return to Virginia on 11 April.

*"The Gray Fox," Robert E. Lee. After Gettysburg, Lee spent most of his energy fending off the constant advances and attacks of his Federal enemy.*

Three days later, Longstreet's command had been moved via rail to Charlottesville, Virginia, where it would be marched to Gordonsville, southwest of Lee's camp. On 29 April, Lee visited the First Corps for what was an emotional reunion. The troops prepared as best they could for the meeting with their beloved army commander as soldier Augustus Dickert related, "Everything possible that could add to our looks and appearances was done to make an acceptable display before our commander in chief. Guns were burnished and rubbed up, cartridge boxes and belts polished, and brass buttons and buckles made up to look as bright as new. Our clothes were patched up and brushed up, so far as was in our power, boots and shoes greased, the tattered and torn old hats were given here and there a 'lick of promise,' and on the whole I must say we presented not a bad-looking body of soldiers."

# Robert E. Lee

No other leader has been better loved in the South or more identified with the Confederacy than Robert E. Lee (1807-1870). His amazing record of victories made him legendary and ranked the "Gray Fox" as one of the greatest military minds in American history.

Lee came from a distinguished heritage: scion of an aristocratic Virginia family, son of a Revolutionary War hero, Richard Henry "Light Horse Harry" Lee, and related to two signers of the Declaration of Independence. His illustrious father, however, suffered the ignominious fate of financial disaster such that he was forced to flee the country to escape creditors.

Lee graduated from West Point in 1829 ranked second in his class with nearly impeccable grades. He served in a variety of military posts before entering in the Mexican War. There he displayed valor as well as ability in Winfield Scott's march from Vera Cruz to Mexico City and won three brevets. His postwar service included the position of superintendent of West Point, commander of the *2nd U.S. Cavalry* and leadership of a force sent to put down John Brown's revolt at Harper's Ferry.

Lee's tremendous ability was recognized in both the North and South when the Civil War broke out. Though Lee was offered command of Federal armies shortly after Fort Sumter, he maintained an allegiance to his native Virginia, not to the United States. The South extended high rank as well, command of Virginia's state troops. He was then named a brigadier general in Confederate service in May and was later given third highest ranking generalcy in the Southern army, just behind Samuel Cooper and Albert S. Johnston.

Despite his talent, Lee suffered an inauspicious career early on in the war. He was sent to rescue the collapsing Confederate forces in what is now West Virginia, but the situation there was hopeless even for him. Fortifications along the Carolina and Georgia coasts then occupied Lee until March of 1862 when he was called to Richmond to serve as an advisor to Jefferson Davis during McClellan's slow assault up the Virginia Peninsula. The entire fortune of Lee's career and

When Lee rode forth to inspect his troops, artillery stationed nearby opened up with a 13-gun salute. The soldiers almost lost control at the sight of their august general in gray. Dickert described the scene, "Hats and caps flew high in the air, flags dipped and waved to and fro, while the drums and fifes struck up 'Hail to the Chief.' General Lee lifted his hat modestly from his head in recognition of the honor done him,

the war changed when the commander of the Army of Northern Virginia, General Joseph E. Johnston, was wounded at the battle of Seven Pines outside Richmond on 31 May. The next day Lee received command of the army he would be associated with during the rest of the war. Late in June, the Gray Fox inaugurated a smashing offensive that came to be known as the Seven Days Battles during which McClellan was swiftly driven back from Richmond by a series of defeats.

Lee then engaged in a long offensive throughout August and September which included his first invasion north of the Potomac. However, the inconclusive battle of Antietam on 17 September forced him to fall back to Virginia in defeat. Lee then parried two Northern offensives, one at Fredericksburg (13 December 1862) and the other at Chancellorsville (1-4 May 1863), the latter Lee's most spectacular victory. He then crossed the Potomac again only to be severely defeated in the three day battle near Gettysburg on 1-3 July 1863. Once again, he fell back to Virginia to await the next Northern move.

Lee's next opponent was Ulysses S. Grant who forced the Army of Northern Virginia back to Richmond. The aggressive Grant engaged Lee throughout 1864 at the Wilderness, Spotsylvania, Cold Harbor and Petersburg. Despite winning victories in all these battles, Lee was constantly on the defensive due to his enemy's continuous pressure. On 2 April 1865, Lee was forced to abandon Richmond for a long march to Appomattox which ended in surrender seven days later.

Lee spent the remaining years of his life as president of Washington College. The grand general refrained from much social activity and cared for his ailing wife. He was supposedly offered the position of Grand Wizard of the Ku Klux Klan, but refused to accept it.

Without Robert E. Lee's ability, the war certainly would not have gone on for as long as it did. He did the best with the forces he had and instilled such a fear into his opponents that it resembled terror. Despite his mistakes, Lee's superlative tactical skill was unquestionable, though he can be faulted for not giving as much attention to strategic aspects of the war as he should have.

---

and we knew the old commander's heart swelled with emotion at this outburst of enthusiasm by his old troops on his appearance." Some men rushed forward to touch the general's horse or the bridle or stirrup as if he were a king or saint. When one participant remarked how proud Lee must have felt to bask in such adulation another replied, "Not

*President of the Confederacy, Jefferson Davis.*

proud, It awes him." Lee evidently lost his iron composure for a few moments as tears could be seen streaking down his face.

With the men of Longstreet's command at Gordonsville, Lee could now field three corps against the future assault by Grant. The Second Corps under Lieutenant General Richard S. Ewell was quartered to the northeast of Lee's headquarters at Orange Court House in the vicinity of Adairsville. Ambrose Powell Hill's command, the Third Corps, was stationed with Lee. The formidable Confederate cavalry under Major General James Ewell Brown Stuart was wintering near Fredericksburg. All told the Army of Northern Virginia had between 61,000 and 63,000 troops for the coming campaign. Other forces nearby included 11,500 men in the Shenandoah Valley under Major General John C. Breckinridge, 6,000 troops guarding Richmond and the 10,000 men of Pickett's Division in Southern Virginia and North Carolina. Around 15,000 men under the creole General Pierre Gustave Toutant Beauregard protected the Georgia and Carolina coasts.

From his simple headquarters at Orange Court House, Lee pondered how to best meet the threat of Grant's future aggression. His inclination was to throw the Federals off balance by taking the offensive, but poor weather, lack of supplies and Federal numbers all connived to deny Lee's hopes to take the initiative into his own hands. Thus he was forced to be content with merely holding the Rapidan line until the Federals made their move and waiting for any openings he could find. Lee could be comfortable with waiting; he had successfully defeated other "On to Richmond" campaigns before, leaving a list of Northern commanders, McClellan, Pope, Burnside and Hooker, with their reputations severely tarnished. Once the enemy did move, it would be imperative that they be defeated before they reached the James River and the vicinity of Richmond. Lee was painfully aware of this fact, stating, "If he gets there it will become a siege, and then it will be a mere question of time."

There was no reason to doubt that Lee could not win a similar victory against Grant's hordes when campaigning resumed in the spring of 1864. Lee could always count on the Army of Northern Virginia, a force of disciplined and hard fighting veterans steeled against the harm of privation, to wage battle effectively against Yankee armies when they crossed the Rapidan. However, the abilities of his primary lieutenants were in question. All three of his corps commanders were infected by different illnesses which, if inflamed, could cause serious difficulties during the coming campaign. Longstreet's infirmity was a mental one, he had become terribly embittered by his inability to attain a major victory during his tenure of independent command out West. This seething indignation lashed out at two of his senior generals: division commander Major General Lafayette McLaws and Brigadier General Evander Law. McLaws was an able leader, but Longstreet unfairly used him as a scapegoat for the defeat suffered at Fort Saunders during the campaign in East Tennessee and had the unfortunate general relieved from command. During the Wilderness campaign, the helm of McLaws' Division would be under South Carolinian Joseph B. Kershaw, a crack brigade leader who had seen action from the very first day of the war at Fort Sumter. The tangled dispute between Longstreet and Law became so serious that Longstreet threatened to resign if the brigadier was not court-martialed. Law's Brigade was left behind in East Tennessee until the situation was sorted out while the rest of the First Corps returned to Virginia. Fortunately, Lee was able to influence the Confederate War Department to send the badly needed troops of Law's Brigade to rejoin the rest of the corps in Virginia so that they too could participate in the upcoming campaign.

The commander of the Second Corps, Richard Ewell, suffered from the pain of a wound incurred at the battle of Groveton on 28 August 1862 which had resulted in the amputation of a leg and now sported a wooden replacement. The pain of this injury was compounded by the continuing affects of an illness acquired during the Mine Run campaign of late winter of 1863.

Lee's remaining commander, Hill, suffered from prostatitis resulting from venereal disease he had contracted 20 years previous. Almost constant pain left the general fatigued and depressed. In March, Hill's continuing illness forced him to turn over his command to a subordinate for a short period of time. As spring progressed towards summer, and the contest between Lee and Grant sharpened, Hill's condition only got worse.

(By mid-May, all three corps commanders would be lost to Lee. Longstreet fell grievously wounded from shots fired by his own men on the second day of the Wilderness on 6 May; Hill's illness took its toll on him and forced the general to relinquish his command just before Spotsylvania; and during the fighting at Spotsylvania on 12 May Ewell was injured by a fall from his horse and would no longer command troops on the field of battle.)

Compounded with the uncertainty over his commanders, was Lee's concern about reinforcements. The Confederacy was busily exerting itself to supply its armies with manpower through a series of desperate measures to meet the plentiful ranks of the North: all troops with enlistments up in 1864

# Religion in the Confederate Army

Religion has always played a role in the history of the United States, from the Pilgrim landing to the tele-evangelists of our own day. Religious revivals show on the record of the Republic as well. During the War Between the States religious feeling was extremely strong in the Confederate camps. Its intensity led to several revivals spurring conversions, baptisms and affirmations of faith.

Before the war, many churches had already split into Northern and Southern factions over such issues as slavery. The predominant religious sects, Presbyterian, Methodist, Baptist, Lutheran, Episcopal and Roman Catholic, all remained active in the states that split away from the Union, all preaching a theology that supported Southern attitudes. When the war came, it was viewed by both sides as a religious struggle. Indeed, Lincoln put it best in his second inaugural address when he said, "Both [sides] read the same Bible, and pray to the same God; and each invokes his aid against the other....The prayers of neither have been answered fully. The almighty has his purposes."

In the Southern ranks, religion literally went to war as preachers donned uniforms to fight in the ranks and exhort the troops. Some were in high ranks: Episcopalian Archbishop Leonidas Polk was a lieutenant general in the Army of Tennessee, Thomas J. "Stonewall" Jackson's aide de camp was a Pres-byterian minister and William N. Pendleton was an Episcopalian preacher who served as a brigadier general and Lee's chief of artillery (early in the war he was a captain of the Rockbridge Artillery during which he named four of his cannons Matthew, Mark, Luke and John).

As the war dragged on after the first major confrontation at First Bull Run on 21 July 1861, men in the Confederate ranks of the Army of Northern Virginia began to turn to vice, swearing, drinking and gambling. After Lee took over command of the force on 31 May 1862, he encouraged religious activities such as prayer and called chaplains to enter military service. Other commanders such as Brigadier General John B. Gordon also championed religion by advising men to turn towards Christ. Perhaps the deepest influence was the devoutly religious Stonewall Jackson who also asked chaplains to come into the army. A devout Presbyterian, Jackson so adhered to his faith that he attempted to avoid going to battle on Sundays if he could help it. He constantly praised God for his victories rather than taking personal credit. A day after his success at First Bull Run where he won his famous sobriquet, he wrote his wife, "Yesterday we fought a great battle and gained a great victory, for which all the glory is due to God alone....My preservation was due, as was the glorious victory, to our

God, to whom be all the honor, praise and glory....Whilst great credit is due to other parts of our gallant army, God made my brigade more instrumental than any other in repulsing the main attack."

The deeply religious nature of Southern life, people and frequent calls to turn to Christ led to entourages of religious figures to coming to camps and proselytization through religious literature. Clergy in the ranks swelled to such an extent that two corps of the Army of Northern Virginia could boast 36 Methodists, 20 Baptists, 6 Episcopalians, 3 Catholics and 1 Lutheran serving as pastors to the soldiers. The Confederacy's some 2,000 Jewish troops were served by at least 2 volunteer Rabbis. Visiting preachers also conducted services and led religious meetings.

The distribution of religious tracts was a common activity of the religious movement. Over the war years thousands of Christian tracts were passed out to the ranks. In 1863, a religious association reported the distribution of more than 7,000,000 pages of tracts, 45,000 hymn books, 15,000 Bible readers and 15,000 copies of the Bible, testaments and Gospels. The American Bible Society, a Northern institution, also distributed 800,000 Bibles during the war, 100,000 of which went to Southern troops.

Fear of death obviously played a major part in the religious attitudes of soldiers. Before going into battle, troops often threw away objects of sin, such as playing cards. It was far better to go into battle with a Bible since stories abounded of such books catching bullets and sparing soldiers' lives from the effects of deadly missiles.

In the Southern ranks religious revivals took the form of emotional meetings and get-togethers where sermons were given and the faithful described spiritual experiences. These meetings usually took place on Sundays in whatever accommodations the troops could provide. When troops were not actively campaigning, churches were built in camp. When in the field, anything might suffice. Hundreds of soldiers made professions of faith including several generals, such as Braxton Bragg, Richard Ewell, Richard H. Anderson and Robert Emmet Rodes. The Fighting Bishop Leonidas Polk baptized three of the most famous generals in the Army of the Tennessee during one of these periods of religious fervor, Joseph E. Johnston, John Bell Hood and William J. Hardee.

The biggest revivals usually were held during the winter months when troops were idle. One great revival took place during the turn of 1863 to 1864 and was interrupted when Yankees launched an offensive. A renewal of activity occurred in the winter of 1864-1865 and was brought to an end by the final battles of the war.

*Hungry Confederates try to supplement their meager rations with some game.*

were ordered to serve for the duration of the conflict; the practice of substitution was abolished and stronger conscription measures were introduced. The spectrum of the draft age was also widened to include boys of 17 and men of 46 to 50 to swell the ranks of reserve units. When the Federals began to strip their garrisons of men for the spring campaign, the Confederates did the same.

Despite these measures, Lee was not able to get a significant number of reinforcements. Many of the ones that did arrive in camp were of poor quality, as Confederate J.F.C. Caldwell remembered, "Some of them, certainly, made excellent soldiers; but between discharges then or subsequently, their ill health, and aversion to duty, we made very little out of them." Once again, Lee would have to rely on his superior generalship and the dogged determination of his troops to overcome the Yankee strength in manpower. The odds against him were made all the worse when Lee learned from a spy that the thousands of troops in the *IX Corps* were on their way to reinforce the *Army of the Potomac.*

By mid-April Lee began to prepare his forces at hand for the offensive he knew must come. On 18 April, troops along the Rapidan were ordered to send their excess baggage to the rear and prepare for action. Several days later, the grass was green again and Lee could begin to have the artillery and cavalry horses, spread out for forage during the winter, concentrated. Throughout April and early May, those units not with the Army of Northern Virginia were ordered to rejoin the command, including Pickett's Division and Robert F. Hoke's brigade, then in North Carolina, and Brigadier General Robert D. Johnston's brigade at Hanover Junction. Pickett's Division and Hoke's Brigade would be unable to rejoin the army as Federal activity would force both commands to remain south in defense of Richmond.

Lee wrote of the coming action to his niece Margaret Stuart during one of the last days of April: "...I dislike to send letters within reach of the enemy, as they might serve, if captured, to bring distress on others. But you must sometimes cast your thoughts on the Army of Northern Virginia, and never forget it in your prayers. It is preparing for a great struggle, but I pray and trust that the great God, mighty to deliver, will spread over it His almighty arms, and drive its enemies before us...."

Of all Confederate commanders, General Longstreet had an idea of what to expect from their new adversary Grant. "Old Pete" had schooled with him at West Point, been present at his wedding and served with the future Union general during the Mexican War. When an officer gloated about the ease with which Grant would be beaten, Longstreet replied, "...I tell you that we can not afford to underrate him and the army he now commands. We must make up our minds to get into a line of battle and to stay there; for that man will fight us every day and every hour until the end of this war." The Confederates of the Army of Northern Virginia would discover the validity of "Old Pete's" claim through bitter experience.

On 2 May, with all in preparedness, Lee and his staff climbed Clark Mountain. The 600 foot height offered an excellent vantage point to view the lands of northern Virginia and the Federal camps north of the Rapidan. Two roads led from the enemy encampments to the river crossings at the Germanna and Ely's Fords. From there they entered the tangled forest of the Wilderness where Lee had defeated Hooker almost a year previous. Lee pointed towards the Rapidan crossings and said, "Grant will cross by one of those fords." The Federals were indeed crossing the Rapidan at Germanna Ford and Ely's Ford only two days later. Soon after that Lee's army was organizing to sally forth and meet the enemy on the field of battle once again.

# The Draft

Before the Civil War, Americans had maintained a suspicion and intolerance for a standing military. The Army and the Navy were seen as more of a threat to the Republic than a steadfast guardian, a necessary evil to be supported at a minimum level. When war came, the small ranks of the military needed to be swelled in order to accomplish the repulse of an invader or the invasion of an enemy state. Citizen soldiers, who were thought to have innate combat abilities, were to join the fray, giving the military the force it needed to win. To accomplish this task, the government relied on the militia or volunteers. By the decade of the Civil War, both sides found it necessary to increase the numbers of their troops through a more severe measure, conscription.

After the bombardment of Fort Sumter, war fever gripped both the North and South as patriots signed up to fight for States Rights or Union. The numbers of these volunteers was so great that the services of many of these hopeful warriors were refused. However, it wasn't long before the grim reality of a long war inevitably eroded the foolish romantic notions of the citizenry and both sides began to find their supply of volunteers drying up. If citizens wouldn't volunteer of their own free will, they were to be coerced to do so. Unlike the draft of more modern wars, the conscrip-

tion was not intended to be the basic source of manpower for the military. Instead, it was viewed more as an incentive to influence citizens to avoid the shameful stigma of being a draftee by freely volunteering to serve.

The South was the first to act. Many of the troops in the rolls of the Confederacy early in the war had enlisted for one year, and as 1861 passed on into 1862 their terms of service were up before the job was done. Incentives were offered to keep soldiers in the ranks, including a $50 bounty, 60-day furlough, the right to choose regiments in which to serve and elections of officers. Even still, this was not enough to keep the Confederate armies in the field up to strength to repel the more numerous Yankee hordes. In April 1862, the Confederacy passed its first conscription act. This made all males between the ages of 18 and 35 eligible to be drafted. Those who were drafted were given 30 days to enlist on their own accord. If they did, they would be allowed to join new regiments. Those who waited would be assigned to existing regiments of veterans who would doubtlessly be hostile to such skulkers.

The law also included controversial measures to avoid being drafted. Exemptions were made to protect persons with services essential to the government such as state officials, certain industrial and transportation workers, clergy, apothecaries and teachers. Another way to avoid serving the Confederacy was substitution. This age-old practice in military history allowed a person to avoid service if he provided someone that could fight in his stead.

The conscription immediately won the disapproval of many politicians and citizens who saw the law as an assault on liberties and states rights. Some politicians blatantly flouted the measure by increasing the number of public servants who were safe under exemption while new schools and apothecaries sprung up. Matters were not helped when the practice of substitution became scandalously expensive. Newspapers began to advertise prospective substitutes at huge prices, some costing as much as $6,000.

Despite the outcry, the Confederacy passed another conscription act in September extending the draftable age to 45. The measure also included a controversial provision which allowed the exemption of 1 white male for a plantation owning 20 slaves. While this was to allow white supervisors to remain on Southern plantations to ensure their productivity, it was harshly condemned as a sop to the wealthy. This gave rise to the saying that the soldiers were in a "rich man's war, but a poor man's fight," even though relatively few people sought this exemption. The law was later amended so that slaveowners had to pay $500 for the exemption and the number of slaves to qualify

was reduced to 15. In February of 1864, the manpower shortage forced the Confederates to desperate measures such as expanding the draft to include boys of age 17 to men of 50. The conscription laws were effective in mobilizing the manpower of the Confederacy and more significantly they did not prove to be as open to corruption and disruptive to morale as the measures that were adopted by the North.

The Union government began to take steps towards conscription early in the war, but only adopted concrete measures almost a year after the South had done so. On 17 July 1862, the Militia Law of 1862 was passed placing every male between the ages of 18 and 45 in the militia and subject to serve for a period of up to 9 months if the President gave his authorization. In August the President exercised his powers under the act, calling for the states to provide 300,000 militia troops to serve a 9 month period. This was in addition to a levy of 300,000 volunteers from the states a few months earlier. One volunteer was allowed to count as four from the militia However, the states managed to avoid Federal involvement by enlisting a substantial number of volunteers over the number desired by the government.

By the winter of 1862-1863, the Federal government came to realize that it could not rely on patriotic fervor alone to supply its armies with the necessary troops to achieve victory. Enlistments were low and the number of men in the ranks was being worn down by losses on the battlefield, disease, excessive desertion and the expiration of terms of service. To cope with the problem, the government passed the Enrollment Act of 1863. Under the law, if states couldn't meet their quotas of volunteer enlistments, a draft of the male population from ages 20-35 would be drawn from a lottery to meet the balance.

Like the Southern system, conscription was viewed as a measure to spur enlistments, not draft an army. To help avoid reliance on the draft, Federal, state and local authorities offered bounties of large cash awards as incentives to increase enlistments. Also like the Southern conscription laws, there were several ways to avoid the draft. Exemptions included medical disability and only sons with families dependent on their labor. Substitution was allowed, though the North employed a commutation fee to avoid the extreme prices of furnishing a substitute that had occurred in the South. Under this system, a person could pay $300 to avoid service. Unfortunately, the Northern system was prone to corruption and resulted in more strife than volunteers. Individuals abused the medical qualifications by claiming infirmities with false documents and some went as far as to undergo self mutilation to avoid service. Bounties led to the existence of bountymen, villains who would enlist for the money, desert and then enlist again to repeat the process.

Unscrupulous substitute brokers provided unhealthy men for service; the more venturesome of this sleazy class went so far as to shanghai foreigners and other unfortunates into Federal arms.

The system caused widespread resentment. Democrats, especially the pro-peace Copperheads, attacked the measures as an assault on liberty. The heinous intentions of the Lincoln government were exposed when it suspended the right of habeas corpus and subjected anyone to martial law who discouraged enlistments, resisted the draft or supported the enemy. The process of substitution and commutation led Northerners to also view the war as "a rich man's war, and a poor man's fight," for it was perceived that only the wealthy could pay the large sums to avoid service. Discontent frequently led to anger and riots against the draft in many Northern cities. The most destructive was in New York on 11-14 July 1863—the worst in U.S. history—it resulted in around 75 deaths and millions of dollars of damage. The problems stemming from the draft were hardly worth the effort; of the some 250,000 drafted, only 6 percent actually served. Of the draftees in the ranks during the Wilderness campaign, many were shunned by their comrades who had enlisted of their own accord.

After the Civil War, the normal means of recruiting troops came under attack. By World War I, practices such as commutation and substitution were dropped in favor of a more egalitarian system of selective service. From thence forth, America's wars were fought by millions of men picked by a lottery system, a practice which was readily accepted by the once anti-militarist civilian populace.

## Number of Men Volunteered or Conscripted for Union Service

| Date of Call, Act of Congress, or Draft | Term of Service | Number Furnished |
|---|---|---|
| 15 Apr. '61 | 3 months | 91,816 |
| 3 May/25-26 July '61 | 6 months | 2,715 |
| | 1 year | 9,147 |
| | 2 years | 30,950 |
| | 3 years | 657,868 |
| May/June '62 | 3 months | 15,007 |
| 2 July '62 | 3 years | 421,465 |
| 4 August '62 | 9 months | 87,588 |
| 15 June '63 | 6 months | 16,361 |
| July '63* | 3 years | 35,582 |
| 17 October '63/ 1 February '64 | 3 years | 281,510 |
| 14 March '64* | 3 years | 259,515 |
| 23 April '64 | 100 days | 83,612 |
| 18 July '64* | 1,2,3,4 years | 385,163 |
| 19 December '64* | 1,2,3,4 years | 211,752 |
| Various from territories and Southern states | 1,2,3,4 years | 172,744 |
| Various from territories and Southern states | 60 days-1 year | 15,509 |
| Emergency men and militia, '63 | 2-3 weeks | 120,000 |
| Total | | 2,898,304 |

* Calls with draft

## CHAPTER II

# Enlightened War

$T$he 87th anniversary of the birth of the Republic, 4 July 1863, was a banner day for the Union. In the East, the formidable Robert E. Lee had been defeated on the fields around Gettysburg at the hands of Major General George Gordon Meade, the new commander of the *Army of the Potomac*, and was soon on the retreat from Pennsylvania. Lee's second invasion proved to be nothing but a tragic waste of effort and manpower. In the West, Ulysses S. Grant accepted the surrender of General Pemberton's garrison of around 20,000 Confederates holding Vicksburg, Mississippi after an arduous two-and-a-half month siege of the city. Shortly afterwards, the Southern garrison at Port Hudson, Mississippi fell. The Union was now in control of the Mississippi River leaving the region of the Confederacy west of its waters cut off from the rest of the South.

The North had finally redeemed its fortunes after the defeats of Fredericksburg, Chancellorsville and the embarrassing raids of Confederate cavalry forces and Bragg's army in the West. Yet, despite the South's setbacks of 4 July, the North could still very easily lose the war. This fact was demonstrated in Meade's failure to engage Lee during his retreat from Gettysburg and the ineffectual posturing of the Mine Run campaign during late November and early December of 1863. Lee and his Army of Northern Virginia continued to awe Federal commanders even in defeat. By the end of the year, the army had only driven as far south as the Rapidan leaving a vast amount of rebellious territory to be brought to

# The Corps

The corps is a loose structure smaller than an army consisting of two or more divisions. It was a concept used by Napoleon, who divided his legions into numerical corps, often identified with the name of a particular commander, to give him better control of his large forces. As Confederate and Union armies swelled with troops, both sides employed corps as the war continued.

The North's adoption of corps contained some controversy. In 1862, McClellan held command of the *Army of the Potomac* and the post of general in chief. His reluctance to engage in an offensive had strained his relationship with the President who was eager for some sort of action. While McClellan planned to divide his army into corps after he took to the field in order to bring combat proven leaders to the fore, Lincoln arbitrarily created corps through a presidential war order in March. These new commands were to be led by generals also selected by Lincoln.

Some 25 Federal corps were created during the war which were consolidated, reorganized and renumbered in a most confusing manner. During the Second Bull Run campaign in August and September of 1862, the *Army of the Potomac* and the *Army of Virginia* each had *I*, *II* and *III* corps. Before the Antietam campaign of September, these *Army of Virginia* units were consolidated into the *Army of the Potomac*. In another confusing incident, the *XI* and *XII* corps of the *Army of the Potomac* were sent West in September of 1863 and were combined into the *XX Corps* of the *Army of the Cumberland*. A *XX Corps* of that army had been in existence since January 1863, but was combined with the *XXI Corps* to form the *IV Corps*. During the battle of Gettysburg, Meade had to contend with seven corps in the *Army of the Potomac* along with a cavalry corps. So many subordinates made directing a battle extremely difficult. It is no wonder that Meade decided to streamline his organization before the Wilderness campaign into three corps.

Over the course of the war, the army made organizational changes. Cavalry brigades, which had been under the control of infantry brigades, divisions and corps, were organized into corps of their own. While artillery had been controlled by brigade and division commanders in the war, an artillery brigade became a staple feature in the Union corps. Both these features strengthened the efficiency of the cavalry and artillery arms of the Un-

heel. At the current pace it might well have taken a decade to completely best the South.

By February 1864, the authorities in Washington decided to rejuvenate the war effort by appointing a senior general with

ion forces and also became features of the Confederate army.

Corps were led in the Union army by an officer with the rank of major general. To undertake the directions of the army commander, the corps commander had a staff for administration, signaling and the dispatch of orders. A staff could include a chief of staff, assistant adjutant general, aides de camp, a commissary officer and a quartermaster officer. Though a corps commander held a great many more responsibilities than one who led a brigade, oftentimes his staff was not much larger or different from that smaller unit.

A distinctive feature of the Federal corps was a badge or symbol that signified the command. For instance, the badge of the *II Corps* was a trefoil or three leaf clover; the *IX Corps* insignia displayed a cannon crossed with an anchor over a shield, and the one for *XV Corps* was a cartridge box. The practice was started by Major General Phil Kearny as a way to identify troops and instill pride in the unit.

The corps became a part of Confederate military organization a day after the battle of Antietam on 18 September 1862. Up until the conclusion of the Seven Days of battles, the Army of Northern Virginia was composed of separate divisions, many commanded by division commanders who were jealous of each other's powers. After the battles on the Virginia Peninsula, Lee divided up his army into separate commands, consisting of several divisions commanded by a major general. Lee's choices to lead the commands were his top subordinates: James Longstreet and Thomas J. "Stonewall" Jackson. When the Confederate Congress gave the authorization to create corps, it also created the rank of lieutenant general for the commanders of such units. Two more corps were eventually created in the Army of Northern Virginia as the war progressed. While Confederate corps were given numerical organizations, they were often known by the last name of their commanders.

The Confederates never had the profligacy of infantry corps that occurred in their adversary's armies. There was never more than four corps in the Army of Northern Virginia while the Army of Tennessee only had two to three. This gave Southern army commanders easy control over their units due to the lack of personalities they had to deal with when issuing commands.

When later wars of greater magnitude dwarfed the efforts exerted during the Civil War; with massive armies of millions of men, the corps became an integral part of the U.S. Army.

the restored rank of lieutenant general. Only George Washington had ever held the full title before and it never had been offered again out of deference to the first President (not concerned with such an act of homage, the Confederacy had

# Ulysses S. Grant

Born Hiram Ulysses (1822-1885), Grant managed to get himself accepted to the United States Military Academy at West Point through his father's influence. A mistake on the letter of recommendation furnished by his Congressman listed Grant's name as Ulysses Simpson, but the young man evidently did not mind the error and adopted the new name for the rest of his life. Grant was an adequate student at the Academy, graduating 21st out of the 39 graduates of the class of 1843. He then went on to serve as lieutenant with the *4th U.S. Infantry* and fought with both Zachary Taylor and Winfield Scott during the Mexican War. Action in combat led to laurels of two brevets, but from there Grant's career slipped slowly towards oblivion. After duty in California, Captain Grant resigned from the Army in 1854 only to face failure after failure in various civilian professions. When the Civil War broke out the future general in chief of all the armies was a mere clerk in a leather goods store in Galena, Illinois.

Once in the military again, Grant's star began to rise though a slow start awaited him. He was assigned as a drill instructor for troops around Galena while he sought a commission for service. In June of 1861, he became a colonel in the *21st Illinois* infantry regiment before winning a brigadier generalcy, thanks to the backing of political sponsor Congressman Elihu Washburne. Grant then took command of the Department of Southern Illinois based at Cairo. In November of 1861, the general boldly moved against a Confederate force at Belmont, Missouri, in an engagement he initially won, but was later forced to retreat. While the action was not successful, Grant had impressed his superiors. The campaigns against Confederate Forts Henry and Donelson in February 1862 presented the general with more opportunities to prove his worth. He was able to accomplish the seizure of both positions, resulting in hundreds of captive troops and a new nickname; Grant's initials now stood for "Unconditional Surrender" for the terms he offered the commander of Fort Donelson. After this success, Grant narrowly avoided disaster at the battle of Shiloh and eventually routed the enemy.

Grant then spent the next year engaged in his classic Vicksburg campaign. He attempted many different schemes to assault the key city on the Mississippi only to find every one flustered by nature, logistical difficulties and Confederate raiders. Despite his frustrating failures in every effort, his activity impressed Lincoln. When someone suggested that the President relieve Grant, he responded, "I can't spare this man, he fights." In April of 1863, Grant risked all by cutting his own communications to undertake an offensive south of Vicksburg. The ploy worked. He defeated the Confederate forces that opposed him and besieged Lieutenant General John Pemberton's command inside the Mississippi town. Pemberton finally surrendered with some 20,000 troops on 4 July 1863 after a two-and-a-half month siege.

Grant's tremendous victory eventually led to a promotion to the Military Division of Mississippi consisting of the combined departments of nearly all the troops west of the Appalachians and east of the Mississippi River. In this position, Grant led the *Army of the Tennessee* and the *Army of the Cumberland* in the decisive victory over Braxton Bragg's forces at Chattanooga on 23 to 25 November 1863. The victory propelled Grant's prestige to the heights of the Union military leadership making him best choice for Lincoln's senior general.

In March of 1864, Grant received the newly revived rank of lieutenant general and the post of general in chief. He then proceeded to develop a brilliant strategy which called for numerous thrusts into the heartland of the Confederacy to exhaust the enemy's armies and material. While his protege William T. Sherman advanced into Georgia, the lieutenant general stayed with the *Army of the Potomac* as it maneuvered its way south, engaging in many severe fights along the way at the Wilderness and Spotsylvania. Though Major General George Gordon Meade was the effective head of the *Army of the Potomac* and Grant claimed to give him a free hand, the general in chief had a direct influence in the conduct of the maneuvers and battles of the force. His gravest mistake of the entire war occurred when he ordered an ill-advised frontal attack by the *Army of the Potomac* against a strong Confederate position at Cold Harbor. The result was a slaughter as 7,000 men fell in roughly 30 minutes. Still Grant besieged Lee's army at Petersburg from which the valiant Confederate would march to surrender at Appomattox on 9 April 1865.

Grant was the Union's primary war hero when the war ended. Following in the tradition for America's victors in war, Grant ran for President and served two terms from 1869-1877. Unfortunately, his brilliance on the battlefield did not translate into any perspicacity in the state house as scandal dogged Grant throughout his administration. After his tenure in office, the general-president toured the globe before returning home to engage in business. Unwise decisions led the once great general to disaster and left his family close to poverty. Fortunately, Grant was able to retrieve his honor and support his family through writing. His personal memoirs, finished in 1885 as he was dying of throat cancer, are a classic of military history.

While it has been claimed that Grant was not the greatest of all Union generals, certainly he conducted the war with marked intelligence, diligence and an uncanny degree of flexibility. The seizure of Vicksburg demonstrated his flair for risk and maneuver while battles during his march overland to Richmond displayed a more deliberate nature. Whatever critiques have been lodged against him, Grant's brilliant grand strategy finally won the war for the Union.

restored the rank in September of 1862). One general had come close to such an honor; Winfield Scott, America's greatest general after Washington, attained the rank only through brevet status. As the most victorious Union general of the war, Ulysses S. Grant appeared to be the best candidate to receive the rank and appointment. Indeed, the bill to revive the rank was sponsored by Grant's friends, the most notable being Congressman Elihu Washburne from Illinois. Washburne was closely linked to Grant's rise. After Grant's offers to serve the Union were turned down, the congressman managed to secure him a colonelcy and then the rank of brigadier general, thus starting the foremost Yankee hero of the war on his path to glory. Though Lincoln realized that Grant was equal to the post of general in chief, he was somewhat concerned the general might harbor presidential aspirations and use the post for personal advantage, a serious apprehension since the President was up for reelection that year. After the bill passed the Senate on 24 February, Lincoln's worries were relieved when he received confirmation that Grant was only interested in military matters. A good acquaintance of the general gave the President a letter he had received from Grant which read, "I already have a pretty big job on my hands, and my only ambition is to see this rebellion suppressed. Nothing could induce me to think of being a presidential candidate, particularly so long as there is a possibility of having Mr. Lincoln re-elected." Upon reading this Lincoln exclaimed with relief, "I wanted to know; for when this Presidential grub once gets to gnawing at a man, nobody can tell how far in it has got."

Grant's arrival in Washington on 8 March has since become a legend of his unpretentious nature. The capital had witnessed many generals who acted with pomp and arrogance, who were later found utterly incompetent when they finally took to the battlefield. Grant arrived with no great fanfare that his predecessors might have enjoyed, his entourage being two staff officers and his teenage son, Fred. Grant signed the Willard's Hotel register book with the modest inscription, "U.S. Grant and son, Galena, Ill." Richard Henry

*President Abraham Lincoln, though originally concerned about appointing Grant lieutenant general and general in chief, maintained a trusting relationship with him through the rest of the war.*

Dana spotted Grant at Willard's Hotel and wrote that though the "generalissimo" displayed a common appearance, he also had an aura of firm determination, a quality he would need in the difficult months ahead. "I saw that the ordinary scrubby-looking man, with a slightly seedy look, as if he was out of office and on half-pay with nothing to do but hang around the entry of Willard's, cigar in mouth, had a clear blue eye, and a look of resolution, as if he could not be trifled with, and an entire indifference to the crowd about him. Straight nose, too." Though the general attempted to keep a low profile, his reputation caused him to be the object of some curiosity of many onlookers at Willard's. His dinner was even interrupted by three cheers from those at the tables around him.

Later in the day, Grant went to the White House to meet the President personally for the first time. Horace Porter, an aide to Grant during the coming campaign, was in the Blue Room before the general entered. Porter noted the appearance of Lincoln, worn ragged by exhaustion from the trials required of him during the nearly three years of bloody civil strife,

> He was in evening dress, and wore a turned-down collar a size too large. The necktie was rather broad and awkwardly tied. He was more of a Hercules than an Adonis. His form was ungainly, and the movements of his long angular arms and legs bordered on the grotesque. His eyes were gray and disproportionately small. His face wore an expression of sadness, the deep lines indicating the sense of responsibility which weighed upon him; but at times his features lightened up with a broad smile, and there was a merry twinkle in his eyes as he greeted an old acquaintance and exchanged a few words with a tone of familiarity. He had sprung from the common people to become the most uncommon of men.

When Grant arrived at the White House, he humbly proceeded towards the president in a group of visitors. Lincoln spotted the general, recognizing his face from photographs, advanced toward him and exclaimed, "Why, here is General Grant! Well this is a great pleasure I assure you." Lincoln seized the general's hand for a hearty vigorous shake in welcome which lasted for several minutes.

The general was soon crowded by the curious who became quite unmanageable in their efforts to get a look at the man who would soon hold the fate of the Union in his hands. Secretary of State William Seward managed to have the affair transferred to the larger East Room, but this measure had little effect on the uncomfortable situation. When the crowd began to chant "Grant! Grant! Grant!" Seward got the general to stand up on a sofa in hopes the crowd might be placated by a look at him. Instead, the shouts increased as the multitude rushed up, some eager for a chance to shake his hand. Lincoln and his Secretary of War, Edwin M. Stanton, adjourned to a cabinet room to speak privately with Grant. They had to wait a while for it took an hour for the general to make his way through the crowd and even then only with the help of several ushers.

Grant received his new commission the next day in a small ceremony at the White House, a blissful change from the

*Grant received his new commission from President Lincoln in a
small ceremony at the White House on 9 March 1864.*

chaotic events of the previous day. The action effectively
replaced Major General Henry Halleck who had been general
in chief since July of 1862. Though Halleck was a military
intellectual of the first rank whose mental capacities were
praised by his comrades, he never really demonstrated effective leadership during his tenure as general in chief though he
was a superb "clerk in chief." Halleck usually attempted to
avoid major operational decisions by involving himself with
administrative duties, staff work and giving advice to the
President and other commanders. Grant wisely assigned him
to the new position of chief of staff with the charge of the
duties he had primarily occupied himself with as general in
chief. While bureaucratic Halleck concerned himself with the
tedium of administration, paperwork, explaining military

*The headquarters of the* **Army of the Potomac** *at Brandy Station.*

policy and actions to civilians along with other incidental matters, Grant was free to oversee strategy.

On 10 March, Grant arrived at the headquarters of the *Army of the Potomac* at Brandy Station, Virginia. The reception was an inglorious one. Rain drenched the band, officers and few onlookers who turned out to see the new general from the West. Though Grant came with the immense prestige of his victories at Fort Donelson, Vicksburg and Chattanooga, the members of the *Army of the Potomac* were decidedly unimpressed. To them, he had only faced mediocre enemy commanders like Bragg and Pemberton. Beating Robert E. Lee was a different matter altogether.

Upon meeting with Meade, the commander of the *Army of the Potomac* selflessly pressed Grant to relieve him in favor of his own hand picked officer. Grant later wrote of the incident in his memoirs, "He said to me that I might want an officer who had served with me in the West, Sherman specially, to take his place. If so, he begged me not to hesitate about making the change. He urged that the work before us was of such importance to the whole nation that the feeling or wishes of no one person should stand in the way of selecting the right men for all positions. For himself, he would serve to the best of his ability wherever placed." Grant was impressed by Meade's gesture of humility, writing later, "This incident gave me even a more favorable opinion of Meade than did his great victory at Gettysburg the July before. It is men who wait to be selected, and not those who seek, from whom we may always expect the most efficient service." Though Grant had once contemplated replacing Meade with one of his Western subordinates, the general in chief kept the victor of Gettysburg in his position.

One of the first major decisions Grant faced as general in chief was where to conduct the war effort: in the West where he directed his brilliant campaigns or in the unfamiliar East close to Washington and its political pressures. William T. Sherman, Grant's favorite and most talented subordinate, fervently argued for the former course in a letter dated 10 March:

> Do not stay in Washington. Halleck is better qualified than you are to stand the bullets of intrigue and policy. Come out West; take to yourself the whole Mississippi Valley; let us make it dead-sure, and I tell you the Atlantic slope and the Pacific shores will follow its destiny as sure as limbs of a tree live or die with the main trunk! We have done much; still much needs to be done. Time and time's influences are all still with us; we could almost afford to sit still and let these influences work. Even in the seceded states your word *now* would go further than a President's proclamation, or an act of Congress.
>
> For God's sake and for your country's sake, come out of Washington,....Here lies the seat of the coming empire; and from the West, when our task is done, we will make short work of Charleston and Richmond, and the impoverished coast of the Atlantic.

Despite Sherman's passionate points, Grant came to the conclusion that he would only be able to conduct the war effort from the East. His political friends, Washburne among them, advised that he could only command from there since the potential Rebel threat to the capital was too great to allow anything else. The public and politicians were also expecting a showdown between the North's greatest general and Lee on the territory between the enemy capitals. If the new lieutenant general conducted his affairs far away from the Army of Northern Virginia, he might appear to be frightened of "Bobby" Lee. Grant had come to realize soon after his arrival in Washington that he had no choice except to remain in the East. "...when I got to Washington and saw the situation it was plain that here was the point for the commanding general to be. No one else could, probably, resist the pressure that would be brought to bear upon him to desist from his own plans and pursue others."

Though Halleck and his predecessors as general in chief, Winfield Scott and George Brinton McClellan, had commanded from within Washington, Grant astutely realized the advantages to setting up his headquarters outside of Washington next to the headquarters of the *Army of the Potomac*. Outside of Washington he would be away from political pressure, but close enough to keep in constant contact with authorities there. He would also be able to shield Meade from coercion by politicians and others, but at the same time directly press that general to stay on the offensive while he directed other theaters. This was an important consideration since there was a feeling among Western generals that the *Army of the Potomac* had never really been pushed to achieve victory. Whatever the truth of that opinion, the new lieutenant general was going to see that the force was kept in motion. Grant set up his headquarters at Culpeper, six miles south of Meade's position at Brandy Station. The pages of Northern newspapers joked that the general in chief was now closer to the enemy than the commander of the *Army of the Potomac*.

Grant's decision to stay with the *Army of the Potomac* before and during the upcoming campaign proved his determination to take on the Confederacy's biggest and best led army along with Northern political pressure. The problem in doing so was an uncomfortable dual command structure for the *Army of the Potomac* with both Lieutenant General Grant and Major General Meade as its immediate heads. Despite his rank over Meade, Grant did his best to leave the command of the army to his subordinate and wrote in retrospect in a report of 22 July 1865, "I may here state that commanding all the armies as I did, I tried, as far as possible, to leave General Meade in independent command of the Army of the Potomac. My instructions for that army were all through him, and were general in their nature, leaving all the details and the execution through him." Still, the state of affairs was uncomfortable as Grant wrote in his memoirs, "Meade's position afterwards proved embarrassing to me if not to him." Despite Grant's best attempts to give Meade a free hand with the *Army of the Potomac*, it was perhaps inevitable that Grant often meddled with the command of the army by making operational and tactical decisions, even to the point of giving orders that directly conflicted with his subordinate's directives.

Grant's stay with the *Army of the Potomac* did not negate his tremendous responsibilities of directing the entire Federal war effort, tasks that were perhaps the most formidable that any American military leader had faced up to that time. All at once he found himself commanding around 745,000 troops spread out over 19 military districts. The situation required him to hold the territory gained after three years of war while subduing those huge stretches of territory which still remained defiant. At that time the Mississippi River was under Federal control and guarded from its mouth to St. Louis. East of the Mississippi, all of Tennessee was in National hands, despite Rebel raids, along with West Virginia and Northern Virginia north of the Rapidan and east of the Blue Ridge. In addition, garrisons had been established on the Atlantic coast of the Confederacy including Fortress Monroe and Norfolk in Virginia; Plymouth, Washington and New Berne in North Carolina; Beaufort, Folly and Morris islands, Hilton Head, Fort Pulaski in South Carolina and Georgia; and Fernandia, St. Augustine, Key West and Pensacola in Florida. West of the Mississippi, Federal forces held the line of the Arkansas River and points in Louisiana on the Mississippi River including New Orleans.

Of the primary Federal forces actively in the field, the *Army of the Potomac* was on the north side of the Rapidan facing off against the Army of Northern Virginia. As of 10 March, the forces in the Department of West Virginia (covering the new state to the Allegheny Mountains) were under the command of the inept military mind of Major General Franz Sigel. Political General Benjamin Butler, one of the most hated Union generals in the South, held a command at Norfolk on the mouth of the James River. William Tecumseh Sherman had taken Grant's old command of the Western theater, called the Military Division of the Mississippi, controlling the territory from the Appalachians to the Mississippi and the command of the *Army of the Tennessee*, the *Army of the Cumberland*, and the *Army of the Ohio*. Major General Nathaniel Banks was in Louisiana with a large force, including 10,000 troops borrowed from Sherman, busily engaged in his disastrous operations up the Red River. Throughout the war, Federal commands in the East and West had all been working for a common purpose but, for the most part, had acted independently of each other. This folly was to change under Grant's command.

Throughout the months of March, April and May, Grant evaluated the military situation, concentrated troops and planned how he would wield the huge armies at his command. One lingering hindrance to Grant's plans was the possibility that the Rebels might abandon or siphon forces from one point on their line to support another one in the belief that, in Grant's words, "a defeat with one victory to sustain them is better than a defeat all along their line." Such had been the case in September of 1863 when a lull in activity in the East had allowed Longstreet's Corps to reinforce the Army of Tennessee at Chickamauga and almost annihilate the Federal forces there. Grant desired to avoid such an occurrence by having all the Union forces possible moving in offensives at the same time to pin down the Confederate armies and deny them the initiative to attack and raid.

In the East, Lee's Army of Northern Virginia was to be the objective of the *Army of the Potomac*. Grant desired to keep that force so occupied that it would be unable to reinforce the Army of Tennessee. At the same time, Sherman's three armies in the West would press against Johnston's force to prevent a concentration against the Federal forces in the East. While these mighty commands were so engaged, Sigel, Butler and Banks would also be nibbling away at Confederate territory while further occupying enemy forces. Sigel was to advance down the Shenandoah Valley to deprive that breadbasket from Confederate use. The Valley had also proved to be a pathway for an enemy invasion of the North, but Sigel's activity there would plug up this route thus protecting Union territory. Operating in close proximity to Sigel would be a cavalry force under Major General George Crook whose targets would include the Virginia & Tennessee Railroad as well as industries and agriculture in southwestern Virginia. This incursion would threaten a major Confederate artery of communications along with access to supplies and would distract the enemy from Sigel's moves. Butler would threaten the Confederate capital itself. He was to be reinforced by troops stripped from coastal garrisons for a move up the James River to operate against Richmond and the railroad junction town of Petersburg. It was hoped Banks would be finished with the Red River operation in time to assist Sherman by moving on the vital port of Mobile, Alabama. To Grant's and Sherman's exasperation Banks was severely defeated and forced to retreat. The disastrous situation made his assistance to Sherman an impossibility.

With so many offensives, the Confederates would be under ceaseless exhausting pressure. There would be no chance to attack or route forces from one area to another. This was to deny or delay Lee from receiving substantial reinforcements even from Confederate forces nearby such as Pickett, Breckinridge and Beauregard. At the same time, manpower, supplies and treasure would gradually be destroyed by Union forces or exhausted by Confederate armies until the South was compelled to accept total surrender and ultimate defeat. Sherman wrote of this strategy, "That we are now to act on a common plan, converging on a common centre, looks like enlightened war." Lincoln described the strategy in layman's terms, "As we say out West, if a man can't skin he must hold a leg while somebody else does."

Grant had enough confidence in Sherman to give his protege a free hand in directing the Western campaigns. However, the lieutenant general took it upon himself to develop the strategy for beating the Army of Northern Virginia. The territory Grant would campaign on was not ideal for an army on the offensive. South of the Rapidan the ground was cut by streams and heavily timbered in some areas making it difficult to cross. The roads there were poor, and even worse after a good rain, making any movement for an army supplied by wagon transport exceedingly difficult. Grant had thought about the possibility of avoiding Lee altogether by transporting a force by sea to the coast of North Carolina. There it could launch a raid into the heart of the Confederacy destroying resources and railroads while encouraging slaves to leave their masters for freedom and soldiers to desert the army to protect their homes. As appealing as this plan might be, it was not politically feasible; it smacked too much of avoiding a fight and too much resembled McClellan's failed campaign up the Virginia Peninsula in the spring and summer of 1862. Worse still, it appeared to leave Washington dangerously open to an enemy attack.

Forced to fight Lee directly, Grant's hope was to pin the Army of Northern Virginia down by constant advances to take the initiative and ensure that the enemy general would be unable to engage in any of his wily maneuvers to defeat the Union army, invade the North, or threaten Washington. To do this, Grant sought to get between Lee and Richmond. The general in chief again pondered an amphibious movement, this time to the Peninsula, but dismissed the idea for the same reasons that blocked the operation into North Carolina. Instead he would have to move south over difficult terrain in the hopes of turning one of Lee's flanks, thus forcing the enemy to retreat or fight on Grant's terms.

The next question was which flank to turn. Turning Lee's left appeared attractive. In doing so, Grant could move on to land which would maximize the use of his larger numbers of infantry, cavalry and artillery as he fell upon Lee's communications. Lee would then find himself in an untenable position

*Federal wagons at Culpeper, Virginia, where Grant set up his head-
quarters. The* **Army of the Potomac** *required a massive train of
some 4,000 such vehicles. Moving and guarding the wagon train
was a constant concern for Federal planners throughout the Wilderness campaign.*

between the *Army of the Potomac* and Butler's command.
However, this plan entailed abandoning supply lines to live
off a land lacking supplies and forage, or relying on huge
wagon trains or the Orange & Alexandria Railway which
would have to be guarded against the area's formidable Rebel
raiders.

Moving against Lee's right seemed to offer better opportunities. The close proximity to Chesapeake port facilities and a

plethora of rivers presented the chance for the waterborne transport of supplies to short hauling distances to the army as it moved south. Since the Confederacy didn't have a navy that could interfere with this operation, the Union supply line would be practically invulnerable. Yet, this move also contained problems as well for the tidewater region was especially wooded in some places. In May of 1863, Major General Joseph Hooker had entered the dense woodland of the Wilderness to be severely humiliated there by Lee. Fighting in that region would negate Federal superiority in manpower and weaponry while giving the Confederates the advantages of operating off interior lines and possibly allowing them to head north on an invasion.

During Grant's first interview with the President, military amateur Lincoln offered his advice on the shape the offensive should take to the amusement of the general. Grant recalled of this incident, "He brought out a map of Virginia on which he had evidently marked every position occupied by the Federal and Confederate armies up to that time. He pointed out on the map two streams which empty into the Potomac, and suggested that the army might be moved on boats and landed between the mouths of these streams. We would then have the Potomac to bring our supplies, and the tributaries would protect our flanks as we moved out. I listened respectfully, but did not suggest that the same streams would protect Lee's flanks while he was shutting us up." What the President might have lacked in strategic thought, he made up in prudence. Since Lincoln realized it was not in his nature to keep military secrets, he urged Grant to keep whatever plans he made to himself, a request the general easily granted. Later in a discussion with his personal secretary William O. Stoddard, Lincoln said Grant was his first real general, explaining, "You know how it's been with all the rest. As soon as I put a man in command of the army he'd come to me with a plan of campaign and about as much as say 'Now, I don't believe I can do it, but if you say so I'll try it on,' and so put all the responsibility of success and failure on me. They all wanted me to be the general. It isn't so with Grant. He hasn't told me

*The headquarters flag of the* **Army of the Potomac** *had a golden eagle in a silver wreath. When Grant first saw the royal banner, he remarked sarcastically, "What's this! Is Imperial Caesar anywhere about here?"*

what his plans are, and I don't want to know. I'm glad to find a man who can go ahead without me."

By 29 April Grant had decided that the ability to supply his army over water was worth the risk of an engagement in the Wilderness. He informed Halleck of his intentions to move out on 4 May unless Lee decided to move first. On that day Grant planned to slip through the Wilderness and get between Lee and Richmond causing the Confederates to either attack or retreat. This operation, the Wilderness campaign, turned out to be the first step in Grant's Overland Campaign which would take him on a path to Richmond inevitably paved with the blood of thousands of Northern and Southern soldiers.

Though Lee's army was the ultimate goal, Grant was also eager for the chance to link up with Butler and take Richmond, an important political and psychological objective. However, he was also wary of forcing Lee into the standoff of a siege at the enemy's capital (a prospect which the Confederate general did not find all that attractive either). For Grant, a siege would take precious time to break thus risking war weariness in the North defeating a successful cause. Still, he prepared for this eventuality by ordering Meade to have siege equipment readily available when the Federal army reached the James River.

The instrument Grant would use to accomplish the defeat of the Army of Northern Virginia and the capture of Richmond, the *Army of the Potomac*, had changed significantly since its victory on the fields and farms of Gettysburg. At the time of that battle, the army consisted of seven corps. Two of these, the *XI* and *XII*, had been sent west and two more, *I* and *III*, were disbanded with their troops being transferred into three remaining entities, the *II*, *V* and *VI Corps*. Meade had asked the War Department for the reorganization since he felt there was not a sufficient number of commanders to lead such a large number of units and the strengths of infantry regiments were depleted by previous campaigns. This decision may have seemed astute at the time, but three large commands would prove quite unwieldy in a future confrontation in the thick woodland of the Wilderness. Meade's chief of staff Andrew A. Humphreys argued this point in his book, *The Virginia Campaign of 1864-1865*: "In a country so heavily wooded as that in which the operations were to be conducted, five infantry corps of about 15,000 each would have been a more judicious organization, owing to the difficulty of communication between the corps commander and the subordinate commanders in a battle in such country, and the consequent difficulty of prompt and efficient control of extensive lines of battle, especially at critical moments, or when unforseen exigencies occurred." This action also caused a great deal of the consternation amongst the troops who strongly identified with their old units. The corps had a

*Federals of the* 18th Pennsylvania Cavalry *in camp north of the Rapidan.*

strong sense of competition, camaraderie and pride, all of which were sacrificed by the reorganization decision. In their anger, some of the members of the old *III Corps* erected a mock cemetery out of fence rails confiscated from a "secesh" farm. Within it was a tombstone reading:

SACRED
to the
MEMORY OF THE OLD
3d
CORPS
Killed by General Order No. 9
March 1864
Actuated by
Personal Malice, Spite, and Jealousy
"HOW SLEEP THE BRAVE"

The remaining corps formed a formidable legion. The *II Corps* was under the command of one of the Union's best corps commanders, Winfield Scott Hancock. After Gettysburg its three divisions had been consolidated into two and it was reinforced by two divisions from the now defunct *III Corps.* The *V Corps* under Major General Gouverneur K. Warren consisted of four divisions, two comprised of troops from the old *I Corps.* The *VI Corps* under the able John Sedgwick also

# Philip Sheridan

The place of the fiery Yankee cavalryman Philip Sheridan's (1831-1888) birth is open to speculation, but this son of Irish immigrants is believed to have come into the world in Albany, New York. Eager for a military life, he managed to attain entrance to the United States Military Academy at West Point by changing his birth date by a year to get early admission. Sheridan's stay there was marred by a lukewarm academic performance, he graduated 34th out of a class of 49 in 1853 (a class which included the likes of Union generals James B. McPherson and John M. Schofield and Confederate John B. Hood) and suffered a year's suspension for threatening a fellow cadet with a bayonet.

Sheridan was an officer on frontier service before the Civil War broke out. A captain in 1861, his early appointments in the war were staff positions, no place for a person of Sheridan's fighting temperament. On 25 May 1862, the Irish officer became colonel of a cavalry regiment and steadily rose through the ranks as he recorded an impressive combat record. By September of that year, he was a brigadier general in charge of a brigade and by March of 1863, he was a major general with a retroactive date of commission back to 31 December. At the battle of Stone's River on 31 December 1862 to 2 January 1863, Sheridan's division delayed a Confederate onslaught that had broken the right of the *Army of the Cumberland*, action that surely saved the force from complete destruction. More combat laurels were won at Chickamauga, where his division suffered 37 percent casualties, and at Chattanooga where his troops broke the Confederate line on Missionary Ridge.

Sheridan went East with Grant to take command of the *Army of the Potomac*'s cavalry, a position that

contained *III Corps* troops. Altogether Grant's command would total almost 100,000 soldiers.

An anomaly in the command structure of Grant's army was the *IX Corps*, commanded by Major General Ambrose E. Burnside, notable for leading the *Army of the Potomac* into the disastrous bloodbath at Fredericksburg in December of 1862. This contained 20,000 troops in four divisions including one of African-American soldiers. Most of the *IX Corps* had seen service in East Tennessee from March 1863 to March 1864, after which it had been sent to Annapolis, Maryland. Because of Burnside's rank, the *IX Corps* would enter the new campaign not under Meade, but Grant. This awkward arrange-

would allow him to come to the fore as one of the North's leading generals. Though kept on a leash during the Wilderness campaign, Sheridan finally won the chance to go on several raids, one of which resulted in the death of Confederate cavalry wizard Jeb Stuart at Yellow Tavern. Sheridan later led the infantry of the *VI* and *XIX Corps* into the Shenandoah Valley against Confederate Jubal Early's force there. He won several victories including Cedar Creek (19 October 1864) in which he rode 20 miles to rally his broken troops, an incident that became a Civil War legend. After Sheridan completed his work in the valley, including a vicious scorched earth policy, the region was no longer of use to the Confederates.

"Little Phil," as he was called, returned to the *Army of the Potomac* during some of the war's last battles in the East. He commanded the victories at Five Forks (1 April 1865), netted some 8,000 Confederate troops at Sayler's Creek 5 days later and·pursued Lee's army to its surrender at Appomattox.

Sheridan continued on in the military after the war with a distinguished and sometimes controversial record. He led a force of 50,000 troops to the U.S.-Mexico border to intimidate the French out of their imperialist adventures in North America and held command of the Fifth Military District, comprised of Texas and Louisiana, during Reconstruction. When Grant became President in 1869, Sheridan advanced to the rank of lieutenant general. He then oversaw the subjugation of the Plains Indians and engaged in various administrative posts before becoming commanding general of the Army in 1884. He died, a full general, shortly after writing his memoirs.

Sheridan has gone down in history as one of the finest Union commanders to emerge during the Civil War. Though a cantankerous and possibly spiteful character, his aggressiveness was second to none.

---

ment, basically allowing the existence of an independent corps, was bound to cause problems in the coming battles. If Meade desired to use the *IX Corps*, he would first have to petition Grant who then would issue the proper orders, a tedious chain of command which could prove dangerous in moments requiring quick decisions and action.

The command of the cavalry arm of the *Army of the Potomac* underwent some changes as well. Grant was dissatisfied with the Eastern army's troopers even though the force had vastly improved from its farcical state early in the war to the sometimes equal of their Confederate counterparts. Grant had nothing against the current commander Major General

*The fiery Philip Sheridan, one of the Union's finest cavalry commanders. His fighting qualities were not evident during the Wilderness campaign as most of his* **Cavalry Corps** *was protecting the* **Army of the Potomac's** *wagons.*

Alfred Pleasonton, but when Henry Halleck offered the chance to employ the hard fighting Philip Sheridan in the East, the lieutenant general responded, "The very man I want." When someone remarked to Grant of the five foot six inch cavalry man "The officer you brought on from the West is rather a little fellow to handle your cavalry," the general in chief replied, "You will find him big enough for the purpose before we get through with him."

Federal forces in the East were preparing for the new campaign by the end of April. On the 27th, Ambrose Burnside left Annapolis with his *IX Corps* heading for Meade's position. The next day, his command was spotted by a Confederate agent while parading through Washington who reported the news to Lee. On the same day, Meade was directed to ready his troops for the advance. Butler was informed on the 28th that he was to be ready to move up the James on 4 May. Sherman was directed to move on 5 May. Sigel was told to begin his offensive in conjunction with the activity of the other commands.

By the time the *Army of the Potomac* was prepared to head south, a joke had spread through its ranks. It ran along the lines that events in the near future would decide if Grant's first name was Ulysses or "Useless."

# Parole, Exchange and Prison

One of the darker sides of the Civil War was the sad conditions that awaited prisoners of war at the multitude of prison camps whose names were infamous: Libby Prison in Richmond, Elmira in New York and, the worst of all, Andersonville in Georgia. The situation in the camps went from bad to worse when active campaigning began in 1864 due to the collapse of the parole and exchange system which had been used to handle prisoners of war throughout the years of strife.

When the war began, it was expected to be a short affair, so no one gave much if any thought to the housing and care of enemy soldiers captured in battle. During the first several months, the number of prisoners of war was small and they could be accommodated in existing jails, obsolete forts or buildings converted into prisons. Keeping prisoners became a problem as battles grew larger and more frequent. The fights at Forts Henry and Donelson,

Shiloh, the Peninsula campaign and the Seven Days Battles brought in hundreds of prisoners on both sides, more than could possibly be cared for in the makeshift prisons of the North and South. The problem led to negotiations for a cartel based on the European military practices of exchange and parole.

These discussions were a sticky issue for the North. It was important to solve the prisoner of war (POW) issue, but the Union did not recognize the legitimacy of the Confederacy; to open negotiations was tantamount to a recognition of the South as a foreign belligerent power, not an area in rebellion. Despite this point of contention, an agreement was reached and signed by Major General John A. Dix for the Union and Major General Daniel Harvey Hill of the Confederacy on 22 July 1862. Under this system, soldiers remained out of combat until exchanged for a soldier of equal rank or a number of soldiers of lesser status.

## Exchange Cartel

| Person Exchanged Army Rank/Naval Rank | Value |
|---|---|
| General commanding in chief/ admiral | Officer of equal rank or 60 privates or seamen |
| Major general/ flag officer | Officer of equal rank or 40 privates or seamen |
| Brigadier general/ commodore | Officer of equal rank or 20 privates or seamen |
| Colonel/naval captain | Officer of equal rank or 15 privates or seamen |

| | |
|---|---|
| Lieutenant colonel/ naval commander | Officer of equal rank or 10 privates or seamen |
| Major/lieutenant commander | Officer of equal rank or 8 privates or seamen |
| Captain/lieutenant or master | Officer of equal rank or 6 privates or seamen |
| Lieutenant/master's mates | Officer of equal rank or 4 privates or seamen |
| /Midshipmen, warrant officers, masters of merchant ships and commanders of privateers | Officer of equal rank or 3 privates or seamen |
| Non commissioned officers/ 2nd captains, lieutenants, or mates of merchant ships or privateers and all petty officers | Person of equal rank or 2 privates or seamen |
| Private/seaman | Private or seaman |

For those troops who could not be immediately exchanged, they were to be paroled 10 days after their capture. These troops gave a solemn oath not to fight until they were formally exchanged.

The exchange and parole system worked well for almost a year though with several significant defects. Many soldiers saw the practice as a way to escape combat and offered themselves up as prisoners to the enemy. Some of those soldiers paroled left the ranks never to return. Others found duty in non-combat garrison positions, or service against truculent Indians, a violation of the agreement since this policy freed up other soldiers for combat. More unfortunate soldiers ended up in camps to await their paroles which were little better than prisons.

Despite these problems, the practice was much more beneficial for soldiers than the alternative of languishing away in enemy prison camps. An ominous fate awaited thousands of prisoners on both sides as the Union willingness to uphold the agreement deteriorated over time. One major factor irritating Union leaders was the refusal of the Southerners to treat African-American soldiers in the Union uniform as prisoners of war.

As the war progressed, the Union increasingly became drawn to the idea of enlisting blacks in the fight against the "Slavocratic" South. Lincoln was given permission by the Congress to allow blacks to join the army in July of 1862. The Emancipation Proclamation went into effect on 1 January 1863, and thousands of bondsmen fled the South to Northern controlled areas, a significant number of whom joined the Union Army. In all 200,000 African-Americans served in Federal ranks during the war. In May of 1863, the Confederacy issued a heinous proclamation declaring that Federal African-American troops were to be re-enslaved, possibly even executed while their white officers were also under threat of death if captured. The Union government reacted by suspending the Exchange Cartel and held Southern prisoners against the threat.

Paroles continued in the field, however, especially when thousands of troops were captured in the Mississippi garrisons of Vicksburg and Port Hudson. In the former, Grant netted around 20,000 men and at the latter Major General Nathaniel Banks took some 7,000 at Port Hudson. Grant paroled the prisoners, writing, "It saves, probably, several days in the capture, and leaves troops and transports ready for immediate service." This might have been an imprudent deci-sion for the Confederates were arbitrarily declaring their troops exchanged. Thus four months later, Grant became especially annoyed when enemy troops captured and paroled at Vicksburg, but not formally exchanged, were recaptured at Chattanooga.

The South's refusal to treat blacks as prisoners of war and its use of the parole system to reinforce its ranks led to General in Chief Grant's refusal to accept exchanges on 17 April 1864. As a result, some Yankee troops captured in the Wilderness found themselves incarcerated in Andersonville and Southerners were imprisoned in facilities in Northern states. Most of these places were overcrowded and unsanitary leading to the deaths of thousands; over 30,000 Federals died in such camps and some 26,000 Southern prisoners perished in the North.

# CHAPTER III

# The Wilderness

*T*en miles west of Fredericksburg, south of the Rapidan River, north of Spotsylvania Court House was the infamous Wilderness, a forbidding woodland consisting of impenetrable tangled underbrush, dense woods, gullies, streams and a handful of clearings. A few roads provided adequate passage through the area, though many were mere wagon tracks. The most important routes, almost parallel to each other, ran from east to west, the northernmost being the Orange Turnpike and the southernmost the Orange Plank Road. Routes also led from the Germanna Ford and Ely's Ford on the Rapidan south through the woodland, intersecting both the Turnpike and the Plank Road.

On 30 April 1863 Major General Joseph Hooker had led the *Army of the Potomac* into the Wilderness to fight what became the battle of Chancellorsville. Over the next few days, he suffered a devastating defeat, one of the bloodiest and worst experienced by the Union during the war. Lee, wielding a numerically inferior army, deftly managed to bring Hooker's advance to a halt and then initiated his most brilliant offensive humiliating his befuddled and outgeneraled adversary. On 6 May Hooker retreated with his army to the north, his ranks reduced by some 17,000 men in casualties and his days as an army commander numbered.

Now Grant was leading the *Army of the Potomac* back to nearly the same ground where it had faced disaster almost a year before. The man who received the unenviably difficult task of formulating the maneuver through the Wilderness was Meade's chief of staff, Major General Andrew Atkinson Humphreys. Humphreys was a talented engineer and field commander who had also served on the staff of George B. McClellan. By the time of Antietam, he was at the head of a division in the *III Corps* and had seen action in many of the prominent battles of the war thus far, such as Fredericksburg and Gettysburg. In the latter battle he managed to keep his command organized as the rest of the corps was shattered by a powerful Confederate assault. Though a fierce fighting commander, he gave up the role as a leader of troops in order to serve on Meade's staff with the rank of major general.

The task given to Humphreys seemed well nigh impossible. *The Army of the Potomac* would have to advance to the south, east of the Army of Northern Virginia, on the poor roads leading south from the Rapidan River fords. With the Confederates making use of the imposing Clark Mountain as a nest from which to observe Federal movements, the enemy could easily spot any offensive. Once alerted, columns of Confederate troops would be on the march east down the Orange Turnpike and Orange Plank Road to catch the Federals in a general engagement within the Wilderness. There the Yankees would be at a severe disadvantage; the knots of thickets would disorganize attacks against the enemy and artillery would be nearly useless. As the Confederates were more familiar with the area, they would use this knowledge to immeasurable advantage to further nullify the Federal strength in manpower and resources.

Humphreys was well aware of the many dangers that the Wilderness contained, but he was of the opinion that they might easily be surpassed. In reviewing the Mine Run campaign of the previous November, he came to the conclusion that the *Army of the Potomac* might be able to steal a march on the Southerners if it moved out at midnight. If the army could make a forced march of 30 miles in 24 hours, it might escape the danger of fighting in the Wilderness and get beyond Lee's right flank. While Humphreys' plan appeared tenable, there was one major difficulty: moving the army's *Reserve Artillery*, ambulances, thousands of beef cattle and the unwieldy sup-

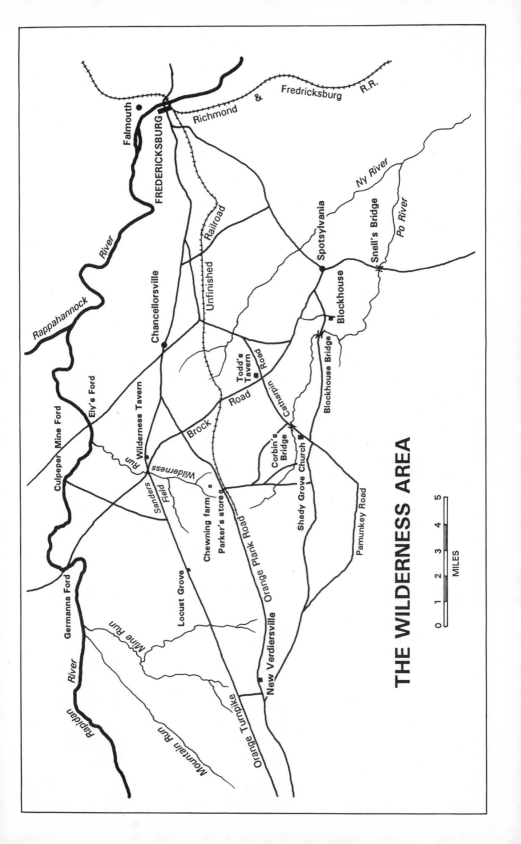

# THE WILDERNESS AREA

MILES
0 1 2 3 4 5

# The Wilderness

The Wilderness was an unlikely place to hold a battle, especially for a force on the attack. The terrain there was some of the most difficult troops on the move ever faced, with thick woods that could hide defending forces, conceal enemy movements and leave an advancing army stranded or lost in its deep reaches. Indeed, the original Union operational plan for the Wilderness campaign of May 1864 called for a swift movement through the woods to avoid a confrontation there. A day after the march of the *Army of the Potomac* began, though, Grant decided to risk an engagement with the Army of Northern Virginia there and his adversary Robert E. Lee obliged.

The Wilderness was a thick and tangled woodland of timber and underbrush cut by numerous streams and interspersed by a few clearings. The woods had originally been a hunting ground for American Indians before the white man came. The area then was cleared by settlers who tried to develop a small iron industry in the area, but the attempt failed. Without much human concern for the area, a dense growth of underbrush grew up of low-limbed pines, scrub oak, hazel and prickly vines. By 1861, the place had a haunting atmosphere, that caused one writer to say of it, "It is a region of gloom and the shadow of death."

The Wilderness contained a few human habitations of farmers, with names like Sanders, Lacy, Tapp and Chewning, who attempted to make a living in the foreboding woodland. The woods were cut for their fields and clearings. Numerous buildings also scattered about the area: the Chancellorsville house, destroyed in the battle of Chancellorsville on 1-3 May 1863, Todd's Tavern, the Wilderness Church and the Wilderness Tavern. The Wilderness Tavern was once a busy stage stop long before it became a landmark of a bloody battle. By May 1864 it was a rickety shack surrounded by weeds and brush.

Several tracks cut through the almost impenetrable woodland. The Orange Turnpike extended from the town of Orange to

ply trains of over 4,000 wagons through the Wilderness before the Confederates were on the scene. Humphreys himself noted this difficulty in his book, *Virginia Campaign of 1864 and 1865*, "There was no question of the practicability of the troops, with their fighting trains, accomplishing, this as they were quite equal to, and ready for, a continuous march of thirty miles or more in twenty-four hours, by which they would have got substantially clear of the Wilderness; they

Fredericksburg. About three miles to the south was the Orange Plank Road, so named because it was paved with wooden planks. Further to the south was the Old Fredericksburg/Catharpin Road. This broke off from the Plank Road towards the southeast and then eastward to Shady Grove Church. From there it went northeast intersecting with the Brock Road at Todd's Tavern before connecting with the Plank Road west of Fredericksburg. Roads also ran from the fords over the Rapidan south. From the Germanna Ford, the Germanna Plank Road intersected the Orange Turnpike and Plank Roads, between which it was known as the Brock Road.

The nature of the Wilderness made it an awful place to fight a battle. Attacks of both sides were difficult and confused. Union Brigadier General Alexander S. Webb wrote, "Tangled thickets of pine, scrub-oak, and cedar prevented our seeing the enemy, and prevented any one in command of a large force from determining accurately the position of troops he was ordering to and fro. The appalling rattle of musketry, the yells of our own men were constantly in our ears. At times, our lines while firing could not see the array of the enemy not 50 yards distant." A cannoneer in the First Company, Richmond Howitzers, William Dame, wrote of the battle in the woods on 5 May, "The crushing pealing thunder kept up right along, almost unbroken, hour after hour, all through the long noon and longer evening, until just before night, it slackened and died away. It was the most solemn sound I ever heard, or ever expect to hear, on earth. I never heard anything like it in any other battle. Nothing could be seen, movements of troops, in sight, to distract attention, or rivet one's interest on the varying fortunes of a battlefield...out of the dark woods, which covered all sight, rolled upward heavy clouds of battle-smoke, and outward, that earth shaking thunder, now and then fiercely sharpened by the 'rebel yell,'—as our men sprung to the death grapple."

Today portions of the Wilderness battlefield are part of the 5,900 acres of the Fredericksburg and Spotsylvania County Battlefields Memorial National Military Park.

had often made such marches when called to do so; but the question was of practicability of moving the great trains of the army that distance simultaneously with the troops so as to keep them under cover of the army."

The safety of the wagon train was to be a constant source of woe for the Federals in the upcoming campaign. In his plan, Humphreys could only guarantee that the ponderous train would still be in the act of crossing on the second day of the

*The tangled terrain of the Wilderness north of the Orange Turnpike. The thick undergrowth made infantry attacks extremely difficult and rendered artillery all but useless.*

*Architect behind the Union move through the Wilderness, Major General Andrew A. Humphreys.*

movement when the Confederates would be in the area in force. Sheridan and his troopers became victims of concern over the train. Throughout the upcoming battle they would chomp at the bit for action while most of the cavalry remained idle protecting the wagons instead of engaging the enemy.

On 2 May Humphreys issued the final plan for the first day of movements to take place on 4 May. The plans called for two columns to advance into the woodland. The westernmost group consisted of the *V Corps* followed by the *VI Corps*. Preceded by the cavalry division of Brigadier General James H. Wilson, these corps were to cross the Rapidan at Germanna Ford and follow the Germanna Plank Road to the Wilderness Tavern. To the left and east would advance another column with Chancellorsville as its destination. This body consisted of a vanguard of Brigadier David Gregg's cavalry division, the *II Corps* and the *Reserve Artillery*. Wagon trains were divided into two columns with one to cross at Ely's Ford and another farther west to cross at the Culpeper Mine Ford. Those that passed over the river on the first day would park around Dowdall's Tavern. The safety of the wagons left north of the river belonged to the cavalry division of Brigadier General Alfred T.A. Tobert. Burnside's *IX Corps* was at Warrenton in the event the *Army of the Potomac* was held up in its crossing. Once Meade's troops were across the Rapidan, the *IX Corps* would advance across Germanna Plank Ford on 5 May to cover the *Army of the Potomac's* rear.

The troops were ordered to be prepared to be on the move by 2400 on 3 May. On the third, the Federal camps were stirring with the necessary activity that preceded a march. Beleaguered orderlies could be seen riding off in various directions delivering orders and messages. Soldiers were supplied with ammunition and rations for the coming days of marching and battle. Many Yankees had pondered and were still giving a thought to what lay in store for them when they marched south once again. Edwin O. Wentworth of the *37th Massachusetts* wrote to his wife before the offensive:

> Some say we will not see much fighting here, but that the army on the Peninsula will do the work and we be kept as a feint to its movements. I do not have much faith in such reports. I guess our corps will have as much fighting as we will care about. But I have strong hopes the coming campaign may close the rebellion. If it does not do so wholly, I think it will decide it in our favor and not leave much fighting for another year. For my part, as much as I dislike to see a battle, I want to have the work go on. I know there has got to be just so much done; and, as it is a disagreeable task, I want to get through with it as speedily as possible. I hope we may strike the rebellion at the heart of the coming summer. I believe we will be in Richmond ere long; and when *we have that you may safely calculate the war is near over.* But it would probably cost thousands of lives.

It would cost Wentworth's life, he would be killed at the battle of Spotsylvania, his skull shattered by an enemy bullet.

Pennsylvanian Harold C. George later wrote of his feelings before the march:

> The main of the Army of the Potomac had been inactive in camp for a long time, and the breaking of the winter's camps, and the beginning of a march toward the Rapidan was of itself sufficient to cause ones pulse to get a more rapid "move on."
> Everyone knew too that going in that direction that they would not see the rising or setting of the sun often before it

*Federal drummerboys beat the long roll as the* Army of the Potomac *begins its advance.*

meant a meeting with General Lee's Army. Of course we had a...larger army, under a new commander "Grant," but if the truth is told, the Army of the Potomac was never enthused much over Grant. I honestly believe our army would have been more sanguine of victory in meeting the rebel army if commanded by any of our Eastern generals, that had been in this army from the beginning, and understood both armies, and knew from experience the methods and caliber of the leader of the enemy's army. The men of the Union army firmly believed from the first, just what the next 60 days proved, viz. that Grant didn't have the least idea what he was up against.

On the night of the third, Grant characteristically smoked a cigar as he discussed the future movements of the army with his fellow officers and staff. The lieutenant general emphasized the point that Lee's army would be the objective of the campaign, more so than Richmond. However, the Federal commander left no doubt as to the importance of the Confederate capital. At one point during the evening he pointed at a wall map, passing his forefinger around the points indicating Rich-

# The Mine Run Campaign

After Gettysburg, George Gordon Meade allowed Robert E. Lee's Army of Northern Virginia to slip across the Potomac to safety. Both the *Army of the Potomac* and their Confederate enemies then entered a period of relative inactivity for three months before engaging in some ineffectual sparring before they settled down for the winter. One of these efforts was the Mine Run campaign of late November and early December.

Meade had driven Lee's forces across the Rapidan after an engagement at Rappahannock Station on 7 November and had decided to make a move against his adversary's new position. He planned to head across the river into the Wilderness and then move against Lee's right flank. The advance began on 26 November only to dete-

riorate when the lead command, the *III Corps* under the cautious Major General William H. French, acted sluggishly. This hesitancy gave Lee the time to react to the threat to his flank and make proper dispositions for its defense. Instead of finding a vulnerable line, Meade then found a strongly fortified Confederate line seven miles long facing him on the west bank of the Mine Run.

All was not yet lost for the Federals. When the *II Corps* under Gouverneur Warren arrived south of Lee's position, the general, who would later become known for his reluctance to attack, believed that he might be able to get around the Confederate position. Meade planned a major attack and Warren tried to make the maneuver on the night of 29 November. He found to

mond and Petersburg and said, "When my troops are there, Richmond is mine. Lee must either retreat or surrender."

The first troops to move out in the great offensive were the troopers of Wilson's *3rd Cavalry Division*. Wilson's division was undertaking one of the most dangerous missions of the campaign: scouting out territory which would soon contain Confederate troops feeling their way east to discern their enemy's intentions. Despite the importance of Wilson's mission and the likelihood it might be engaged, he commanded the smallest cavalry division of the *Army of the Potomac* (the larger ones were engaged primarily with guarding the army's wagon trains). It reached the Rapidan in the early morning darkness of 4 May along with wagons carrying pontoons to bridge the waterway. By 0200, the Federal cavalrymen of the

his consternation that the enemy had lengthened his fortifications. Since the attack would be without purpose, Meade canceled it and both armies faced each other waiting for the next move.

On 2 December Lee took the initiative with a plan similar to the one used at Chancellorsville. He hoped to detach a force to hit the Union forces in flank to deal them a severe defeat. However, while Meade's forces may have been slow on the offensive, they deftly pulled off a speedy retreat across the Rapidan without incident. An angry Lee remarked of this event, "I am too old to command this army. We should never have permitted those people to get away."

The Mine Run was just another unimportant affair of no major impact for either side. After the campaign, the Confederates could only wait for the *Army of the Potomac* to take up campaigning the next spring when the weather improved. However, the activities of the Mine Run did loom on planners in both armies during the Wilderness campaign of May 1864. Major General Andrew A. Humphreys of Meade's Staff, who drew up the plans for the Wilderness operation, used the Mine Run campaign as a model for movements of the *Army of the Potomac* through the Wilderness. When the Federals crossed the Rapidan on 4 May, Lee entertained the belief that the Federals might be planning a similar operation to the one they had undertaken the previous November. More importantly, the inconclusiveness of Mine Run proved the need for a fierce commander in the East who would push the *Army of the Potomac* until victory was won. That man was Ulysses S. Grant.

*3rd Indiana* were across the river scattering a picket of the 1st North Carolina Cavalry. The Southerners rode off to give warning to Ewell of the Federal activity. All of Wilson's troops were across almost five hours later and disappeared into the formidable woodland of the Wilderness. In the wake of Wilson's advance came the troops of Warren's *V Corps* bringing bridging equipment of their own. These troops began to cross at 0700. Further to the north was Sedgwick's *VI Corps* which began moving out at dawn.

Gregg's cavalry moved out later than Wilson, starting out for Ely's Ford along with their bridging equipment at 0200. The cavalry crossed the Rapidan before dawn and pushed on down the Ely's Ford Road past Chancellorsville to Aldrich's farm at the junction of the Catharpin and Orange Plank

*Troops and wagons of the* **Army of the Potomac** *cross the Rapidan at Germanna Ford. Lee's army did not contest the crossing and the Federals were able to lay pontoon bridges at Germanna and Ely's Fords early in the morning of 4 May 1864.*

Roads. From there Gregg dispatched feelers in all directions: to the southwest towards Shady Grove Church, south to Spotsylvania Court House, and east to Hamilton's Crossing. Hancock reported the arrival of the *II Corps* at Ely's Ford at 0630 as he followed Gregg's path south. The troops began to cross as more bridges were thrown across the river to accommodate the mighty advance.

The march of the thousands of troops in the powerful Federal columns was an awe inspiring sight. One soldier likened the vast lines of men to a "prodigious serpent." Though the Yankees were moving out in spring weather, the dust and heat of the march combined to make the long trek an uncomfortable one. The historian of the *88th Pennsylvania* remarked, "...the men were constantly enveloped in a stifling cloud of dust that covered them from head to foot, causing them to resemble gray-backs rather than honest blue coats." It wasn't long before soldiers began to shed some of their gear to lighten their burdensome loads. One soldier remarked, "The beginning of this campaign was like all those which had preceded it; and thousands of overcoats and blankets were scattered in the woods and fields through which the soldiers passed." The rookie troops were especially guilty of this wasteful practice. They started out with so many objects believed to be essential, only to dispense with the once cherished possessions as the march grew difficult. Grant was surprised by the wastefulness and called it "...an improvidence I had never witnessed before."

The Confederates had been aware that something might be up even before the *Army of the Potomac*'s march had begun. On 2 May, an unusual amount of dust in the air had been spotted proving that the Federals might soon be on the move. On the night of 3-4 May, sentinels at Clark Mountain peered through the darkness to discover shadows of the enemy moving in front of their flickering camp fires. Though motion could be seen, there was no way of telling where Grant's troops might be going. The news was soon reported to Lee.

By 0500, the morning fog cleared to lift the veil masking the Federal troops marching to the Rapidan fords on their trek around the Confederate right. The discovery was hurriedly flagged to Ewell's camp and then passed on to army headquarters. Lee responded by dispatching two of Hill's divisions east down the Orange Plank Road sometime shortly after 0900 with a detachment of cavalry preceding them. The remaining division under George T. Anderson was left at Rapidan Heights to guard the rear. Ewell, less Brigadier

*Confederate troops of the Army of Northern Virginia. Though they suffered through a long winter of deprivation, soldiers such as these performed admirably in the field during the Wilderness campaign.*

General Stephen D. Ramseur's brigade sent across the Rapidan to investigate the situation north of the river, was on the Orange Turnpike heading east towards Locust Grove at 1200. Instructions were sent to First Corps headquarters at Mechanicsville ordering Longstreet to join the rest of the army. Able to decode the messages from a signal station at Clark Mountain, the Federals were soon aware that the enemy was bestirred.

Now aware that the Yankees were finally engaged in an offensive, Lee had to determine the intentions of his newest adversary. This was a perplexing problem since the enemy could be involved in one of several possible operations: a move against the Old Mine Run entrenchments west of the Wilderness, a push east towards Fredericksburg, or perhaps a run south for open country. Despite cavalry probes on the scene of the enemy advance, Lee could not be certain which course Grant had embraced. At 1030, Longstreet communicated to Lee his beliefs about Grant's intentions, arguing the enemy's plan might be to lure the Confederates east towards Fredericksburg with the *Army of the Potomac* while Butler's army placed itself in an advantageous position in the Army of Northern Virginia's right or rear. Originally, Lee had planned for Longstreet's First Corps to follow Hill's line of march, but "Old Pete" suggested a change to meet the contingency he suggested. He proposed his advance to take a route farther to the south on the Old Fredericksburg-Catharpin Road and then head north on the Brock Road. This would protect the Confederate flank if Butler became a threat and also alleviate the amount of troops on the Orange Plank Road which Hill was using. By 1600 Longstreet's troops were finally on the move—they were some 40 miles away from the rest of the army and would not be available for some time. If Grant turned and faced Lee with vigor, the absence of one full corps from the Army of Northern Virginia could prove disastrous.

Before the march, Confederate soldiers quickly prepared their affairs for the first major campaign of 1864. The many responsibilities and arrangements attendant with the order to break camp were performed quickly as South Carolinian J.F.C. Caldwell related, "In pursuance of a previous order, the officers' tents were torn down and cut up for distribution among the men. Knapsacks were packed, blankets rolled up, half-cooked dough or raw meal thrust into haversacks, the accumulated plunder of nine months thrown into the streets, accoutrements girded on, and in a half an hour we were on the march." Men had been ordered to have cooked three days of rations, but many soldiers improvidently chose to enjoy their prepared provisions all at once and rely on fortune for future meals. The troops themselves were in fighting trim despite the privations of winter, their meager belongings rolled up in blankets with the ends tied together and hung from left shoulders and under right arms. One member of the army claimed that his comrades could pack up their things within two minutes and live with all their possessions carried on their backs.

On the morning of the fourth, the *3rd Division* of the *Cavalry Corps* of the *Army of the Potomac* under Wilson advanced down the Germanna Plank Road to halt at the Wilderness Tavern near the intersection with the Orange Turnpike. Once there Wilson sent out some troopers down the Orange Turnpike towards Locust Grove to feel for the enemy advance sure to be coming. It wasn't long before the staccato shots of carbine fire revealed contact with the enemy: Stuart's cavalry men, in fact, on a reconnaissance mission of their own. The eyes and ears of Lee's army were in the vicinity. A Federal detachment sent south to the Brock Road also uncovered enemy troopers.

Once infantry of Brigadier General Charles Griffin's division arrived at the Wilderness Tavern, Wilson was free to take up his advance once more by proceeding further south down a wagon track towards Parker's Store on the Orange Plank Road. When Wilson reached this destination around 1400, probes were sent south towards the Catharpin and Pamunkey roads and west down the Orange Plank Road towards Mine Run. Wilson and his troops then spent the night of 4 May at Parker's Store and took up the advance the next day.

Meanwhile, the infantry of Warren's *V Corps* reached their objective for the day and went into bivouac positions. At about the time Wilson arrived at Parker's Store, Griffin's troops advanced west down the Orange Turnpike before halting and throwing out pickets. Brigadier General Samuel Crawford's *3rd Division*, the *Pennsylvania Reserve Division*, followed Wilson's path south for a short distance before halting for the day on the fields of a farm carved out of the rough terrain. Warren's other two divisions under Brigadier General James S. Wadsworth and Brigadier General John C. Robinson went into camp nearby. By 1505, the commander of the *V Corps* reported his men were in camp "washing their feet." The *VI Corps* encamped in the wake of Warren's advance, two-and-a-half miles to the northwest of the Wilderness Tavern near the Flat Run. The *3rd Division* under Brigadier General James Ricketts crossed the Rapidan around 1800 and remained near the Germanna Ford to guard the crossing until the *IX Corps* came up the next day.

The *II Corps* had the misfortune of camping on the haunted battleground of the battle that had taken place in the Wilderness a year previous. By 1500, the corps was in position around the remains of what once was the Chancellorsville mansion. Somber reflection plagued many soldiers as they passed over the old entrenchments, forgotten impedimenta and, worst of all, bleached bones uncovered from their hasty burial by time and weather. One soldier recalled, "The numerous breastworks that were thrown up by both armies to hold their positions, the shattered oaks and the splintered limbs, and fragments of weather-stained clothing and equipments reminded men of that sanguinary struggle. Many of the Union dead had been exhumed, or remained unburied; jaws arms, and legs were bleaching upon the soil; and the wasps and moles made their nests in some of the skulls." For some troops it was even possible to find the remains of a fallen comrade. Members of the *11th New Jersey* stumbled on a skull broken by a minie ball or shell. It still wore the cap once worn by a living soldier. An examination under the visor revealed the stamped name of Sergeant Daniel Bender of *Company H* of the same regiment.

Grant and Meade crossed the Rapidan sometime around 1200 to establish his headquarters in a decaying farmhouse overlooking the Germanna Ford. Meade set up his center for operations in the area and by 1300 had been informed of Confederate cavalry activity south of Fredericksburg. He responded by ordering Tobert's division south of the river for the next day to join Gregg in protecting the wagons and guarding against any threat on the Federal left.

Grant sat down on the steps of his new headquarters to watch Sedgwick's ranks tramp across the Rapidan bridge in the early afternoon sun. Pleased with the way events were

*The ruins of the Chancel-lorsville house. Once a fine brick hotel, it served as Hooker's headquarters in the battle of Chancel-lorsville. It burned down during the fight, but was still a landmark for the Wilderness campaign.*

passing he lit a cigar and after a few moments of silence said, "Well, the movement so far has been as satisfactory as could be desired. We have succeeded in seizing the fords and crossing the river without delay. Lee must by this time know upon what roads we are advancing, but he may not yet realize the full extent of the movement. We shall probably soon get some indications as to what he might do." A newspaper reporter then stepped forward to ask, "General Grant, about how long will it take you to get to Richmond?" The general in chief jubilantly replied, "I will agree to be there in about four days—that is, if General Lee becomes party to the agreement; but if he objects, the trip will undoubtedly be prolonged."

By 1300, Grant was informed of the contents of a decoded Confederate message from Clark Mountain telling of the Federal movement. Lee's command was probably already on the move. Grant was excited by the news and exclaimed, "That gives me the information I wanted. It shows that Lee is drawing out from his position, and is pushing across to meet us." He then requested writing paper which he placed on a

*Bleached bones and skulls, remnants of the battle of Chancellors-*
*ville. Soldiers who camped in the Wilderness in 1864 found such*
*discomforting sights from the battle of the previous year.*

book laid out on his knee to write a message to Burnside
ordering his troops up to relieve Ricketts' division upon their
arrival at the Germanna Ford. It read, "Make forced marches
until you reach this place. Start your troops now in the rear
the moment they can be got off, and require them to make a
night march." At 1350, Halleck received information from
Grant on his progress, "The crossing of the Rapidan is
effected. Forty-eight hours now will demonstrate whether the
enemy intends giving battle this side of Richmond."

Grant did not have much reason to feel at ease. His troops
were still in the Wilderness where Lee could bring on a
general engagement to his advantage. While the Federals
were only five miles from more advantageous positions that

*The victor of Gettysburg and commander of the* **Army of the Potomac,** *Major General George Gordon Meade. Throughout the Wilderness and subsequent campaigns Meade was handicapped by an awkward command structure, but nevertheless continued to be an effective leader.*

would easily allow them to march out of the Wilderness on the second day of the movement, the necessity to keep the multitudes of supply wagons close by forced the army to halt before better objectives could be reached. Of some consolation was the fact that the troops would be fresher from the early halt if the enemy forced a contest the next day.

To strengthen the resolve of his troops, Meade issued a declaration telling them what was at stake and what was needed to attain victory:

> Soldiers: Again you are called upon to advance on the enemies of your country. The time and occasion are deemed opportune by your commanding general to address you a few words of confidence and caution. You have been reorganized, strengthened, and fully equipped in every respect. You form a part of the several armies of your country, the whole under the direction of an able and distinguished general, who enjoys the confidence of the Government, the people, and the army. Your movement being in co-operation with others, it is of the utmost importance that no effort should be left unspared to make it successful. Soldiers! the eyes of the whole country are looking with anxious hope to the blow you are about to strike in the most sacred cause that ever called men to arms.
>
> Remember your homes, your wives and children, and bear in mind that the sooner your enemies are overcome the sooner you

# George Gordon Meade

George Meade (1815-1872) was born outside the country in Cadiz, Spain, while his family was there for business. Meade graduated from West Point 19th out of 56 classmates in the class of 1835. His military experiences included engineering duties such as surveys, the construction of lighthouses and port development. His military experiences included the Seminole War and the Mexican War, in which he won a brevet rank.

Meade established himself as a competent commander early in the war. He won a brigadier generalcy of Pennsylvania volunteers and led a brigade during the battles on the Virginia Peninsula, where he was wounded at White Oak Swamp, and later at Second Bull Run. He then commanded a division in the *I Corps* at Antietam and Fredericksburg under "Fighting Joe" Hooker. Soon after the latter battle, he received a promotion to the rank of major general. He briefly commanded a grand division until the formation was discarded and then led the *V Corps* at Chancellorsville on 1 to 4 May 1863.

Dissatisfaction with Hooker paved the way for Meade to assume command of the *Army of the Potomac* just three days before its epochal confrontation with the Army of Northern Virginia at Gettysburg. When Lee learned of Meade's promotion, he supposedly said, "...Meade will commit no blunder in my front, and if I make one, he will make haste to take advantage of it." Meade led the great confrontation with tremendous competence

will be returned to enjoy the benefits and blessings of peace. Bear with patience the hardships and sacrifices you will be called upon to endure.

Have confidence in your officers and in each other. Keep your ranks on the march and on the battle-field, and let each man earnestly implore God's blessing, and endeavor by his thoughts and actions to render himself worthy of the favor he seeks. With clear consciences and strong arms, actuated by a sense of duty, fighting to preserve the Government and the institutions handed down to us by our forefathers—and true to ourselves—victory, under God's blessing, must and will attend our efforts.

For the moment, the *Army of the Potomac* was more concerned with advancing than battle for their generals planned to continue the march south on the fifth at 0500. Wilson's cavalry was directed to move on Craig's Meeting House while placing parties on the Orange Turnpike, Orange Plank

by fielding Lee's heavy blows, though he would be criticized for being passive during the battle and the subsequent Confederate retreat, a fact of special annoyance to the President. When Meade allowed Lee to escape across the Potomac, Lincoln exclaimed, "Your golden opportunity is gone and I am distressed immeasurably because of it." Meade offered to resign as a result, but Lincoln thought better of accepting and both he and Halleck soothed the feelings of the hot tempered general.

Meade led the *Army of the Potomac*'s ineffective campaigns during the fall and winter of 1863. In March of the next year, Grant took command of all the Federal armies. He decided to pay special attention to the *Army of the Potomac* by accompanying it during its advance against Lee and Richmond. Though

Meade still held command of the army as its last leader, he effectively shared command with Grant and carried out his orders. At Appomattox, Meade supposedly briefly met with Lee who expressed surprise at this former adversary's gray hairs. Meade responded, "I'm afraid you are the cause of most of it, sir." After the war, Meade served in various administrative posts until his death in 1872.

Meade was a superior commander of steady and constant ability. He maintained a fierce temper that became legendary among his comrades, but cared about his men, solicited advice and worked well with Grant in a difficult relationship that would have collapsed if he had proved less concerned about the Republic than his self-importance.

Road, and other routes leading from the west to guard against the Confederate advance. The *V Corps* was to march from the Wilderness Tavern to Parker's Store with its right extended to the Wilderness Tavern, the destination of the *VI Corps*. The *II Corps* would move from Chancellorsville to Shady Grove Church on the Catharpin Road by moving past Todd's Tavern. There it would extend its right west to the *V Corps*. In the rear would be the *IX Corps* and the Federal cavalry under Gregg and Tobert. The former would cross the Rapidan and take up a position between the *VI Corps* at Wilderness Tavern and the Germanna Ford. The latter would guard the wagons and be prepared for any move from the enemy cavalry at Hamilton's Crossing.

Grant and his lieutenants remained in good spirits throughout the evening in a camp which ignored the stringent rules of rank that belonged to other armies. Grant's aide Horace Porter wrote of the scene, "Perhaps no headquarters of a general in supreme command of great armies ever presented so democratic an appearance. All the officers of the staff dined at the table with their chief, and the style of the conversation was as familiar as that which occurs in the household of any private family. Nothing could have been more informal or unconventional than the manner in which the mess was conducted. The staff-officers came to the table and left it at such times as their duties permitted, sometimes lingering over a meal to indulge in conversation, at other times remaining to take only a few mouthfuls in all haste before starting out upon the lines. The chief ate less and talked less than any other member of the staff and partook only of the plainest food."

Grant, himself, retired to his spartan personal quarters before 2400. Porter described his commander's living facilities during the great campaign, "Its only furniture consisted of a portable cot made of a course canvas stretcher over a light wooden frame, a tin wash-basin which stood on an iron tripod, two folding camp-chairs, and a plain pine table. The general's baggage was limited to one small camp trunk, which contained his underclothing, toilet articles, a suit of clothes and an extra pair of boots."

To the west, the Confederates also prepared for an evening's rest. Ewell went into camp in the vicinity of Locust Grove. Heth's Division of Hill's command went into camp east of New Verdiersville while Wilcox's Division of the same corps camped to the west of the town. Lee went into camp at the Rhodes House in between both divisions. Characteristically, despite his position and place in the Southern cause, the commander refrained from commandeering the house for his personal use and had tents set up for the night. Longstreet reported to Lee that his troops had marched a distance halfway between the Army of Northern Virginia and Mechanicsville. He hoped to make for Richard's Shop on the Catharpin Road by the next day.

On the night of 4 May, Lee issued belligerent instructions to

Ewell at 2000: if Grant turned east, Ewell was to follow; if Grant turned west, Ewell was to block him. Ewell was also told, "The general's desire is to bring him [the enemy] to battle as soon as possible."

"Just the orders I like," the commander of the Second Corps said of his responsibilities for 5 May, "go straight down the road and strike the enemy wherever I find him."

# CHAPTER IV

# Grant Attacks

$B$y the morning of 5 May, Lee was confident the Federals could be defeated in a similar manner as the year before. Artillery officer Brigadier General Armistead L. Long described Lee's mood that morning as jovial: "The General displayed the cheerfulness which he usually exhibited at meals, and indulged in a few pleasant jests at the expense of his staff officers, as was his custom on such occasions. In the course of the conversation that attended the meal he expressed himself surprised that his new adversary had placed himself in the same predicament as 'Fighting Joe' had done the previous spring. He hoped the result would be even more disastrous to Grant than that which Hooker had experienced. He was, indeed, in the best of spirits, and expressed much confidence in the result—a confidence which was well founded, for there was much reason to believe that his antagonist would be at his mercy while entangled in these pathless and entangled thickets, in whose intricacies disparity of numbers lost much of its importance."

While Lee's forces were closing on the enemy several miles away, he had become wary of engaging in an all out confrontation just yet. His forces were heavily outnumbered and Longstreet still had a formidable distance to cover before he would be close enough to support the two other corps of the Army of Northern Virginia. Lee revised his hostile plan in favor of using the Second and Third Corps of his army, along with Stuart's cavalry, to get into a position to observe Federal movements and divine their plans. When Longstreet's forces finally came up, his command would be used as a flanking force to roll up the Federal left. Other commands such as Anderson's Division of Hill's Corps and Stuart's cavalry might be able to assist "Old Pete" in this operation.

Confederate forces spent the morning concentrating and moving towards the as-of-yet unsuspecting *Army of the Potomac*. Cavalry units were heading towards Shady Grove Church to the southwest of the enemy columns while Fitzhugh Lee's troopers were riding west from Fredericksburg towards Spotsylvania. Ewell took up his advance once more heading eastward down the Orange Turnpike, feeling cautiously for the presence of the enemy. To the south on the Orange Plank Road marched A.P. Hill's divisions preceded by elements of Stuart's cavalry. When these Confederates passed by the old entrenchments from the Mine Run campaign on their march, they knew then they were not going to await the Federals behind fieldworks, and a full scale engagement awaited them further up the road. To the west was Anderson's Division of Hill's men moving on the Plank Road. Its mission of guarding the Confederate rear had been fulfilled and it now rushed to join the rest of Hill's command. Longstreet's troops were across the North Anna River that morning on their trek to Richard's Shop on the Old Fredericksburg/Catharpin Road. Another detached force, R.D. Johnston's brigade was on its way from Hanover Junction and was half the distance of its 66-mile journey to join the rest of the army.

One of the first encounters of the future fight took place sometime before 0600. The lead brigade of Ewell's Corps, under Brigadier General John M. Jones, ran into pickets of Griffin's division of the *V Corps* in the vicinity of the Wilderness Tavern. Jones fell back two miles after the contact to the junction of the Orange Turnpike and the Culpeper Mine Road. Lee received the report of Ewell's contact with the enemy on the Orange Turnpike at 0900. When the Confederate general found himself faced with the unhappy prospect of engaging the enemy with an almost three mile gap of Wilderness terrain between his forces on the Orange Turnpike and the Orange Plank Road, he issued cautious instructions to Ewell ordering him to keep pace with Hill.

Meanwhile, Grant was cheerfully confident of the successes of the first day of the offensive. Events soon went awry however, evaporating any optimism for an easy campaign, primarily because Brigadier General Wilson had failed to provide a proper screen for the rest of the army. Wilson's cavalry division left its bivouac at Parker's Store around 0500 to head down a path leading to the Catharpin Road. Inexplicably and in direct disregard of his instructions, he left no troops on the Orange Turnpike and only had the *5th New York Cavalry* under Lieutenant Colonel John Hammond remain on the Orange Plank Road near Parker's Store. While the two main avenues of the Confederate advance were improperly guarded, the rest of the division rode south and ended up completely missing the enemy advance, allowing the infantry to discover for themselves that the Confederates were on the scene. At the same time, Wilson's cavalry managed to get into a pointless running fight with enemy troopers on the Catharpin Road.

The *V Corps* took up its advance that morning with extreme caution. The troops slowly advanced on the right of the road, the direction from which the enemy would come, while the wagons moved down the left side. The troops were closed up and told to be ready for battle. In the lead was *3rd Division*, followed by Brigadier General Wadsworth's *4th Division* and Brigadier General Robinson's *2nd Division*. In the rear was Griffin's *1st Division*. In the tracks of the *V Corps* was the *VI Corps* under "Uncle John" Sedgwick with Brigadier General George W. Getty's *2nd Division* in the lead, followed by Brigadier Horatio G. Wright's *1st Division*. The troops of these units were moving towards the Wilderness Tavern. The remaining *3rd Division*, under Ricketts' command was still guarding the Germanna Ford awaiting Burnside. Around 0500, the *II Corps* began to organize and before 0730 Hancock's troops left the area of the ruins of the Chancellorsville mansion to follow a track leading southwest to Todd's Tavern.

*Major General Gou-*
*verneur K. Warren led*
*the outbreak of hostili-*
*ties in the Wilderness by*
*engaging the Confeder-*
*ates on the Orange Turn-*
*pike. Warren was known*
*to be slow, reluctant to*
*attack, and had a pen-*
*chant for giving un-*
*wanted advice.*

The Federal movement was thrown into confusion a few hours after it began by the sudden appearance of Confederates of John M. Jones' brigade before 0600. Colonel D.T. Jenkins reported the fact to *V Corps* headquarters in a dispatch which read:

> The rebel infantry have appeared on the Orange Court-House turnpike and are forming a line of battle, three quarters of a mile in front of General Griffin's line of battle. I have my skirmishers out, and preparations are being made to meet them. There is a large cloud of dust in that direction.

Warren was shocked when this information was reported to him as ordnance officer Morris Schaff recalled, "I do not believe that Warren ever had a greater surprise in his life, but his thin solemn, darkly shallow face was nowhere lightened by even a transitory glare." The general halted his command to dispatch a reconnaissance mission, ordering Griffin at 0620 to send troops to the west to find out what the enemy was up to. By 0700 Griffin gave orders to the commander of his *3rd Brigade*, Joseph J. Bartlett, to launch the probe. Two regiments, the *18th Massachusetts* and the *83rd Pennsylvania*, encountered Ewell's Confederates in force. In the course of the skirmish-

# Gouverneur K. Warren

Gouverneur K. Warren (1830-1882) saw his star rise during the Civil War and then tragically crash before its conclusion. Born in Cold Spring, New York, Warren graduated from West Point in 1850 to serve in the engineers and as an instructor of mathematics at West Point.

Warren commanded troops early in the war, starting out as a lieutenant colonel of the *5th New York* which he led at the disaster at Big Bethel on 10 June 1861. During the Peninsula campaign almost a year later, he had attained command of a brigade in the *V Corps*. Warren saw action at Second Bull Run, Antietam and Fredericksburg and was promoted to brigadier general. During the spring of 1863, Warren won an appointment to the staff of the *Army of the Potomac* and the post of chief engineer. Warren's claim to fame came the second day of the battle of Gettysburg on 2 July 1863 when he became aware of the significance of Little Round Top and organized a defense of the height, an act credited with saving the *Army of the Potomac* from severe defeat during that epic battle.

After Gettysburg, Warren, now a major general, took command of troops once more, this time at the helm of the *II Corps*. Warren participated in the Mine Run campaign during the winter of 1863 and recognized a strengthened Confederate line which caused Meade to call off an otherwise costly assault. The commander of the *V Corps* during Grant's offensive for Richmond, Warren's service was not always exemplary. He was known to be overly cautious at times with a penchant for giving unwanted advice to his fellow generals and superiors. Grant gave Major General Philip Sheridan permission to relieve Warren during the battle of Five Forks on 1 April 1865 and Warren's mistakes during the battle caused Sheridan to exercise his right to do so. All of a sudden the corps commander's career was in ruins.

After the war, Warren served in a few posts, but was primarily interested in having his name cleared of dishonor. Fourteen years after the fact a court of inquiry was set up to deliberate the matter and met for two years with such distinguished witnesses as Grant, Sheridan and Confederate Fitzhugh Lee. Warren won his final battle too late—he died an embittered man on 8 August 1882 while the court's findings clearing his name were not published until several months later.

ing, Charles A. Wilson, an anonymous soldier like so many who fell during the war, won the cruel distinction of being the first death in a battle that would soon result in thousands of casualties.

The leadership of the *Army of the Potomac* soon learned of the discovery of the enemy, who had arrived on the field many hours before they were expected. Meade received the news at 0715 as he headed to the Wilderness Tavern from Germanna Ford. He proceeded to *V Corps* headquarters where he confirmed Warren's decision to halt, ordered him to launch an attack, and also sent a dispatch for the *II Corps* to halt at Todd's Tavern. After this flurry of activity, Meade notified Grant of his intentions:

> The enemy have appeared in force on the Orange Pike, and are now reported forming line of battle in front of Griffin's divison, Fifth Corps. I have directed General Warren to attack them at once with his whole force. Until this movement of the enemy is developed, the march of the corps must be suspended. I have, therefore, sent word to Hancock not to advance beyond Todd's Tavern for the present. I think the enemy is trying to delay our movement, and will not give battle but we shall soon see. For the present I will stop here, and have stopped our trains.

In the moments after the discovery of Ewell's Confederates, Meade had discarded the primary Union plan and adopted a course which he, Grant, and the rest of the Federal leadership had labored so hard to avoid, a confrontation in the Wilderness. Once Grant was informed of Meade's intentions, he heartily approved of them, sending the following dispatch from his headquarters at the Germanna Ford,

> Your note giving the movements of the enemy and your dispositions received. Burnside's advance is now crossing the river. I will have Ricketts relieved and advanced at once, and urge Burnside's crossing. As soon as I can see Burnside I will go forward. If any opportunity presents itself for pitching into a part of Lee's army, do so without giving time for disposition.

Grant evidently had also lost whatever qualms he had about pursuing a fight in the Wilderness.

The three Federal corps now spent a large amount of time trying to adjust to the new situation. Warren attempted to close up the rest of his divisions with Griffin's left in preparation for the attack. The *VI Corps* was not immediately affected by the change in plans and thus continued its march south towards the Wilderness Tavern. The *II Corps* had moved a

*The Wilderness Tavern, the site of the Federal headquarters during the battle in the Wilderness.*

short distance beyond Todd's Tavern when it received Meade's orders to halt around 0900. Pickets were thrown out while the rest of the men stacked arms and boiled coffee.

The immense difficulties that would be faced in the ensuing battle were quickly beginning to irritate Gouverneur Warren as he tried to organize the attack of his troops down the Orange Turnpike. He attempted to build a line perpendicular to the road, causing him to force his divisions to come up on Griffin's left through the Wilderness terrain. The ranks had to contend with dense thickets, rolling streams, and marshy ground. Axes and hatchets were used to cut paths through the almost impenetrable brush, but only Wadsworth's division was able to get close enough to Griffin's flank to assist that command in an attack. Warren had urged Wadsworth on by pointing into the thick woods and saying, "Find out what is in there." Robinson's division was unable to make it to the developing line in time and thus was put in reserve.

Crawford's division provided Warren with an even more serious difficulty. Brigadier Samuel Crawford himself was a proven fighting commander. A member of the Fort Sumter garrison, this surgeon turned commander had shown himself a leader on the fields of Cedar Mountain and Antietam. On the first day of the battle of the Wilderness, he found himself

*Major General Jeb Stuart at the head of his fine cavalry. Stuart's command spent the Wilderness campaign sparring with Federal troopers and came close to annihilating Wilson's 3rd Cavalry Division on 5 May. Stuart would be mortally wounded at Yellow Tavern less than a week later.*

on the horns of a dilemma. Around 0800, the Pennsylvanians of the *3rd Division* had advanced to the Chewning farm on a high plateau close to the Orange Plank Road and a mile to the northeast of Parker's Store. Once there, Crawford could hear cavalry fighting in the distance. It soon proved to be more than just a skirmish for, as matters were coming to a head near the Wilderness Tavern, a battle was brewing to the south as well. Cavalry commander Wilson reached the Catharpin Road near Craig's Meeting House at 0800. A probe sent to the west soon revealed Confederate cavalry and a full blown battle then developed around the meeting house as the Federals engaged the enemy with their seven-shot Spencer repeating carbines. Stuart heard the firing as well and left Hill's advance to join the battle with even more Confederate troopers.

While Wilson joined the Confederates in battle around Craig's Meeting House, Hammond's *5th New York Cavalry*

# Spencer Carbine

The Civil War saw the introduction of repeating rifles to warfare. Though a muzzleloading singleshot musket was most likely to be used by a soldier on either side from the beginning to the end of the war, hundreds of thousands of breechloading repeating rifles and carbines were procured and handed out to the ranks. Of the latter, one of the most prominent was the Spencer carbine which proved a handy instrument to cavalry troops fighting in the Wilderness campaign.

The Spencer carbine was patented almost a year before the Civil War on 6 March 1860 by Christopher M. Spencer. It became the first repeating firearm regularly issued to troops in the field. Throughout the war 100,000 39-inch Spencers were issued, thousands of others were purchased by individuals and 12,000 of a longer 47-inch rifle version were passed out to troops.

The Spencer could fire seven cartridges kept in a tubelike magazine which fitted into the butt of the gun. These bullets were attached to copper casings which contained the powder. The charge was ignited when the hammer of the gun struck and set off the mercury fulminate

charge on the rim of the cartridge. This was a definite improvement over the paper cartridges and the percussion cap used to fire the common musket and muzzleloaders of the time.

To load and fire the gun, the trigger guard acted as a lever which if pulled down ejected an expended shell by lowering the breech block. When the trigger guard was pulled back up another round was fed into the firing chamber by a spring in the magazine. The trigger was manually cocked. An experienced soldier was said to be able to get 20 shots off in a minute, 10 times the rate of fire for a man using the more common Springfield muzzleloading musket.

The Spencer found the most use with the cavalry arm of the Union army. In 1863, it began to be found in the hands of Union troopers, giving them a technical and firepower edge over their Confederate foes. In addition, the Spencer also gave the Yankee cavalrymen the ability to take on infantry. This was in evidence when Lieutenant Colonel John D. Hammond and his *5th New York Cavalry* delayed the advance of an entire brigade of Confederate infantry.

enjoyed a rather uncomfortable surprise. Hill's leading unit, Brigadier General William W. Kirkland's brigade, ran into the New York troopers. Hammond deployed his men to meet the Confederate advance as Kirkland's North Carolinians attempted to force their way eastward. The Federals' Spencer carbines belied their strength as the troopers peppered away at the advancing ranks of Confederates. Their annoying fire was enough to force Kirkland to send men through the thick brush on either side of the road to touch the flank of the enemy regiment. Hammond's men held as best they could under this pressure, but were slowly forced to fall back. Still their tenacious defense was enough to convince the Confederates that they were up against a full Federal brigade.

Crawford realized that with fighting to the south near Parker's Store, the heights of the Chewning plateau, dominating a large area including the Orange Plank Road, would prove invaluable. He thus decided to deploy his division until he could learn more about the situation on the Orange Plank Road and informed army headquarters of his decision, "I have advanced to within a mile of Parker's Store. There is brisk skirmishing at the Store between our own and the enemy's cavalry. The general's order is received and I am halted in good position." The dispatch arrived at *V Corps* headquarters, but Warren was out. When Meade finally learned of Crawford's dispatch around 0915, he gave orders for Wilson to investigate, evidently ignorant of the fact that his cavalry division was heavily engaged. This lack of any serious concern over the news of Confederate forces on the Orange Plank Road seems almost inexplicable. Both the *II Corps* and Wilson's cavalry division were south of the road and both could easily be cut off if the Hill's troops were able to push aggressively east.

Victims of the Federal indifference to their plight, Hammond's *5th New York* was continually pushed back, allowing Kirkland's troops to reach Parker's Store. Crawford's probes in that direction revealed Confederates feeling his own positions. At 0915 Crawford reported in a dispatch which reached Meade's headquarters an hour later, "The enemy are working around to get upon the plank road. No firing at this moment." At about the same time, reports were being received of enemy troopers on the Culpeper Mine Road to the north. It ominously appeared as though the enemy was on both flanks of the *Army of the Potomac*.

Eager to have Crawford join the contest that would take place on the Orange Turnpike, Warren sent Major Washington Roebling of his staff to press for that division's move north. When Roebling joined Crawford, he too realized the seriousness of the situation on the Orange Plank Road and agreed with Crawford's decision to hold the plateau. Both Roebling and Crawford petitioned Warren to hold the Chewning farm, with Warren's aide writing his commander, "It is of vital importance to hold the field where General Crawford is. Our whole line of battle is turned if the enemy get possession of it. There is a gap of half a mile between Wadsworth and Crawford. He cannot hold the line against an attack." At 1115, Warren received this query from Brigadier Crawford, "Shall I abandon the position I now hold to connect with General Wadsworth, who is about a half a mile on my right; he having moved up to connect with Griffin." Warren had become famous for his realization of the vital importance of Little Round Top at Gettysburg. Here in the woods of the Wilderness, Warren was more preoccupied with his own advance down the turnpike, not the necessity to divert his attention to a far away landmark despite its importance. He dismissed Crawford's concerns by ordering the division commander to give up the position and head north to participate in the coming attack. The brigadier general reluctantly obeyed and at 1200 reported with an ominous dispatch, "The connection with Wadsworth is being made. The enemy hold the Plank Road and are passing up."

As the tension in the Wilderness began to swell for both sides, Grant decided to take a much more firm grip on matters once he entered the Wilderness to join Meade. By 0840 he had tired of waiting for Major General Burnside to come up and headed off to the headquarters of the *Army of the Potomac*. He left instructions for the *IX Corps* to leave a division to cover the crossing and move forward the rest of his troops in the wake of Sedgwick's advance. Grant met with Meade near the Wilderness Tavern around 1000. The situation he found there was almost disastrous. Warren's offensive against the Rebel force on the turnpike was held up for some three hours and

*After giving orders to launch an all-out attack in the Wilderness, Grant whittled on a stick while awaiting the fruits of his decision.*

would take much more time before it was completely ready; enemy forces appeared to be on both flanks of the army; and they might even be using their knowledge of the web of trails through the Wilderness to launch an attack on either flank to wreak terrible havoc. Unwilling to hand Lee the initiative for such a move, Grant ordered the only division ready to attack, Griffin's, to make his assault immediately without proper support. Wright's division of the *VI Corps* was commanded to join the attack by moving down the Culpeper Mine Road to link up with Griffin's right. Getty's division, which had reached the Wilderness Tavern, was sent to take care of the situation on the Orange Plank Road by moving south on the Brock Road. Once on the Plank Road, Getty was to advance west towards Parker's Store. Hancock was to advance north from Todd's Tavern to assist in Getty's advance. With that business taken care of Grant settled down to whittle on a stick and await the fruits of his daring movements.

Grant was now acting less the role of general in chief and more as an army commander. The fact that the *Army of the*

*Potomac* effectively had two heads caused more serious confusion in an incident involving the *3rd Division* of the *VI Corps* under Brigadier General James B. Ricketts. Grant had ordered Ricketts' forward once it was relieved when the *IX Corps* reached the Germanna Ford. When the *IX Corps* finally came up, Ricketts also had orders from Meade to hold roads leading west on the army's right flank. The general decided to hold firm until he received information resolving the conflicting orders from the two commanders of the *Army of the Potomac*. Grant cleared up the problem at 1030 by ordering Burnside's troops across the river and Ricketts' forces to be relieved and held in reserve.

As the Federals were fumbling to launch an attack, the Confederates of Hill's Corps continued to draw closer east. Despite the efforts of Hammond's troopers, Heth's Division of Hill's Corps forced them back with Brigadier General John R. Cooke's brigade of Tarheels relieving their comrades of Kirkland's command. The *2nd Division* of the *VI Corps* made its way down the Germanna Plank Road, eventually heading south on the Brock. Getty and his staff arrived at the intersection of the Brock and Plank Roads in advance of his troops just in time to find retreating elements of the *5th New York Cavalry* who reported that enemy infantry were just behind them. Though enemy troops could be seen lurking in the brush to the west, Getty boldly decided to hold the intersection with a paltry force of staff officers and orderlies until his troops came up. For a few moments the situation was palpably tense. Firing from the enemy grew in intensity as Hill's troops bore down on the small obstacle blocking their path. Had events gone differently, the Confederates would have opened the battle of the Wilderness with a captured brigadier general as a trophy. But it was not to be. The leading brigade of Getty's division arrived to throw a line across the road in advance of the enemy ranks. The Federals blasted into the woods forcing the Rebels to become more cautious. They fell back in the face of the fire as the Federals threw out skirmishers. The soldiers advanced only 30 yards before they found Rebel dead. Getty had had a close call indeed. Harold C. George in the *139th*

*The birdlike Lieutenant General Richard S. Ewell, commander of the Confederate Second Corps. Ewell managed to block Federal attacks down the Orange Turnpike on 5-6 May.*

*Pennsylvania* regiment found a North Carolina sergeant who had been killed instantly, shot through the heart. He leaned against a sapling, his rifle still in hand. An examination of his belongings revealed an unfinished letter to his wife in which he told that a battle would take place soon and many would fall.

Confederate activity on the Plank Road nearly caused cavalry commander James Wilson to lose his entire division. The attack of Hill's Corps on the *5th New York Cavalry* had cut him off from the rest of the army and by mid-day through the early afternoon, Confederate cavalry forces drove the division east from Craig's Meeting House up the Catharpin Road in an endeavor to entrap his entire force. Sheridan dispatched Gregg's division to save the endangered force and Wilson's Federal troopers rallied on these reinforcements at Todd's Tavern around 1445.

Meanwhile, the Second Corps began to set up a position on the turnpike. The hour of 1100 brought another report from

# Richard Ewell

Richard Ewell (1817-1872) was born in Georgetown in the District of Columbia before his family moved to Prince William City, Virginia. He graduated from West Point in 1840 to serve in the Dragoons. Up to 1861, most of his service was against the Indians, though he did fight in the Mexican War where he won a brevet rank of captain. He left the Army as such on 7 May 1861 and joined the Confederate forces as a colonel.

Originally a cavalry officer, Ewell was a brigadier general in command of an infantry brigade during Bull Run. He was later transferred to serve with Stonewall Jackson during his famous Shenandoah Valley campaign. Though Ewell thought his new commander insane, he eventually came to appreciate his genius. A wound at Groveton on 28 August lost Ewell a leg but won him a wife, as he fell in love with the nurse who attended him. From thence forth, Ewell's injury forced him to endure the inconvenience of having to be lifted and strapped into his saddle.

Ewell returned in May of 1863 and took command of Jackson's old corps after Stonewall's death. Ewell did not enjoy spectacular service in his new role. He led some ineffective attacks against Culp's Hill on the second and third days of Gettysburg, but performed with more competence at the Wilderness and Spotsylvania. During the latter battle he was removed from command after being injured in a hard fall from his saddle. He left combat to supervise the defense of Richmond and after the city fell, he was captured at Sayler's Creek on 6 April 1865.

Ewell was one of many Confederate commanders who found themselves promoted beyond their abilities. While excellent at the helm of a division, he was often too timid when leading a corps and too reluctant to act decisively on his own. He was known to his troops as "Old Bald Head" or "Baldy Dick."

Ewell to Lee that Federal forces were spotted moving down the Germanna Plank Road past the Wilderness Tavern—these were Getty's troops being sent south for action on the Orange Plank Road. Lee renewed his unaggressive orders calling on Ewell to continue to match Hill's movements and avoid a large confrontation. Since he was already in advance of Hill's march to the south, Ewell had his command build fortifications perpendicular to the turnpike on the west edge of a farmer's clearing called Sanders' Field. Major General Edward Allegheny Johnson's division took the Confederate left with Jones' Brigade, which had first come in contact with Warren's surprised Yankees, just south of the turnpike, and Brigadier George H. Steuart's brigade, the Stonewall Brigade under Brigadier General James A. Walker, and Brigadier General Leroy A. Stafford taking up the left flank north of the road. Major General Robert E. Rodes' division formed Ewell's right while Brigadier General Cullen A. Battle's brigade was in the rear of Jones. To Battle's right were Brigadier General George Dole's and Junius Daniel's brigades who extended the line south. Ewell's reserve included the troops of Jubal Early's command.

As mid-day approached on 5 May, the scene was set for the first major conflict of the opening phase of Grant's campaign to Richmond.

# CHAPTER V

# Battle on the Turnpike

$B$rigadier General Charles Griffin had the reputation for being an aggressive artillerist, known for getting his guns in the thick of action. His abilities won him the rank of brigadier general at the head of infantry brigades in some of the great battles of the war. Though known for his "parade-ground smartness," his troops maintained such an admiration and affection for him that, after an absence, they snatched the returning general off his horse and carried him on their shoulders. Though his pugnacity was unquestioned, Griffin harbored serious doubts about the offensive he was about to undertake. Both he and his subordinates believed they were confronted by a large number of enemy troops and if an attack was to be made they should have proper support. The leadership of the *Army of the Potomac* and the *V Corps* waved away this concern. Grant, Meade and Warren were all pressing for Griffin's assault to be made quickly even at the risk of a lack of proper assistance.

Around 1200, the troops of Griffin's division left the protective works they had thrown up earlier in the day to engage the enemy to the west down the Orange Turnpike. The ranks slowly worked their way through the thick underbrush to get into attack position. The terrain and confusion played havoc with Griffin's organization causing one whole brigade, Colonel Jacob B. Sweitzer's, to become unhinged from the rest of the command when Wadsworth's division moved to join the advance.

The Federals paused to reform when they reached Sanders'

*Fortifications of the Confederate Second Corps at the Wilderness. Though the Union V Corps managed to pierce the enemy position, the Rebels counterattacked and Federal gains were quickly erased.*

Field, an oval-shaped clearing 800 yards long and 400 yards wide, its length bisected by the turnpike. A gully cut through the field, running from the north under a bridge for the road and entering the woods to the south. Brigadier Romeyn B.

Ayres' brigade was on Griffin's right set up north of the turnpike. Brigadier Joseph Bartlett's brigade occupied the left of the division. Sweitzer's brigade went into reserve behind Bartlett while the brigades of Brigadier General Cutler, Colonel Roy Stone and Brigadier General James C. Rice of Wadsworth's division took up the left. Only one of Robinson's brigades would participate in the coming attack, the *3rd Brigade* under Colonel Andrew W. Denison, which supported Wadsworth's division. Altogether, the Federals would have over 12,200 men participating in Griffin's attack.

Around 1300 the Federals moved forward in two compact lines of blue and burnished steel of fixed bayonets. The enemy's line was vulnerable, spread thin but strengthened in the center. Though lacking in numbers, Ewell's line was actually longer than the approaching enemy's which allowed the Rebels to take advantage their unprotected flanks. Ayres' first line easily routed skirmishers out of the gully in the middle of Sanders' Field, only to face confusion when encountering the main Confederate line held by the Stonewall Brigade and Steuart's Brigade. There flanking fire on the Federal right caused Ayres' formation to fall apart. The right held by Regular troops was severely punished and suffered further woes by becoming entangled in vines and bushes. While it was brought to a halt, the left of the brigade, held by the *140th New York*, veered off to the south, crowding the Federal forces in that direction. Two guns of a New York battery were sent forward to assist the attack. Their shots plowed away through friend and foe alike, causing the disorientation of the already confusing battle to increase.

Ayres' second line advanced only to split in two like the first. The *91st* and *155th Pennsylvania* ended up with the Regulars on the right, suffering from heavy fire in the front and in the flank. After a while, the troops from the Keystone State and the Regulars fell back to the rear. The *146th New York* joined up with their comrades of the *140th New York*. Together the New Yorkers pressed onward into the woods against the Confederates, taking heavy casualties on the way. One Rebel recalled the Yankees were, "mowed down like grass before

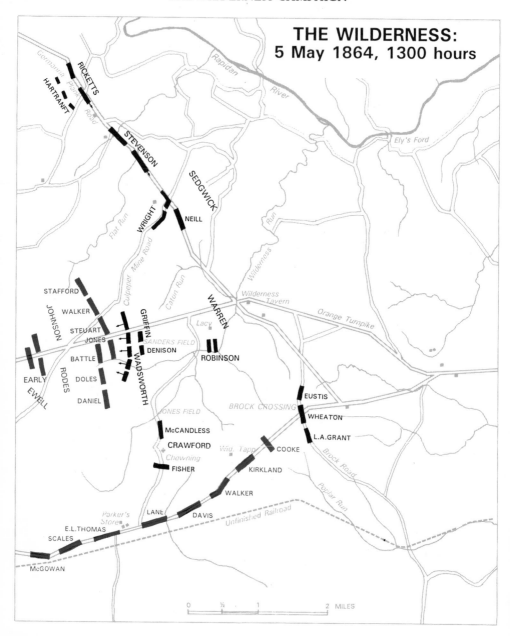

THE WILDERNESS:
5 May 1864, 1300 hours

Germanna Plank Road

RICKETTS

HARTRANFT

Rapidan River

Ely's Ford

STEVENSON

SEDGWICK

WRIGHT

NEILL

Flat Run

Culpeper Mine Road

Caton Run

Wilderness Run

STAFFORD

WALKER

JOHNSON

STEUART

JONES

GRIFFIN

BATTLE

EARLY

RODES

DOLES

WADSWORTH

DANIEL

WARREN

Lacy

Wilderness Tavern

Orange Turnpike

SANDERS FIELD

DENISON

ROBINSON

EWELL

EUSTIS

BROCK CROSSING

WHEATON

JONES FIELD

L.A.GRANT

McCANDLESS

CRAWFORD

Chewning

Wid. Tapp.

COOKE

Brock Road

FISHER

KIRKLAND

Poplar Run

WALKER

Parker's Store

LANE

DAVIS

E.L.THOMAS

SCALES

Unfinished Railroad

McGOWAN

0    ½    1    2 MILES

the sickle." But still they came on, the thick woods being marked by the smoke of battle and interspersed with the roll of the musketry and the cries of those in pain. The retreat of the rest of Ayres' men caused the New Yorkers to suffer flanking fire on the right, but their pressure caused Johnson's men to fall back as well.

Bartlett's advance was somewhat easier. The troops pressed forward coming under increasing fire as they neared the enemy. Holman Melcher of the *20th Maine*, a regiment which had distinguished itself against heavy odds at Gettysburg, likened the fire to a rain:

> We could see spurts of dust started up all over the field by the bullets of the enemy, as they spattered on it like big drops of a coming shower you have so often seen on a dusty road. But that was not the thing that troubled us. It was the dropping of our comrades from the charging line as they rushed across the fatal field with breasts bared to the terrible storm of leaden hail, and we knew that it *would* soon be our turn to run this fire.

Behind the charging ranks rode Brigadier Bartlett himself, a former attorney distinguished in his new profession by the ability to control troops in the thick of fighting; telling his men to charge forward to help their comrades already engaged. He shouted, "Come on, boys, let us go in and help them!" Cutler's command (known as the *Iron Brigade*, one of the best units in the entire Union army) assisted in Bartlett's destruction of Jones. Together, both Union commands broke a hole in the enemy line by pressing up against Jones' Brigade, mangling it and sending it into retreat, its commander killed during the fight. Throughout most of the war, Jones had been a staff officer to some of the best known generals of the South including Jubal Early, Richard Ewell and the indomitable Stonewall Jackson. He eventually came into the command of troops and did quite well. Division commander Ewell later called his loss irreparable. Also a casualty during Bartlett's attack was Jubal Early's son, Captain Richard W. Early, who was serving as an aide to Jones. When Jones' command broke apart, its supporting brigade under Cullen Battle was thrown into confusion by the enemy attack and the rush of Confeder-

*A Confederate line of battle in the Wilderness.*

ates running from the front. The command offered a token resistance before they too ran for the rear.

With the Confederate line collapsing both Cutler and Bartlett pressed on into the smoke-filled woods west of Sanders' Field. As they advanced destructive confusion mounted. Bartlett's brigade continued to push forward as the forces on its flanks either gave way or were stalled. As recounted earlier, most of Ayres' brigade holding the Federal right had melted away. On Bartlett's left, Cutler's *Iron Brigade* was stalled by a brush with Confederates of Dole's Brigade and another of Wadsworth's brigades under Stone became swamped in a marsh near a small stream. Meanwhile Rice's brigade on the southern flank veered somewhat to the northwest, allowing its flank to become a target for Daniel's North Carolinians. Bartlett soon found Confederates on either flank and his situation untenable. After tasting an ephemeral victory, his troops began to break for the rear and safety. Part of the *20th Maine* found itself almost trapped as the enemy began to curl around Bartlett's flanks and get into his rear. They were only saved by a bayonet charge in the direction of their retreat. Bartlett himself bravely rode among his troops.

In Sanders' Field, he miraculously eluded death when his horse was hit by fire as it attempted to jump the gully. The animal flipped in the air, falling on the general who managed to escape unharmed.

After the Union breakthrough, Ewell rode west in great haste to get reinforcements to restore the integrity to his line. He first came upon Brigadier John B. Gordon's brigade of Early's Division which had been held in reserve. Gordon recorded in his memoirs his meeting with Ewell as the situation began to worsen for the Confederates:

> The repulse had been so sudden and the confusion so great that practically no resistance was being made to the Union advance; and the elated Federals were so near me that little time was left to bring my men from column into line in order to resist or repel it by countercharge. At this moment of dire extremity I saw General Ewell who was still a superb horseman, notwithstanding the loss of his leg, riding in furious gallop towards me, his thoroughbred charger bounding like a deer through the dense underbrush. With a quick jerk of his bridle-rein just as his wooden leg was about to come into unwelcome collision with my knee, he checked his horse and rapped out his words with characteristic impetuosity.

Gordon's Brigade formed up at a right angle to the south of the road and pushed forward. The brigade had the good fortune to march right into a gap between Cutler and Rice. Once there, Gordon divided his forces to take advantage of his position. One regiment turned north to roll up Cutler's flank; three others turned south to wreck the right of the rest of Wadsworth's command, and the remaining two were left in front. The attack exploded Wadsworth's line into a total retreat. Stone's Federals, still floundering in a swamp were routed and sent fleeing for the rear. This left Rice's right uncovered and also subject to a flanking attack. In danger of being encircled, it too melted away. Cutler's position became untenable due to the rout to its left as well as the loss of contact with Bartlett on its right. As Confederates could soon be seen dangerously threatening both open flanks, the brave *Iron Brigade* joined in the ignominious retreat.

The troops of the *Iron Brigade* passed through the ranks of some Unionist Marylanders of Denison's brigade in the rear.

Despite the sight of one of the most elite units in the *Army of the Potomac* in flight, the soldiers from the Free State held their ground. The oncoming ranks of Confederates were blocked by this opposition, but they began to touch the flanks of the command sending it slowly back as well.

With both Griffin's and Wadsworth's divisions thrown off the field, the *140th* and *146th New York* also found themselves in a dire predicament. Their flanks were under heavy attack from the Confederates who were even getting into the rear of the Federal regiments almost unopposed. Captain H.W. Sweet, a veteran of the *146th New York*, told of the situation, "We were not only flanked but doubly flanked. We were in a bag and the strings were tied. Those of our regiment who escaped were principally from the right, where the movement of the rebels seems to have been discovered in time to make escape impossible." Unable to hold their ground, the New Yorkers joined the pell-mell flight for the rear.

Large numbers of Federals had been taken in the counter-attack. In one instance the 61st Georgia ran into the *7th Pennsylvania Reserves* which was on its way to bolster the Federal attack. Almost the entire Pennsylvania command surrendered after the Georgians fired an angry volley. In another moment during the confusion of Wadsworth's re-pulse, a colonel approached Richard A. Dempsey, a sergeant in Stone's demoralized brigade, to ask what troops he was looking at. When told it was the Rebels, the officer snorted, "Can't be," and went on to investigate. The sergeant called after him, "All right, colonel, go over, you'll find out. I've been there." Dempsey then recalled later, "...he went, and I went down to the rear, you may bet. He went down to Dixie." As most of the men in Ewell's command were involved in the pursuit, those who were slightly wounded guided prisoners to the rear. Even then, many Federals were told to follow the turnpike west until they could find authorities who could process them.

The Confederates pursued the Federals across Sanders' Field which was now carpeted with the dead and wounded. The air was choked with smoke not only from gunfire, but

*Major General Jubal Early was Ewell's most talented division commander. When Ewell was injured in a fall from his horse during the battle of Spotsylvania on 12 May 1864, Early took command of the Second Corps.*

also from dry leaves and grass set on fire during the battle. The victorious Confederates attempted to round up fearful enemy soldiers left behind from the retreat by driving them from the safety of the places where they sought cover. The 1st North Carolina took the opportunity to run for the cannons placed in the field during the Federal advance and won them from the artillerists and infantry with clubbed muskets and bayonets. Before the Tarheels could lay a full claim to their prize, a mass of retreating Federals came up in their rear forcing them to seek cover. When the North Carolinians emerged to take possession of the cannons, an Alabama brigade sought to acquire the prizes. As the Confederates attempted to settle the dispute, fire from the Federals drove them off leaving the cannons behind. During the night, the North Carolinians returned to the field to bring the pieces back into Confederate lines.

After being ravaged by Ewell's counterattack, Warren attempted to reform his battered lines. Robinson's *2nd Division* had been sent to block the Confederate offensive from pushing any farther. Most of Warren's troops involved in the attack fell back to their defensive positions of the morning. Wadsworth's men fell in on Griffin's left near the Lacy House.

Crawford's division came up to take up Warren's left while Wright's *VI Corps* division approached on the right on its way to attack the enemy left by advancing down the Culpeper Mine Road. Ewell was not interested in pressing the issue, but allowed his troops to fall back to the western edge of Sanders' Field. He countered the appearance of Wright by sending two of Early's brigades, Harry T. Hays' and John Pegram's, to his left. The Confederates then suffered through a routine of rest and responding to reports of Federal advances. After a half dozen false alarms, they approached the call to arms with less energy. In between the Confederates and Federals lay the grim sight of Sanders' Field. A Federal in the *146th New York* saw a field swept with flame burning the dead and wounded who couldn't escape. As the fires licked the bodies, filling the air with the putrid odor of burnt flesh, a comical "pop" could be heard as the contents of cartridge boxes were set off. One Confederate, McHenry Howard, recalled "...the field in our front was strewn very thickly with their fallen mingled with some who were our own. This being territory of neither party, the wounded of neither could be removed or receive attention. Several efforts were made to relieve them but the enemy opened fire whenever we exposed ourselves at the edge of the thicket and the attempts had to be abandoned." Awful scenes could also be found behind the front lines of the Federal army. On the Orange Turnpike the pathetic wounded made their way to the rear, asking over and over, "How far to the 5th Corps' hospital."

An irate General Griffin rode to Grant's headquarters at the Wilderness Tavern to vent his anger over the failure of the attack which he blamed on his superiors. There in front of the army commander, general in chief and their staff, Griffin launched into a furious tirade for not being properly supported, vociferously blaming Wright and Warren for his repulse. Shocked by the display, Grant's chief of staff Brigadier General John A. Rawlins called Griffin's behavior mutinous and demanded his arrest. Grant, who had misheard Griffin's name, asked Meade, "Who is this General Gregg? You should arrest him!" The army commander only responded, "It's Griffin not Gregg; and it's only his way of talking."

While Ewell was engaged, Lee concerned himself with attempting to plug the dangerous gap between his lines and investigating the possibility of having Hill attack down the Orange Plank Road. He had arrived at the Widow Tapp farm at 1200 and set up his headquarters for the battle there. As Lee pondered events with Hill and Stuart, one of the greatest "almosts" of the war occurred when a party of Federals stumbled on the surprised generals during their deliberations. Right then and there the anonymous group had the chance to change the war. But for some unknown reason, the timorous Federals turned out to be just as surprised as the enemy officers and, rather than engage in a fight, melted back into the woods. Quickly digesting this scare, Lee ordered Hill to send Brigadier General Cadmus Wilcox's division to extend the right of the Third Corps north to join with Ewell's command. After 1430 Wilcox's men left via the Tapp farm to take up a position at the Chewning farm.

Lee also attended to a possible offensive down the Plank Road. Between 1500 and 1600, Lee sent a staff officer to investigate if Heth could push down the path to take the intersection with the Brock Road. Heth was a sometimes impulsive commander who had brought on the fateful confrontation at Gettysburg by a rash attack against Federal troops there. He was also supposedly one of the only officers in the Army of Northern Virginia that Lee referred to by his first name. On 4 May, the general proved to be uncertain about the advisability of an offensive move, but told one of Lee's staff officers, "I am ready to try if he says attack." Despite Heth's tepid desire to send his troops into battle, Lee was against a serious engagement until he was sure about Ewell's position who by mid-afternoon was again under attack.

By 1500, Wright's troops were finally in a position to assault the Confederates astride the Orange Turnpike. His line was set up with Colonel Emory Upton's brigade on the left, Colonel Henry W. Brown's brigade in the center and

*Major General Horatio Wright took up the battle against the Second Corps after 1500 on 5 May. Despite some success, he found the enemy position too strong to break.*

Brigadier General David A. Russell's brigade on the right. Thomas H. Neill's brigade, left behind by Getty's division, was to support Russell's advance. Upton observed that his troops passed over the grim butchery of the Warren's battle, "The ground had been previously fought over and was strewn with wounded of both sides, many of whom must have perished in the flames, as corpses were found partly consumed." As Wright's division descended on the Confederate line, Steuart's Brigade sortied to meet it. The Confederate attack fell on Emory Upton's brigade which brushed it off and continued the advance until coming upon Ewell's main line. Once before the ranks of fierce Confederate musketry and artillery, Wright's men came to a standstill, their ranks already staggered and confused by Steuart's attack and the rough terrain. A small success was scored when Hays' Louisiana Brigade along with the 25th Virginia of Jones' Brigade, moved to extend the Confederate left and then advanced against the Federals without support. Hays' command entered into a confrontation with Russell's and Neill's brigades of Yankees expecting some Confederate forces to protect his left; while only the 25th Virginia managed to do so. Five

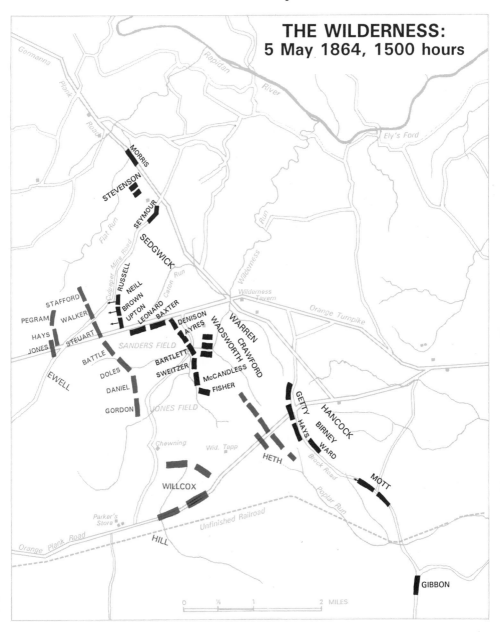

# THE WILDERNESS:
## 5 May 1864, 1500 hours

# Horatio Gouverneur Wright

Horatio Gouverneur Wright was born in Clinton, Connecticut, on 6 March 1820. He graduated from West Point second in a class which included a sizable number of future Civil War generals including John F. Reynolds, Nathaniel Lyon, Don Carlos Buell and Richard B. Garnett. After graduation, he undertook several engineering projects with the Corps of Engineers including the building of harbors and fortifications. He also served as a French teacher and engineering instructor at his alma mater.

In April, Captain Wright found himself involved in the Union war effort soon after the outbreak of war. When Virginia seceded on 17 April, Wright was chief engineer in an expedition to reinforce the garrison of the Norfolk Navy Yard. Though captured, he was released and returned to service in time to participate in the battle of First Bull Run as Samuel Heintzelman's chief engineer.

Wright did not enjoy an illustrious military career during the first two years of the war. He was promoted to brigadier general in September of 1861 and led a brigade in Flag Officer Samuel F. Du Pont's mostly naval effort to capture Port Royal, South Carolina. On 16 June 1862, while still based in South Carolina, his forces along with those under the command of Brigadier General Isaac Stevens attacked a Confederate fort at Secessionville in an ill-advised assault ordered by their superior Brigadier General Henry W. Benham. Wright and Stevens had both argued against engaging in the battle, claiming it was a violation of orders from the commander of the Department of the South, Major General David Hunter, who had given his approval to a reconnaissance in force. The Federals lost some 600 men in casualties.

Wright's next appointment was in the Department of Ohio which was created on 19 August 1862 to cover the states of Ohio, Indiana, Illinois, Michigan, Wisconsin and part of Kentucky. Though Wright

companies from the *5th Wisconsin* slipped around the flank of the Virginians and almost entrapped them. The Confederates were then forced back, with the 25th Virginia suffering the ignominy of losing 300 men and having its colors captured.

Around 1500, Truman Seymour's brigade of Ricketts' *VI Corps* division came up on the Federal right. The general organized his force into two lines before engaging in a personal reconnaissance of the enemy's position. He was elated to find that his command overlapped Ewell's left,

received a promotion to the rank of major general, this was revoked by the Senate.

An assignment as a division commander in the *VI Corps* under John Sedgwick changed Wright's lackluster fortunes. He commanded the division through Gettysburg, Mine Run and the Wilderness campaigns. When Sedgwick was killed in action near Spotsylvania on 9 May 1864, Wright assumed command of the *VI Corps* and was promoted to major general.

The *VI Corps* continued south through Virginia with Grant and the *Army of the Potomac* seeing action in the disaster at Cold Harbor, part of the Petersburg campaign and the Weldon Railroad operation. It was then detached to protect Washington, D.C., from Jubal Early's raid against the city. Following Early's repulse, Wright pursued the Confederates into the Shenandoah Valley. He led his command in Sheridan's *Army of the Shenandoah* during the Federal attempt to deprive the fertile area from Confederate use. The Federals enjoyed victories against the Confederates at Winchester and Fisher's Hill in September of 1864, but almost suffered disaster at Cedar Creek. There, on 19 October, the *Army of the Shenandoah* was under Wright's temporary command during Sheridan's absence. That morning, Early's Confederate army surprised the Federals and routed them. While the Confederate attack faltered, Wright was able to rally his beaten troops which the returning Sheridan then led to victory. Wright was also wounded in the action. Wright and the *VI Corps* were returned to the *Army of the Potomac* with which it served for the rest of the war.

After the war, Wright continued to serve in the military for a year as a lieutenant colonel during which he commanded the Department of Texas. Over time Wright rose to the rank of brigadier general and became chief engineer. Among the many projects he became involved in was the completion of the Washington monument. Wright retired in 1884. He lived in Washington until his death 15 years later.

---

giving him the perfect opportunity for a flank attack. Still smarting from the rout of his forces at the battle of Olustee in Florida the previous February, Seymour might have been blinded by his eagerness for a chance to redeem his reputation. Tragically, he had failed to notice that Pegram's Brigade was deploying on Ewell's left to guard against just such a movement, so that in fact the Rebel line actually overlapped the attacking Yankee one.

Seymour advanced at 1900 with what was supposed to be

a combined attack by the *V* and *VI Corps*, but only Wright's troops to the south joined in the assault. The Federals managed to get within 150 yards of Ewell's line before they came under considerable pressure from Confederate musketry. To add insult to injury, the Confederates were pouring flanking fire into Seymour's exposed flank. Still, the fighting continued until 2100.

The *V* and *VI Corps* had butted up against the line of Ewell's Corps with nothing to show for the fighting except an extensive casualty list. It remained to be seen if the *II Corps* might fare better in an offensive to the south down the Orange Plank Road.

# CHAPTER VI

# "Men Dropped Like the Leaves of Autumn"

*E*lements of the *II Corps* began to reach the Orange Plank Road by 1400. Major General David B. Birney's division was in the advance and went into position to the left of Getty's *VI Corps* division at the intersection of the Brock Road with the Orange Plank Road. Major General Gersham Mott's *4th Division* would arrive to set up on Birney's left an hour later.

Soon after reaching the Plank Road, Hancock received a couple of disconcerting messages from Meade's headquarters. At 1435, he received orders from Humphreys dispatched around 1330 telling the *II Corps* commander to launch an attack:

> The enemy's infantry drove our regiment of cavalry from Parker's Store down the plank road, and are now moving down it in force. A. P. Hill's corps is part of it. How much is not known. General Getty's division has been sent to drive them back, but he may not be able to do so. The major-general commanding directs that you move out the plank road toward Parker's Store, and, supporting Getty, drive the enemy beyond Parker's Store, and occupy the place and unite with Warren on the right of it.

A few minutes later Hancock received information from Humphreys, dated around 1200, of the terrible repulse suffered by Warren. The situation with the *V Corps* was so confused that headquarters could not even tell Hancock where the left of the *V Corps* was and if it could connect with the *II Corps*:

119

*The Orange Plank Road was the site of some of the bloodiest fighting of the Wilderness campaign. Both Yankees and Rebels engaged in bloody charge and countercharge there throughout 5-6 May.*

Wadsworth's division on Griffin's left has been driven in, and Crawford's division has been called in so that his line is thrown back considerably. His left must be more than a mile in rear of where it was before. Its exact position is not reported yet; will send you word as soon as it is known.

After receiving the 1200 dispatch, Hancock immediately reported that he was preparing to attack,

Your dispatches of 12 m. and 1.30 p.m. just received. I am forming my corps on Getty's left, and will order an advance as soon as prepared. The ground over which I must pass is very bad—a perfect thicket.

Hancock prepared to drive west down the Orange Plank

*Major General Winfield Scott Hancock (seated) with his talented division commanders: (from left to right) Brigadier General Francis C. Barlow, Major General David B. Birney and Brigadier General John B. Gibbon.*

Road toward Parker's Store with Getty and available *II Corps* units on that division's left. But then Hancock received a command, issued at 1515, basically instructing him to wrench apart his organization, and piece it together again. Meade, though he was separated from the Federal left, decided to take a direct role in the placement of Hancock's divisions, ordering Getty's division to attack with a *II Corps* division on both of his flanks. The order, written by Humphreys read:

The commanding general directs that Getty attack at once,

121

# Winfield Scott Hancock

Perhaps the best corps in the Union army during the war was the *II Corps*. Its commander through some of its greatest battles was the formidable and hard fighting Winfield Scott Hancock (1824-1886), also known as "Hancock the Superb."

Hancock graduated from the West Point class of 1844 ranked 18th. He served in a variety of military actions before the Civil War including the Mexican War, the Seminole War and the "Mormon War." When the country separated and sides began to take up arms, Hancock was post quartermaster at Los Angeles. He along with several officers took part in an emotional gathering for farewells before comrades departed to serve either the Confederacy or Union. One such was Lewis Addison Armistead who would lead a brigade in Pickett's Charge at Gettysburg against a position held by men under Hancock.

Hancock commanded a brigade of troops as a brigadier general in the Peninsula campaign. By Antietam, he was in charge of a division and later attained rank of major general. Though Hancock participated in Fredericksburg and Chancellorsville, his reputation was sealed as the commander of the *II Corps* of the *Army of the Potomac* at Gettysburg. There Hancock was a major force in the battle. Meade entrusted him with the command of the battle on 1 July and he rescued the Federal cause from defeat by rallying routed Union troops on Cemetery Hill. On the second day, he commanded the left wing of the *Army of the Potomac* and on 3 July, it was Hancock who directed the re-

and that you support him with your whole corps, one division on his right and one division on his left, the others in reserve; or other disposition as you may think proper, but the attack up the plank road must be made at once.

Hancock responded that he had intended to have his divisions attack from Getty's left, but that he would comply with Meade's directive. Time was lost and an already confusing situation was made even worse.

While Meade was pressing Hancock to attack, he was also desperately attempting to motivate Warren to launch an assault in support of the one to be made by the *II Corps*. Warren was reminded that both Robinson's and Crawford's divisions had not seen serious action as of yet and was promised a host of reinforcements, most of which would not

pulse of Pickett's Charge during which he was wounded.

Hancock then led the elite *II Corps* with distinction for most of the rest of the war. It was this force under Hancock's direction which pierced the Confederate line at the Wilderness and Spotsylvania, only to have their gains wiped out by lack of support from other commanders. In November 1864, Hancock's Gettysburg wound continued to bother him, eventually forcing him to relinquish command of the corps. The victorious warrior finished out the war in various posts including the command of the *Veteran Reserve Corps*.

After the war, Hancock ran for President on the Democratic ticket against James A. Garfield in 1880. The race was close with Hancock losing by almost 10,000 popular votes though only garnering 155 votes in the electoral college to Garfield's 214. Hancock died on Governors Island, New York, on 9 February 1886.

Hancock was an impressive force on the battlefield. Horace Porter wrote of his visage during the fight in the Wilderness:

> His face was flushed with the excitement of victory, his eyes were lighted by the fire of battle, his flaxen hair was thrust back from his temples, his right arm was extended to its full length in pointing out certain positions as he gave orders, and his commanding form towered still higher as he rose in his stirrups to peer through the woods. He was considered the handsomest general officer in the army, and at this moment he looked like a spirited portrait from the hands of a master artist, with the deep brown of the dense forest forming a fitting background. It was enough to inspire the troops he led to deeds of unmatched heroism.

be delivered. In a dispatch of 1415 Ricketts' division of the *VI Corps* was reported to be on its way to Warren's aid though only one brigade of the force managed to reach the *V Corps*. Getty's division was even promised although this force was preparing for action on the Orange Plank Road. Meade assured Warren that Hancock would shortly be attacking down the Orange Plank Road, but even this statement was not true. Army headquarters allowed Warren to exercise discretion and issued no peremptory orders to force him into action. A general not overly aggressive by nature, he decided not to advance.

Meanwhile, as 1600 approached, Hancock's troops labored to set up a battle line satisfactory to Meade's directive of 1515.

*Lieutenant General Ambrose P. Hill whose command fought Hancock's II Corps on the Orange Plank Road. During the Wilderness campaign, the general was becoming increasingly ill and would be forced to relinquish his command shortly thereafter.*

Birney's troops had been pulled out of their position on Getty's left, moving to that command's right. Mott's division then edged up to take the place vacated by Birney. At the same time, Getty's division of 7,200 men was to launch its advance down the Plank Road unsupported with its flanks open until the II Corps divisions caught up. Altogether Hancock's assault would combine the efforts of some 17,000 men.

The Confederates in opposition were only three brigades under Heth deployed in a line angling from the southeast to the northwest with a brigade in reserve. A gun was placed in the Plank Road to receive the Federals when they came. All in all, there were 6,700 Confederates to meet the enemy advance.

The Federal attack began when Getty's brigades advanced in two lines around 1600. On the left, south of the Plank Road, was Colonel Lewis A. Grant's *2nd Brigade* composed entirely of men from Vermont. Brigadier General Frank Wheaton's Pennsylvanians and a regiment of New Yorkers were in the center north of the road. To the right was Brigadier General Henry L. Eustis' *4th Brigade*.

The Federals forced through the dense thicket and negotiated their way over streams while being peppered by enemy

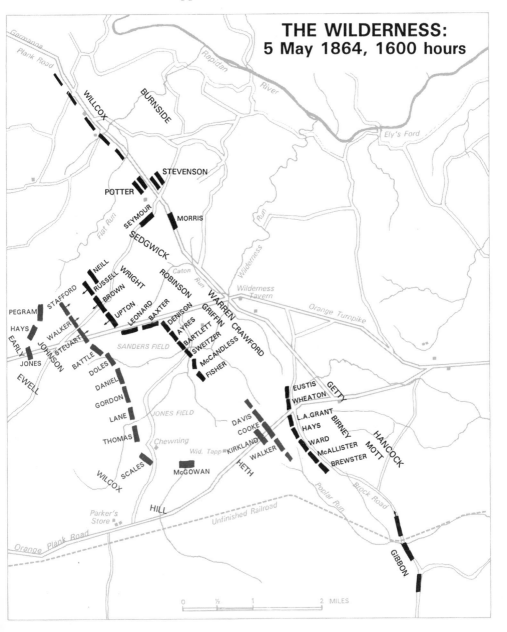

## THE WILDERNESS:
## 5 May 1864, 1600 hours

# Ambrose Powell Hill

Virginian Ambrose Powell Hill (1825-1865) was a respectable 15th in the West Point class of 1847 which included future enemy Ambrose Burnside. Hill's pre-war service included action in the Mexican War, participation in the fights against the Seminoles in Florida and frontier service.

A first lieutenant in the U.S. Army when he resigned in 1861, Hill was commissioned a colonel of the 13th Virginia. Hill went on to become a brigadier general of a brigade during McClellan's Peninsula campaign during which he won distinction at the battle of Williamsburg. A major general by May 1862, he was in command of a division during the repulse of McClellan from Richmond during the Seven Days Battles. His command became known as the "Light Division" for the speed with which it accomplished its movements.

When Hill began having problems with his commander, James Longstreet, he was put under the leadership of Stonewall Jackson. Though his relationship with Jackson was sometimes strained, Hill performed admirably, saving the day for the Confederates at Cedar Mountain (9 August 1862) and Antietam (17 September 1862). He also participated in Fredericksburg in December and assisted in Jackson's destructive flank attack on Hooker's *Army of the Potomac* at Chancellorsville in May of 1863. During the latter battle, Hill took command of Jackson's Corps when its commander was tragically wounded and led the force briefly until he was wounded himself.

Hill recovered, and reached new heights of command when he achieved the rank of lieutenant general in command of the Third Corps of the Army of Northern Virginia. However, illness and his inability to translate his success at division command to a higher level did not win him any great laurels in his new position. He failed to display his penchant for fighting at Gettysburg beyond the first day on 1 July 1863, and on 14 October 1863 his troops suffered a bloody repulse at Bristoe Station. Hill was increasingly pained from severe illness, prostatitis from an infection (quite possibly gonorrhea), along with hypochondria, and was forced to relinquish command from time to time. He was returning from sick leave on 2 April 1865 when his men were breaking under a Union attack at Petersburg. As he rode out to join them, he was shot down by Union soldiers.

Hill made an excellent division commander, but he rarely exercised his brilliance as the leader of a corps. His aptitude may have been affected by his failing health as the war drew towards its conclusion.

pickets who were falling back to the main line. The terrain was so difficult that regiments had to advance in column in some places and one was even forced to crawl into position. Soon the Confederate positions were reached and the Wilderness once again exploded into a blaze of gunfire. Colonel Joseph B. Parsons of the *10th Massachusetts* recalled, "The firing became terrific. Men who had been in all the battles of the war up to that time said they never saw anything like it." One of Parson's men, Alfred S. Roe, recorded that the enemy could not be seen save for the flashes and smoke from their gun barrels. Lieutenant William Ashley of the same regiment was leading his men forward shouting, "Forward, boys!" when he fell dead after he was shot through the head. His comrades later attempted to recover his body, but the constant marches and fighting never allowed them the chance to give the valiant Ashley a proper burial.

All at once Yankees hit the ground for cover. Vermonter Colonel Grant had been a lawyer before the war with no military experience, but had distinguished himself at the head of troops from his home state. In the Wilderness, the brigade commander faced some of the toughest fighting of his career. He wrote of his attack,

as soon as the first volleys were over, our men hugged the ground as closely as possible, and kept up a rapid fire; the enemy did the same. The rebels had the advantage of position, inasmuch as their line was partially protected by a slight swell of ground, while ours was nearly all level ground. The attempt was made to dislodge them from their position, but the moment our men rose to advance, the rapid and constant fire of musketry cut them down with such slaughter that it was found impracticable to do more than maintain our then present position. The enemy could not advance for the same reason.

Eustis reported, "For nearly an hour the fighting was incessant, and the loss was proportionately great, but the enemy was too strongly posted and could not be dislodged." It seemed as though all Getty's men could do was attempt to hold on in the face of the Confederate fire.

Since no *II Corps* troops managed to get on Getty's right in time, the Confederates put Eustis' brigade under a telling

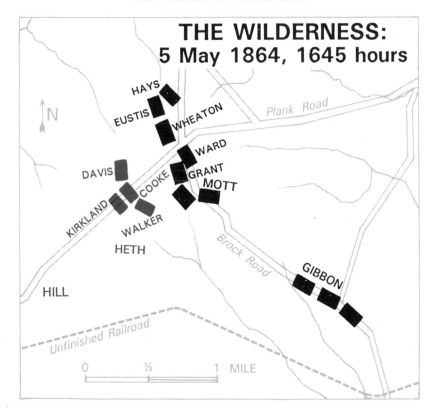

THE WILDERNESS:
5 May 1864, 1645 hours

flanking fire. The *2nd Rhode Island* took the worst of it and fell back in confusion. The next regiment in line, the *10th Massachusetts* then came under flanking fire. Parsons said of the effects of enemy fusillades, "Men dropped like the leaves of autumn.... The ground was literally covered with the wounded, the dying and the dead."

Getty's division suffered a terrible mauling from the enemy fire. Unable to make any headway, its commander appealed to Birney for aid. Birney's division was still struggling to get on Getty's right to assist in the attack, but eventually came forward, sending three regiments of Brigadier General J.H. Ward's brigade to help Grant's Vermonters while the rest of the *II Corps* brigade was held in reserve. Brigadier General Alexander Hays' brigade was dispatched to take position on Getty's right.

Emboldened by the reinforcements, Grant's troops endeavored to press forward with the *5th Vermont* and two of Ward's regiments. Grant recalled the scene in his report,

> I went to Major Dudley commanding the Fifth [Vermont]... and called his attention to the fact that the position of the enemy in his front was less protected than it was in front of the rest of the brigade, and asked him if he could, with the support of two regiments in his rear break through the enemy's line. 'I think we can,' was the reply of the gallant major. I went to the commander of those two regiments, and asked them to support the Fifth in its advance. The men rose and with a cheer answered, 'We will.' The order for the charge was given, and all advanced in good style, and the enemy partially gave way. The two rear regiments were thrown into some confusion, and soon halted and laid down and Major Dudley, finding his regiment far in the advance exposed to a fire flank fire, wisely did the same. Our ammunition soon became well nigh exhausted....

The *20th Indiana* of Ward's brigade managed to come away from the encounter with the colors of the 55th Virginia.

Hays' brigade advanced to Getty's right. The Federals pressed up close to Brigadier General Joseph R. Davis' Mississippians only to be plowed down by their heavy fire. An officer in the *93rd New York* wrote of the enemy fire, "Only by the flash of the volleys of forming lines could we know where was posted the enemy with which we were engaged. The woods would light up with flashes of musketry, as if with lightning, while the incessant roar of the volleys sounded like the crashing of thunderbolts." Hays, a true combat commander, was at the thick of the fighting with his troops, riding up and down the line during the intense storm of enemy fire to exhort his troops to fight. At one point he paused to cheer on his men when a bullet struck him in the head. The gallant general fell to the ground mortally wounded. Hays was a good friend of Grant who had known him at West Point and served with him during the Mexican American War. The lieutenant general was visibly affected when he learned of his friend's death. Grant later wrote of him, "He was a most gallant officer ready to lead his command where ordered. With him it was 'Come, boys,' not 'Go.'"

Mott's division attempted to go in on Getty's left. On the

*Infantry of the II Corps struggles against troops of Lieutenant General Hill's Third Corps. The Confederates managed to hold up against fierce attacks on 5 May, but were severely battered.*

right was the *1st Brigade* under Colonel Robert McAllister and on the left was Colonel William R. Brewster's *Excelsior Brigade* from New York. While Mott's troops tried to advance in columns and deploy into lines, in the confusion of the Wilderness, all their regiments managed to do was to become jumbled or tangled up in other commands. With disorganization mounting and Rebel fire taking its toll, Mott's troops fell back to the safety of the Brock Road. McAllister wrote of the failed attack, "On receiving the enemy's fire, to my great astonishment, the line began to give way on our left...regiment after regiment, like a rolling wave, fell back, and all efforts to rally them short of the breast-works were in vain. To assign a cause for this panic is impossible, unless it was from the fact that a large number of troops were about to leave the service. I think this had much to do with it." Shortly after this incident, Birney's reserve of Ward's remaining troops entered the fray, moving to Getty's left, and picking up some of Mott's men as they advanced.

Meade's aide, Colonel Theodore Lyman, had been dispatched to join Hancock at 1645 with some aides to send reports of the fighting back to headquarters. He found the general at the Brock and Plank Roads intersection astride his horse as musket balls whizzed around him. The sight of the fighting general in the midst of a conflagration of the grandest scale seemed a scene out of a glorious romantic novel or historical epic. Lyman presented himself to the general who did not seem all that optimistic about his offensive. "Report to General Meade," said Hancock, "that it is very hard to bring up troops in this wood, and that only part of my Corps is up, but I will do as well as I can." As events grew more intense, Hancock struggled with herculean effort to maintain the integrity of his attack. An officer rode up to him to report, "Sir! General Getty is hard pressed and nearly out of ammunition!" Hancock shouted back, "Tell him to hold on and General Gibbon will be up to help him." Then an officer rode up telling of Mott's collapse. To this Hancock blared, "Tell him to stop them, sir!!" When multitudes of retreating troops dashed onto the scene, Hancock rode to them, yelling, "Halt there, halt there! Form behind this rifle-pit."

Shortly after 1700, Brigadier General John Gibbon's men marched up to participate in the swelling attack. Colonel Samuel Carroll's brigade in the lead advanced west just north of the Plank Road. His troops passed over Wheaton's men to test the defenses of the Confederates of Kirkland's and Cooke's Brigades. Charge gave way to countercharge and soon both sides took up Indian fighting, firing from the cover of bushes and trees. Alexander S. Webb's brigade attempted to assist Mott's collapsing line. Colonel Joshua T. Owen's brigade came up, moving south of the Plank Road, to assist

*A hard fighter and personal friend of Lieutenant General Grant, Brigadier General Alexander Hays was killed while leading the 2nd Brigade of Birney's division on 5 May. He received a posthumous brevet of major general.*

Carroll, but whatever gains this force could make were lost during a Confederate countercharge. A member of the 44th North Carolina near the Plank Road remembered of the whirlwind of fighting, "The road was swept by an incessant hurricane of fire, and to attempt to cross it meant almost certain death." A Tarheel of the 52nd North Carolina told of the wounded who were fleeing to the rear, "These men were wounded in every conceivable manner—some slightly, others severely and not a few mortally." Confederate cannoneer William Dame also saw the wounded streaming from the fight, some limping, others bandaged and covered with blood, still others were carried on a stretcher. One soldier stopped to tell him, "Dead Yankees were *knee deep* all over about four acres of ground." He said this as blood was running "very freely" from his wounded arm.

When Heth's Division came under attack, Lee called on Wilcox's Division to the north at the Chewning Plateau back to reinforce the troops fighting on the Orange Plank Road. Brigadiers Samuel McGowan's and A.M. Scales' brigades led the movement marching back from the Chewning farm to the Widow Tapp farm and then on to the front. McGowan and Scales were true fighting commanders, both of whom had returned from convalescence from previous wounds in time to lead brigades in the Wilderness. McGowan had been out of combat since he was injured when his brigade was cut up fighting at Chancellorsville the previous year. Scales was wounded on the first day at Gettysburg where his brigade suffered terrible losses. Their previous injuries did not affect their abilities. McGowan advanced his troops up the Plank Road, forcing Heth's ambulances off the road as they went while Scales' troops marched to assist the Confederate right. Before McGowan's troops went into battle, a chaplain in the 1st South Carolina Regiment had time to lead his troops in a short prayer. Confederate J.F.C. Caldwell witnessed the scene, "It was one of the most impressive scenes I ever witnessed. On the left thundered the dull battle; on the right the sharp crack of rifles swelled to equal importance; above was the blue, placid heavens; around was a varied landscape of forest and fields, green with the earliest foliage of spring; and here knelt the hirsute and browned veterans striving for another struggle with death." A severe blast of musketry interrupted the stirring scene and the veterans were then ordered forward into the fray. Caldwell said of the advance, "Balls fired at Heth's division, in front of us, fell among us at the beginning of our advance. We pressed on, guide left, through the thick underbrush, until we reached Heth's line, now much thinned and exhausted. We had very imprudently begun to cheer before this. We should have charged without uttering a word within a few yards of the Federal line. As it was, we drew upon ourselves a terrific volley of musketry."

McGowan's men went up against Carroll's brigade after stumbling about in a thicket while under fire from their own comrades in the rear. The South Carolinians managed to force the enemy back, taking cannons and prisoners in the process. Then a Federal counterattack threatened to surround one regiment which only managed to escape by facing to the rear and heading in that direction. Scales' men maneuvered to get south of the South Carolinians, but were unable to connect with their brigade. McGowan's men were subjected to a severe cross fire and fell back. The captured enemy guns were left behind, but a number of Yankees were herded into Southern lines ahead of retreating South Carolina troops. Scales' men stayed to engage the Yankees only to be forced back from fire on the front and right flank.

Both sides committed cannons and more troops into the deafening whirlwind of gunfire. The *1st Brigade* of Gibbon's division under Brigadier General Alexander S. Webb advanced south of the Orange Plank Road forcing the Confederates back west until it was stymied by the terrain and enemy fire. Wilcox committed his last two brigades under Brigadier Generals Edward L. Thomas and James H. Lane. Learning that Lane's men were on the scene, Lee's excited chief of staff, Colonel Venable, was heard to exclaim, "Thank God! I will go back and tell General Lee that Lane has just gone in and will hold his ground until other troops arrive tonight." A Confederate in the 37th North Carolina of Lane's Brigade remembered the musketry was the heaviest he had heard up to that time and that the whole Wilderness, "roared like a cane brake."

Thomas' Brigade advanced north of the road to relieve Davis' exhausted brigade of Mississippians and North Carolinians, while Lane advanced to the south of the road. As Davis' command fell back its depleted ranks displayed the effects of the tremendous battle. The 55th North Carolina of the brigade lost 34 dead and 167 wounded out of its roster of 340 men. These Confederates would proudly boast that, despite their terrible casualties, the Yankees had not budged their line one foot.

While the Confederates had all but exhausted the manpower available on the right of their line, another Federal division came upon the scene to continue the fight, the *1st Division* of the *II Corps* under Brigadier General Francis Barlow. Barlow had arrived on the Brock Road around 1700, where his men spent some time throwing up entrenchments before they were committed to battle. Barlow left one brigade in the rear as a reserve and forced Colonel Thomas A. Smyth's *Irish Brigade* and Colonel Nelson A. Miles' regiments into the fight before 1900. These were to be supported by Colonel John

R. Brooke's brigade. Altogether, Barlow's three brigades were poised like a sledgehammer of inexorable penetrating force ready to finally break Hill's exhausted line asunder.

The Confederates had reason to wish away minutes and hours as they gazed longingly at the sun still far above the horizon. Colonel Venable expressed this hopeful yearning when he exclaimed, "If only night would come." Though Hancock maintained overwhelming odds and the enemy line was close to cracking, the *II Corps* commander and his staff were not optimistic about the situation. At 1950, Lyman expressed the doubts of the leadership of the *II Corps* in a dispatch to Meade:

> We barely hold our own; on the right the pressure is heavy. General Hancock thinks he can hold the plank and Brock roads, in front which he is, but he can't advance.

As a postscript, Lyman wrote, "Fresh troops would be most advisable."

Barlow's troops fell upon Lane's Brigade in advance of the rest of the Confederate line in the front line by mistake. The Federals curled up both flanks of the brigade, sending the 7th North Carolina on the left reeling off into retreat. Lane's right collapsed and the rest of his troops fled as well. Though Lane's men found it difficult to make their way back to their lines in the gathering gloom of the approaching darkness, they managed to rally with Scales' line. The attacks of Smyth's and Miles' commands failed to attain their desired impact, their impetus petering out before Lane's and Scale's positions. Brooke's command came up after 1900 to assist the Federals battling away in the massive effusion of blood, which continued until 2100. The Federals ended up in a position so close to Lane that Colonel Davidson of the 7th North Carolina accidentally stumbled into the Yankee lines. The Federals pulled him into their position without a word.

The Federals had not expended all their energies however. When Wilcox was found to have retreated from the center of the Confederate line to go to Hill's aid, Wadsworth pleaded with Meade for the chance to use his division to make an attack on Hill's left. Wadsworth got the go-ahead along with another brigade under Brigadier General Henry Baxter. His forces cautiously advanced south against Hill's left around 1800. Baxter's brigade was in the front on the right along with Stone's, whose command maintained the left of the attacking force. Cutler's *Iron Brigade* supported the advance while Rice's brigade was left in reserve.

Hill lacked adequate force to meet this oncoming assault. All that could be managed to meet Wadsworth's troops was a paltry force consisting of 125 members of the 5th Alabama, a provost guard detailed to watch prisoners. Their captives turned over to noncombatants, the Alabamians tramped through the woods making a tremendous ruckus by wildly screaming and firing their weapons. The activity was enough for the timorous Federals. Stone's brigade collapsed, its commander got lost and the rest of Wadsworth's force came to a halt. With this tragicomedy, the first day of the battle of the Wilderness came to an end.

# CHAPTER VII

# Night of the Battle

$T$hough the fighting had ended, the horror of the day of slaughter would linger into the night. Captain John B. Adams of the *19th Massachusetts* in Gibbon's division recalled, "The dead and wounded of both armies were strewn all through the woods, which caught fire. It was a terrible sight...the air was suffocating with the smell of burning flesh." Confederate McHenry Howard remembered,

> Usually there is not much groaning or outcry from wounded men on a battlefield; they do not feel acute pain or else bear their sufferings in silence. But on this occasion circumstances seemed to make their situation peculiarly distressing, and their moans and cries were painful to listen to. In the still night air every groan could be heard and the calls for water and entreaties for brothers and comrades by name to come and help them. Many Federals and Confederates lay within a few paces of our skirmish line, whom we found it impossible to succor, although we tried. I was myself fired on while making two separate attempts to get some in. I well remember that at midnight where I lay down to sleep, and on waking during the night, their cries were ringing in my ears.

Throughout the night nervous trigger-happy sentries fired into the Wilderness against real and phantom targets. The shots caused alarm up and down both lines leading other pickets to send shots into the Stygian darkness.

Some soldiers were active during the night on the northern portion of the lines. These ghouls scoured the field in order to fill their pockets which booty from the dead. The next day revealed many corpses with pockets turned out, haversacks

*A Confederate soldier searches for a fallen friend on the field of battle.*

opened, and articles of value missing. Some Confederates defied the danger of capture and enemy fire to dine on hardtack, bacon, and coffee relieved from those who would no longer need them. One Rebel returned from a pilfering mission with a fine pair of boots and told how the owner opened his eyes during every attempt to remove them. He had to wait all night for the Yankee to die before he could take his prize without worrying about his enemy's haunting stare.

The fighting on 5 May had been a bestial affair with neither side racking up any real gain. Grant had thrown his forces piecemeal up against Lee's two corps only to suffer repulse after repulse. Though his first grand offensive in the East was stymied, Grant was satisfied with events on the fifth and planned to carry on the great fight the next day. He told members of his staff, "As Burnside's corps, on our side, and Longstreet's, on the other side, have not been engaged, and the troops of both armies have been occupied principally in struggling through thickets and fighting for position, to-day's work has not been much of a test of strength. I feel pretty well satisfied with the result of the engagement; for it is evident that Lee attempted by a bold movement to strike this army in flank before it could put into line of battle and be prepared to fight to advantage; but in this he has failed." Grant planned to engage in battle the next day with renewed ferocity and better organization. One fact that played in his mind was information from captured Rebels which told of Longstreet's march to the field. If Grant was to strike, he would have to do so before these thousands of enemy reinforcements arrived. Thus an early attack was planned, the objective being Lee's right, already severely weakened by Hancock's powerful assaults of the fifth. Hancock was to attack early in the morning with assistance from Wadsworth's and Getty's divisions. Burnside's *IX Corps*, not in action on the first day of battle, was to be Grant's trump card to be played against any weakness to arise in the Confederate line, particularly the enemy center left open by Wilcox's march to aid the rest of Hill's Corps.

At 2000 a circular was issued to all corps commanders calling for every man to be available for the grand attack of the next day:

> The commanding general directs that you order all train guards, as well as every man capable of bearing arms, to join your troops at the front before daylight to-morrow morning. For the present the trains must be protected by cavalry, and every man who can shoulder a musket must be in the ranks.

At 2200, Hancock received his orders from Meade:

> You are required to renew the attack at 4.30 o'clock to-morrow morning, keeping a sharp lookout on your left. Your right will be relieved by an attack made at the same time by General Wadsworth's division and by two divisions of General Burnside's corps.

Meade's corps commanders were not eager for an assault targeted for so early in the morning. During a nighttime meeting, the generals attempted to influence their commander to postpone the attack until later in the day. Meade then voiced these concerns to Grant, telling him that because of the terrain, exhaustion of the men, and the need for daylight in moving the troops, 0600 might be a better hour to have the troops advance. Though Meade's concerns were

# Union Cavalry During the Wilderness Campaign

The Union cavalry began the war almost as a joke when compared to the dashing Southern wizards of the saddle who humiliated their enemy counterparts time and time again. By the time of Gettysburg, fighting quality of the mounted arm of the Federal military had dramatically increased. Under the stewardship of the belligerent and caustic Philip Sheridan, the prowess and reputation of the cavalry increased though this was not so apparent during the Wilderness campaign.

The rifled musket had destroyed the effectiveness of a mounted attack against all but the most demoralized or green troops. Indeed, such cavalry charges that were attempted against infantry proved wasteful in lives with little benefit in return. At Gaines' Mill, the *5th New York Cavalry* attempted a counterattack against a successful Confederate offensive only to lose 156 out of 257 men for no purpose. At Gettysburg, Brigadier General Elon Farnsworth was ordered to make a charge which ended in his death and disaster for his command.

The cavalry enjoyed much more success in reconnaissance and raiding roles. These roles could prove vitally important as proven by just a couple of stirring examples. J.E.B. Stuart, one of the South's most flamboyant cavaliers and horseman, led a reconnaissance that took him clear around McClellan's army before Richmond in June of 1862. His successful mission gave Lee the information he needed to launch a destructive flank attack on the Federals which eventually led to their defeat and retreat from the Confederate capital. When Earl Van Dorn's cavalry command struck U.S. Grant's supply base at Holly Springs, Mississippi, on 20 December 1862, the Federal general was forced to suspend his campaign against Vicksburg.

Though the Federals had been successful in using the cavalry for reconnaissance and raiding roles with increasing success throughout the war, for some reason the troopers of the *Army of the Potomac* were bridled by Federal planners during the Wilderness campaign. The cavalry was given reconnaissance duties, but many troopers spent their time protecting the wagons as the army crossed the Rapidan and moved south. While these were invaluable cavalry roles, there was little thought to use troopers in serious combat against the enemy.

A cavalry division under Briga-

valid, Grant had no desire to repeat the mistake of previous Federal generals by giving Lee the advantage of initiative. Hooker made the fundamental error of hesitating at almost the same location a year before and Grant was not going to

dier General James H. Wilson was given the responsibility of screening the Federal movement through the Wilderness, a mission in which Wilson failed utterly and almost disastrously. Wilson had the smallest cavalry division in the *Army of the Potomac*, the size of which belied his most important mission of discovering where the enemy was as it descended on the infantry and supply columns snaking their way south on the poor Wilderness roads. On 4 May Wilson recorded some skirmishing with the enemy pickets and spent the night at Parker's Store. He failed to properly inform army headquarters of enemy movements in the vicinity of Locust Grove on the Orange Turnpike and failed to leave a force to guard against this force the next day. The next day Wilson left a small force, the *5th New York Cavalry Regiment* near Parker's Store in a liberal interpretation of an order by Meade to leave a force patrolling down the Orange Plank Road. As a result, Wilson failed completely in his mission by missing the movement's of Ewell's Corps and Hill's Corps of the Army of Northern Virginia leaving the infantry forces for themselves to discover the enemy on their own. Once the Confederates of Ewell's corps tapped the Federal advance on the Germanna Plank Road, the *Army of the Potomac* was halted and forced into bloody confrontation. Worse still, the advance of Hill's Corps up the Orange Plank Road almost cut Wilson's division off from the rest of the army and left it prey to the cavaliers of Stuart's command.

The next day, the cavalry spent most of its time either guarding the wagon train of the *Army of the Potomac* or sparring with their Southern counterparts. The inability of the Federal cavalry to be used effectively offensively irked its belligerent commander, Philip Sheridan. His resentfulness strained relations with the commander of the *Army of the Potomac* George Gordon Meade. Their difficult relationship led to an argument between the two and an explosion of Sheridan's temper. The irate Irishman went on to claim that if he could have his way, he would organize the cavalry into one force and lead it out to defeat J.E.B. Stuart's command. When Meade told this to Grant, the latter replied, "Did Sheridan say that? Well, he generally knows what he is talking about. Let him start right out and do it." Sheridan did just that. His cavalry went south, engaging the Confederate cavalry at Yellow Tavern on 11 May 1864, a battle in which Stuart was mortally wounded.

follow his predecessor's ignominious path to defeat. Still the lieutenant general acquiesced somewhat by delaying the appointed hour for the assault until 0500 as a compromise.

By 2300, Grant set about to retire. He told his fellows, "We shall have a busy day tomorrow, and I think we had better get all the sleep we can to-night. I am a confirmed believer in the restorative qualities of sleep, and always like to get at least seven hours of it, though I have often been compelled to put up with much less." When the general was told that Napoleon usually took four hours of sleep and maintained his vigor, Grant replied, "Well, I for one never believed those stories." He went on, "If the truth were known, I have no doubt that he made up for his short sleep at night by taking naps during the day."

While Lee could seek solace in the fact that he had managed to repulse the attacks of the *Army of the Potomac* with heavy casualties, he could not find much cause for satisfaction beyond that single fact. Indeed, if Lee managed to tie down Grant in the Wilderness, Grant had managed to do the same to Lee. The Army of Northern Virginia was fighting in an area which benefitted its smaller numbers, but Lee had been forced to surrender the initiative to beat off Grant's and Meade's attacks. Without the ability to engage in an offensive or begin one of Lee's trademark movements to throw back the enemy, the Confederates were going to find themselves in the agonizing position of suffering terrible casualties, not to win victories, but to merely hold off the enemy.

True to form, Lee was not willing to passively assume the defensive no matter the odds. Late on the 5th, he ordered Ewell to attack the next day. The commander of the Second Corps received this dispatch from Lee's aide de camp:

GENERAL: The general commanding directs me to say that the enemy have made no headway in their attack on General Heth, who is near the intersection of the Brock and Plank roads. He hopes to have General Anderson to-morrow morning and General Longstreet also, and he wants you to get General Ramseur and be ready to act early in the morning. The enemy appear to be on the Wilderness Tavern ridge, and if you see no chance to operate against their right, the general proposes to endeavor to crush their left. He wishes you to send back and care for all your wounded, fill up your ammunition, and be ready to act in the morning. General Wilcox has just reported that the enemy, who was drawn up on the Wilderness Tavern ridge, is all moving up to our right. Should that be the case the general suggests to you

*Major General Burnside led the IX Corps during the Wilderness campaign, but he commanded his corps independently of Meade and took his orders directly from Grant. His performance during the battle was poor.*

the practicability of moving over and taking that ridge, thus severing the enemy from his base, but if this cannot be done without too great a sacrifice, you must be prepared to reinforce our right and make your arrangements accordingly.

An hour later, another message was sent to Ewell ordering him to be ready to fight as soon as it was light the next morning,

The enemy persist in their attack on Hill's right. Several efforts have been repulsed, and we hold our own as yet...and unless you see some means of operating against their right, the general wishes you to support our right. It is reported that the enemy is massing against General Hill, and if an opportunity presents itself and you can get to the Wilderness Tavern ridge and cut the enemy off from the river, the general wishes it done. The attack on General Hill is still raging. Be ready to act as early as possible in the morning.

The Confederates did have reinforcements on the way consisting of Longstreet's First Corps, Anderson's Division of Hill's Corps and R.D. Johnston's brigade, all of which were to arrive the next day. Lee's concern for his right in view of Hancock's heavy assault on the fifth and the enemy forces massing against it forced him to revise his planned use of Longstreet the next day. Rather than accept the risks and

## Ambrose Everett Burnside

Probably more famous for his magnificent sideburns than his leadership, Ambrose Burnside (1824-1881) grew up in Indiana, the scion of slave-owning parents from South Carolina who had freed their chattels and moved to the Hoosier State. Young Burnside worked in a tailor shop before his father secured a position at West Point for him.

Burnside graduated with the class of 1847 and went on to serve in the Mexican War and on frontier posts. During the latter he was wounded in action against Apaches. Burnside left the Army in 1853 to undertake a business career in Rhode Island. He developed a breechloading carbine which he attempted to sell to the United States government with no success. His venture went bankrupt, though around 55,000 of the weapons were purchased in the civil strife that was just then on the horizon. Fortunately, Burnside's friend and future commander, George B. McClellan, was able to secure the humbled businessman a job with the Illinois Central Railroad.

Burnside quickly entered the military as the country went to war in 1861. Already a major general in the Rhode Island militia, Burnside organized a regiment and took it to Washington. He later commanded a brigade during the first battle of Bull Run on 21 July 1861. A brigadier general after service in that battle, Burnside subsequently took a brigade in a successful expedition on the North Carolina coast capturing several important ports. His wins there earned him praise from his government, admiration of the public and a promotion to major general.

delays of any fancy maneuvers in the face of a powerful force of an aggressive enemy, Lee decided to have Longstreet take the Orange Plank Road at Parker's Store in order to directly reinforce Hill's battered command. And it was essential that Longstreet make it to the battle in the timely fashion since Hill had been under severe pressure on the fifth, his casualties were heavy and his remaining troops were exhausted. If Longstreet did not make it up in time on the sixth, there were few if any reinforcements left to bolster the Third Corps' battered line when the Federals attacked the next day.

At 2300, Lee informed Secretary of War James Seddon of the battle of the fifth informing him that he still held the field.

> The enemy crossed the Rapidan yesterday at Ely's and Germanna Fords. Two corps of this army moved to oppose him—Ewell's, by the old turnpike, and Hill's, by the plank road. They

In July 1862, Burnside was recalled to serve with the *Army of the Potomac* under his old friend McClellan. Burnside's performance as commander of the *IX Corps* of the army was lackluster at Antietam, but the President was a firm believer in Burnside's talents and had the general replace McClellan as commander of the *Army of the Potomac* that November. Alas, Burnside did not have complete faith in his own abilities and led the army to a bloody disaster at Fredericksburg, Virginia, on 13 December 1862. Burnside was relieved the next month.

However, the disgraced general did not go on the shelf, but was given command of the Department of the Ohio in March of 1863. His controversial tenure there included the arrest and prosecution of peace activists including the prominent Copperhead Clement L. Val-

landigham. Burnside also managed to capture the flamboyant cavalry raider John Hunt Morgan during the Confederate's raid through Indiana and Ohio in July of 1863. He then redeemed his military reputation by thwarting Confederate James Longstreet's attempts to take Knoxville, Tennessee.

Burnside returned East to command the *IX Corps* during Grant's offensive against Richmond in the spring of 1864 when his leadership was adequate at best. After he bungled the attack on the Petersburg Crater on 30 July 1864, the general was removed from command and saw no further service. He resigned from the army on 15 April 1865.

Burnside enjoyed more success in business and politics after the war, serving as a three-time governor of Rhode Island and then as senator for his state.

---

arrived this morning in close proximity to the enemy's line of march. A strong attack was made upon Ewell, who repulsed it, capturing many prisoners and four pieces of artillery. The enemy subsequently concentrated upon General Hill, who, with Heth's and Wilcox's divisions, successfully resisted repeated and desperate assaults....By the blessing of God we maintained our position against every effort until night, when the contest closed. We have to mourn the loss of many brave officers and men.

Into the night, officers and troops from both armies busily prepared for the bloodfest they knew must come when the day dawned on the sixth. Reorganizing units in the dark woodland after the heavy fighting of the first day proved to be an incredibly difficult task. On the Federal side, the anti-slavery Alabamian Major General David B. Birney was to lead the main assault with his own, Getty's, Gibbon's, and Mott's divisions. The combined 20,000 troops of these commands were to descend down the Plank Road to shatter Hill's forces. Birney's force was divided up into three lines: McAllister's, Hays', and Ward's brigades were organized in the first line just south of the Plank Road; the second line contained Brewster and Grant south of the Plank Road, Wheaton astride it and Eustis to the north of it; Owen's and Carroll's brigades in the third line brought up the rear. Ordinary soldier Wilbur Fisk of Getty's *VI Corps* division remembered his attitude towards the plan to renew the attack on the sixth, "I am willing to say that I dreaded it. The officers, too, thought that they were asking us to do more than our share of the bloody work. We were connected to Hancock's corps and Hancock seemed determined to make us work while we stayed with him."

To the north of Birney's assault force was Wadsworth's division regrouping for its part in the assault of the next day. It faced south with the line consisting of Cutler, Baxter, and Rice with Stone in reserve. Altogether, Wadsworth would be contributing 5,000 men to the coming offensive.

A major concern looming on Hancock's mind aside from his attack was the fear that Longstreet would arrive on his left and crush the entire flank, a possibility confirmed by reports from Meade that interrogated prisoners claimed this was indeed the Rebel plan. Some captured troops from Heth's Division even reported that Longstreet was already on the scene. To protect against this threat, Gibbon was given command of Hancock's left with the job of guarding against a possible flank attack by Longstreet when he reached the field. The force under his command included Barlow's brigades and 69 cannon.

The *V Corps* was also involved in regrouping and reshaping its battered lines. Crawford's *Pennsylvania Reserve* regiments were on the left while Griffin was on the right just east of Sanders' Field. Griffin's men were reinforced by 1,000 engineers who had helped build the pontoon bridges across the Rapidan. To the north of the *V Corps* remained Wright's division of the *VI Corps*.

The *IX Corps* was to join in the attack the next day though without various commands detached for other duties. The *Provisional Brigade*, a force of dismounted cavalrymen and heavy artillery regiments scrounged up from garrisons protecting Washington, was left to guard the ground between the Germanna Ford and the *VI Corps* right. While Ferrero's division of African-American troops was on its way to Germanna Ford, its role would be limited to a guarding force and it would not enter real combat. The rest of Burnside's *IX Corps* was on the move from 0200 to get into position on the field of battle between the *V* and *II Corps*. Though Burnside had maintained to Meade that he would be on the march early in the morning, Major James C. Duane, Meade's chief of engineers, bitterly claimed that the bewhiskered general would fail to be on the field of battle in time, "He won't be up—I know him well!" Indeed, the *IX Corps* got stalled on the roads during the night. When one of Meade's staff officers offered to help iron out the snag, Meade refused bitterly noting Burnside's independence, "I have no command over General Burnside." By 0400 the corps was in sight of army headquarters near the Wilderness Tavern.

Ewell was likewise active, preparing for his action of the next day scheduled at 0430, the same time that Grant had originally planned his assault to begin. Ewell was able to enjoy a small force of reinforcements, Ramseur's Brigade which had been dispatched north of the Rapidan in a reconnaissance mission on 4 May. A few adjustments were made to the Second Corps line; Jones' Virginia regiments were placed astride the turnpike between Johnson's and Rode's Divisions and Gordon's Brigade was shifted from the right to the left where it rejoined Early's Division. As the Confederates performed these movements, they made sure to make plenty of noise tromping about to give the enemy the impression that their adversaries were being heavily reinforced.

Meanwhile on the Confederate right, some commanders were apprehensive of the condition of their men and their line in light of a probable enemy offensive on the sixth. The pummeled line lay perpendicular to the Plank Road. McGowan's troops of Wilcox's Division were north of the road with the left flank of the command withdrawn to guard against a possible renewed flank attack by Wadsworth. Cooke's Brigade, one of the few commands that managed to build fortifications, was also north of the road in reserve. Davis' Brigade was on McGowan's left. Scales' and Thomas' brigades extended the line from the road south. Kirkland's and Walker's Brigades were in the left rear while Lane's Brigade was the reserve in the right rear.

Most of Hill's front line was sadly disorganized by the fighting on the fifth, with few of the brigades able to field a proper line and some regiments even separated from their proper commands. Division commander Heth approached Hill in the late evening in an attempt to receive permission to reorganize the confused battle line. The surly Hill refused, arguing the men needed to rest and Longstreet would soon be up on the field. Heth returned two more times, pleading with Hill to change his mind. "Damn it, Heth," the annoyed corps commander angrily responded, "I do not want to hear any more about it; the men shall not be disturbed." Around 2100 division commander Wilcox voiced concerns about the disorganized Third Corps line to Lee. The general commanding maintained that Longstreet would be up by morning in time to replace Hill's divisions.

Heth and Wilcox still remained apprehensive. Wilcox went down the Orange Plank Road in search of signs of the First Corps, but found none. Around 0330, he ordered engineers to start building firm defenses and breastworks. It was daylight before the troops reached his position and the enemy was too close for them to carry out their duties in safety.

The hopes of Confederate survival in the Wilderness rested upon the timely arrival of Longstreet who was still on the march to the battlefield. Longstreet's progress during the fifth had been a disappointment; his command had only made 15 miles from their earlier camp to Richard's Shop. The tardy First Corps, supposed to be at the shop at 1200, arrived there five hours late and was detailed to rest until 0100 the next day. Concerned about the timely arrival of Longstreet, Lee sent cavalry officer Major H.B. McClellan to have the First Corps hasten to reinforce Hill. McClellan's mission was all for naught. When he reached the headquarters of Longstreet's leading division under Major General Charles W. Field, the officer refused to accept the major's instruction. An indignant McClellan returned late at night to report this fact to Lee along with the information that the First Corps would not be on the move until the early morning of the sixth. When the officer offered to ride back to Field with written orders, Lee responded, "No, Major, it is now past 10 o'clock, and by the time you could return to General Field and he could put his division in motion, it would be 1 o'clock; and at that hour he will move."

Longstreet's men were in motion throughout the pre-dawn darkness of the sixth, a movement plagued with difficulty when a guide couldn't find the right road for the columns of troops. Confederate Augustus Dickert remembered of the trek, "Along blind roads, over grown by underbrush, through fields that had lain fallow for years, now studded with branches and briars, and the night being exceedingly dark, the men floundered as they marched." The timely arrival of Longstreet before the thunderstorm of Hancock's attack broke loose on Hill did not appear likely.

# CHAPTER VIII

# Up Came Longstreet

Grant was awake by 0400 for the second day of the battle. His breakfast for the morning was a cucumber doused with vinegar and a strong cup of coffee. A servant brought him 24 cigars, 1 of which the general lit; the rest he put in his pockets. Then he began to pace back and forth awaiting news of the coming attack. The Confederates would make the first move, however, with Ewell's assault against the Federal right.

Around 0430, intermittent picket fire grew in intensity, mingling with cannon blasts as fighting signaled Ewell's attempt to drive back the Federal right. The opening of the day's battle would prove no more than a diversion for the monumental events to take place farther south and the bloodcurdling battle in the Wilderness began to reach new heights of intensity as the day slowly wore on.

Ewell opened his assault with an artillery barrage before troops of Early's Division moved out against Seymour's and Neill's Federal brigades of Wright's division. The Federals responded to the early attack by blasting away at the oncoming lines with musketry shots at close range. Ewell's half-hearted assault managed to drive back the Federal picket line only to stall before the shower of minie balls created by the main line. The attack was quickly suppressed and the Confederates retreated for their own defenses. Seymour's and Neill's men offered pursuit only to be driven back in turn themselves. At 0500, troops of Wright's division assailed the Confederates of Johnson's Division. The Federals attempted

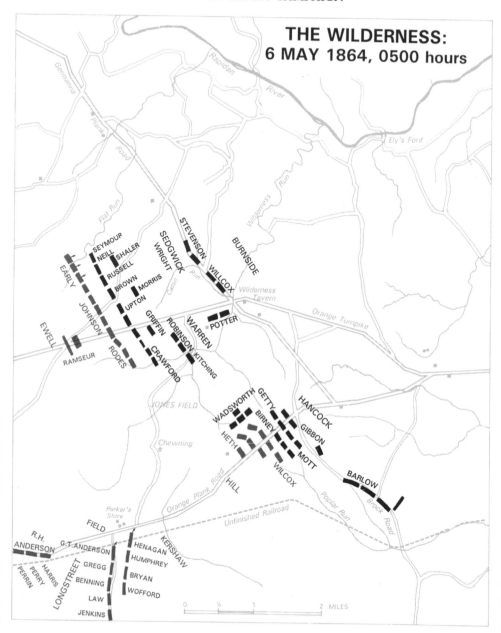

# THE WILDERNESS:
# 6 MAY 1864, 0500 hours

*Yankees of Warren's V Corps receive ammunition. While Hancock pressed the enemy to the south on the Orange Plank Road on 6 May, Warren failed to get actively engaged.*

to force the Confederates from their works in three efforts, but each one was repulsed with a loss.

Further to the south, Warren's troops were tardy in making their assault. The corps commander was both worried and cautious because Burnside was not yet in a position to launch an attack in concert with the rest of the army. The *IX Corps* was still in motion in the direction of the Lacy House to the south of the *V Corps*. Even worse for Warren, Burnside's failure to be on the field in time forced him to send reinforcements to bolster Wadsworth as that general cooperated with Hancock's attack. At 0530, the corps headquarters dispatched this word to Humphreys, "All General Warren's troops are disposed for the assault, except two brigades of Robinson's division which are held in reserve to Griffin and Crawford. The head of Burnside's column is just going on to the field, and in consequence of their not being in position, I have sent the heavy artillery under Colonel Kitching to support General Wadsworth." Still, Warren was urged to move by headquarters.

The *V Corps* was finally underway around 0600. Warren's troops drove up against the enemy works with the support of guns from the light artillery. Griffin's troops marched across the stale carnage of Sanders' Field. To the south were Crawford's Pennsylvanians who were trying to keep up with Griffin's march. At 0625 Warren issued a short report of his activities interspersed with some unsolicited advice:

> General Griffin has moved up close to the enemy's position and driven him from his lines, and I am getting in artillery to open on the enemy. I think it best to not make the final assault until the preparations are made. We are driving them rapidly on the left and prisoners are coming in. General Burnside's column ought soon to be in position to intercept the enemy right.

Throughout the rest of the day, the *V Corps* would fail to actively engage the enemy

To the south, Hancock's grand offensive under Birney was underway at 0500. Blue waves of 25,000 Federals surged forward against makeshift defenses manned by 14,000 Confederates. As during the day previous, the Yankees forced their way through the dense thicket losing organization and casualties as Hill's men unleashed a telling fire. Still, Hancock's ranks managed to come on. All of a sudden the Federals were on top of the enemy works and Hill's right flank trembled under the pressure. To the south Scales' Brigade was punished by the Federals of Ward's men. The *141st Pennsylvania* took the colors of the 13th North Carolina during the short fight as the Tarheels fled for the rear. Scales' entire brigade collapsed leaving a dangerous gap in Hill's line that was soon filled with charging Federals. Once in the breach, the *II Corps* troops turned their fire on the flanks of those units that had once been linked to Scales' left and right. McGowan's Brigade on the right near the Orange Plank Road was also forced to withdraw. Caldwell said of the retreat, "There was no panic and no great haste; the men seemed to fall back from a deliberate conviction that it was impossible to hold the ground, and, of course, foolish to attempt it. It was mortifying, but it was only what every veteran has experienced." Davis' troops attempted to form to meet the assault

# David B. Birney

Oddly enough James B. Birney (1825-1864) a future Union general and son of the prominent Abolitionist James G. Birney, was born in Alabama. His family moved to Ohio and Birney graduated from Andover from which he entered business and the law. Birney practiced in Philadelphia from 1856, but interrupted his work to go to war.

Though having no real military experience, Birney had studied military subjects and was appointed lieutenant colonel of the *23rd Pennsylvania*. He advanced rapidly, attaining the rank of colonel and soon after brigadier general of volunteers. He led a brigade in the *III Corps* during the Peninsula campaign, after which he was court-martialed on a charge of disobedience lodged by Samuel P. Heintzelman and George G. Meade.

However Birney was acquitted and restored to duty in time for the Second Bull Run campaign. At Chantilly he took command of Major General Philip Kearny's division when he was killed after he accidentally rode into the enemy lines. Birney's efforts at Chancellorsville won him a promotion to major general. At Gettysburg, he led his troops in the fight at the Peach Orchard and took command of the *III Corps* upon the wounding of Dan Sickles. In the Wilderness he led a division in the *II Corps* and commanded the forces that broke through the Confederate left on 6 May. He was to have taken command of the *X Corps* but fell ill with malaria and never recovered. His last words were "Keep your eyes on that flag, boys!"

only to be driven off the field; the 55th North Carolina regiment of that brigade was routed before it could even unstack its weapons. To the south Thomas' Brigade, in danger of being cut off from the rest of the Army of Northern Virginia, fled from the deteriorating situation and attempted to find security behind Lane's Brigade. This command had been trying to set up a line perpendicular to the Plank Road when the attack came only to be forced to retire after being struck in the front and left. For many soldiers of the brigade the attack and retreat occurred so quickly that they left the field without even firing an angry shot in reply to the enemy onslaught.

Wadsworth's troops, who had timorously retreated in the face of a small skirmish line the day before, broke like a storm

*View of the fighting on 6 May from the Lacy house looking to-
wards Parker's Store.*

on Kirkland's left flank. The brigade was rolled up and sent
to the rear while Walker's troops were likewise forced back.
Of Hill's Corps, all its brigades had broken save Cooke's
north of the Plank Road which had the luxury of satisfactory
defensive works supported by artillery. Both these measures
tied up the enemy advance when it came.

Wadsworth's success caused severe problems with the
Federal assault. His advance from the north veered in front of
Birney's troops advancing from the east causing a severe
traffic jam. The entire mess was compounded by the formations confused by the terrain and the fight with the Confederates. Wadsworth labored in the confusion to get his brigade
turned around with the *Iron Brigade* facing the front and the
rest of his brigades following.

Getty's *VI Corps* troops detoured south around the jam only
to deviate northwards into Cooke's line which had been
reinforced by members of Kirkland's and Davis' men who

had not yet given up the fight. The Federals were stalled before Cooke's strong position until they were able to tap the flanks of the enemy, sending them reeling to the rear in retreat. As one Confederate of the 33rd North Carolina told it, "the uniformed line was rolled up as a sheet of paper would be rolled up without the power of effective resistance."

Theodore Lyman and several orderlies were dispatched by Meade to join Hancock and give reports of the fighting on the left. Lyman reached the commander of the *II Corps* as he was enjoying the fruits of his success. Gleefully smiling, Hancock told the aide, "We are driving them, sir; tell General Meade we are driving them most beautifully. Birney has gone in and he is just cleaning them out be-au-ti-fully!" Instead of sharing in Hancock's enthusiasm, Lyman told him, "I am ordered to tell you, sir, that only one division of General Burnside is up, but that he will go in as soon as he can be put in position." Hancock's smile and jubilation evaporated with the news. "I knew it!" he bitterly cried, "Just what I expected. If he could attack *now*, we would smash A.P. Hill all to pieces!"

Meanwhile, Lee was treated to a sight he had seldom experienced before: troops of the Army of Northern Virginia engaged in a complete rout. Rivers of panicky Confederates streamed past his headquarters at the Tapp farm down the Orange Plank Road heading west for safety. Lee rode up to the troops in an attempt to bring some sense of order back to his collapsing right. When he came upon McGowan, the general commanding cried out, "My God, General McGowan, is this the splendid brigade of yours running like a flock of geese." "General," the gallant brigadier replied, "They only want a place to form and they'll fight as well as they ever did." Longstreet's arrival was now essential if the entire Army of Northern Virginia was not to be routed. Lee dispatched Colonel Venable down the Plank Road to look for him. When General Wilcox became frustrated with his attempts to get his men to hold, he reported to Lee who also sent him in search of Longstreet to hurry him towards the front. Until the First Corps troops arrived, 16 guns of Lieutenant Colonel William T. Poague's artillery at the Tapp farm

*Lieutenant General James Longstreet's First Corps arrived in the nick of time to throw the victorious Federals back after Hill's command collapsed on 6 May. He then launched a counterattack which rolled back the enemy even further, but fell wounded in the confusion of battle, shot by his own troops.*

were all that stood in the face of the Federal advance. These began to shell the woods to their front as the victorious Yankees advanced.

The first troops Wilcox stumbled upon were those of Kershaw's Division which now held the advance of the First Corps. Major General Joseph B. Kershaw was one of the best brigade commanders in the Army of Northern Virginia, who had proven himself in many of the great battles of the war. At Fredericksburg he helped hold Marye's Heights against the Federals and at Gettysburg he participated in the bloody confusion at the Peach Orchard. Perhaps his greatest test was to come at the Tapp farm. Wilcox hurriedly gave Kershaw Lee's command to move forward before he set off for the rear to find Longstreet. As if to confirm the seriousness of the situation, the First Corps men encountered the sight of their broken comrades fleeing for the rear. A Rebel of the 4th Texas recalled, "Reaching the Plank Road, we found a scene of utter and apparently, irredeemable confusion, such as we had never witnessed in Lee's army. It was crowded with standing and moving wagons, horses and mules, and threading their way through this tangled mess, each with his face to the rear, were hundreds of the men from Wilcox's and Heth's divisions which were being driven from the lines." Colonel William F. Perry leading Law's Brigade remembered, "We were now on the Orange Plank Road, and began to meet the wounded retiring from the field. At first they were few; but soon they came in streams, some borne on litters, some supported by comrades, and others making their way alone. Close behind them were the broken masses of Heth's division, swarming through the woods, heedless of their officers, who were riding in every direction to get attention."

Shortly after 0600 Kershaw threw his men forward, having them set up on the Tapp farm, south of the Plank Road. Colonel John Henagan's brigade was in the lead, taking positions south of the road; save for the 2nd South Carolina, which was positioned north of the Plank Road to protect Poague's guns. The veterans' attempts to form were somewhat hampered by the mob of Hill's broken command. However, Henagan's Brigade let them pass with jeers of "You don't look like the men we left here. You're worse then Bragg's men." Realizing that Longstreet's Corps was on the field to save the day, Hill's troops and the cannoneers yelled, "Here's Longstreet. The old warhorse is up at last. It's all right now."

Then came the pursuing Federals, a conglomeration of Hays', Ward's, McAllister's and Brewster's men. Though tired and disorganized, these smashed into Henagan's line, exploiting a gap that existed between the 2nd South Carolina and the cannons and the rest of Henagan's Brigade. Both Henagan's left and the 2nd South Carolina suffered severely, the latter losing its colonel and lieutenant colonel, forcing the command of the regiment to devolve to a captain. Kershaw brought up Brigadier General Benjamin Humphreys' brigade to bridge the gap, forestalling immediate disaster and Brigadier General Truman H. Bryan and his brigade went in on the right of the line. Poague's guns chimed in against the Federals, firing telling blows with grapeshot.

# James Longstreet

South Carolinian James Longstreet (1821-1904), one of Lee's most able subordinates, did not seem fitted for the grand destiny he later achieved after graduating from West Point a poor 54th out of a class of 62 in 1842. One of his friends during his schooling at the academy was future Federal Lieutenant General Ulysses S. Grant whose wedding Longstreet attended. He then served on various frontier posts and proved himself in extensive service throughout the Mexican War.

Longstreet resigned on 1 June 1861 to take a commission as a brigadier general in Confederate service. After commanding a brigade in the first battle of Bull Run, Longstreet attained the rank of major general at the head of a division. His service in the Peninsula campaign was mixed, but he later proved his abilities during the Seven Days Battles. His rise during this period was tempered with tragedy as the general suffered the crushing loss of three daughters to scarlet fever in the first winter of the war.

Lee gave Longstreet his complete faith and of several divisions, which the general led at Second Bull Run and Antietam. In the former battle, Longstreet launched a smashing attack which rolled up the flank of the Federal army and sent it into a panicky retreat. Longstreet was a lieutenant general by Fredericksburg, but was denied an opportunity to share in the Confederate victory at Chancellorsville, for most of his command had been sent south to protect Richmond.

Longstreet returned to the Army of Northern Virginia to participate in the Gettysburg campaign where his controversial role during the battle continues to spark heated debate even today (some even go as far as blaming him for the Confederate

---

Just as the Federals were being battered by Kershaw's Division, a force driven by Wadsworth appeared on the Confederate left. Field's Division arrived in time to meet this threat. The hard fighting Texas Brigade under John Gregg advanced to protect Poague's guns and blast the enemy while the rest of the divison was still forming. Lee reportedly told Gregg as the command prepared to fight, "The Texas Brigade always has driven the enemy, and I want them to do it now. And tell them, General, that they will fight to-day under my eye—I will watch their conduct. I want every man of them to know I am here with them!" When it appeared as though Lee

loss there). In September of 1863, Longstreet departed from Lee's command once again, this time to participate in the Confederate victory at Chickamauga. There Longstreet was dissatisfied, like so many others, serving under the commander of the Army of Tennessee, Braxton Bragg. He was able to get his force detached to engage in a campaign of his own against Knoxville which failed utterly. The entire sorry incident left Longstreet embittered against several of his subordinates who he believed had failed him.

Longstreet returned to serve with Lee against Grant's campaign at Richmond. He came up just in time to save the Army of Northern Virginia in the Wilderness on 6 May 1864 and send the advancing forces of the Federal *II Corps* back reeling in defeat. While Longstreet was in the process of rolling back the Federal line even further and possibly even coming close to forcing Grant's army into retreat, he

was mistakenly shot and wounded by his own troops. Longstreet returned to duty in November and served out the rest of the war with Lee, fighting against inevitable surrender.

After the war, Longstreet angered many of his former comrades by becoming a Republican and serving in President Grant's government, including a stint as ambassador to Turkey. His memoirs *From Manassas to Appomattox* are a fascinating account of the war from the Confederate viewpoint.

Longstreet was by far one of Lee's greatest corps commanders, second only to Stonewall Jackson himself. Though an advocate of taking a defensive position in many battles, Longstreet oversaw many of the finest counterattacks of the war at Second Bull Run, Chickamauga and the Wilderness. While superb at the helm of a corps under Lee's direction, Longstreet failed to demonstrate any great ability in independent command.

---

was preparing to endanger himself by taking part in their attack, the men of the Texas Brigade cried out for their beloved general to go to the rear. Shouts of "Go back, General Lee! Go back! We won't go unless you go back!" rose through the air competing with the noise of the musketry and cannon fire. Reportedly, a sergeant came forward to take the reins of Lee's horse while Gregg implored his commander to go to the rear. Colonel Venable managed to get Lee's attention turned to command matters when he noted Longstreet was on the field to the right of the Texans. Lee and the staff officer rode out to talk with him, but as the army commander left; he

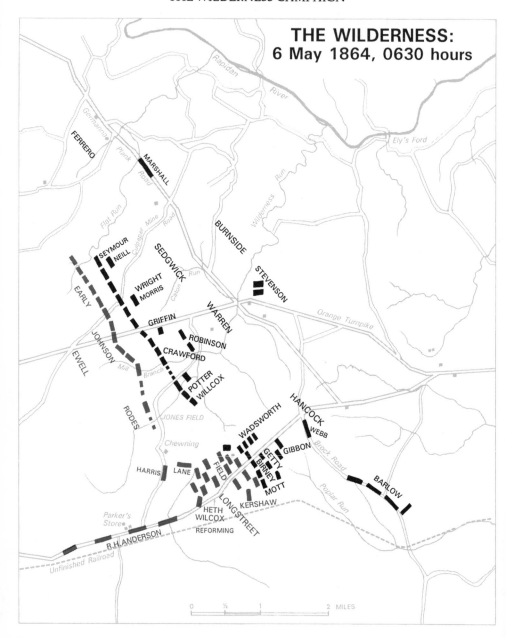

# THE WILDERNESS:
## 6 May 1864, 0630 hours

supposedly told the Texans, "I'll go, my men, if you will drive back those people." When Venable got a chance to tell Longstreet of the incident which had just occurred, the corps commander then joined in urging Lee to go to the rear and safety. Meanwhile the Texans plowed down the ground north of the Orange Plank Road, advancing 400 yards to attack the enemy. The enemy poured on an extremely telling fire of musketry, causing severe casualties among the Texans and thinning their ranks. In the end the men from the Lone Star State, without support and endangered of being trapped, were forced to retreat 200 yards after losing two-thirds of their strength as casualties.

Despite these losses, the rest of Field's Divison was on the ground at 0630 to dispatch the Yankees. First came on Brigadier General Henry Lewis Benning's brigade which only managed to suffer the same fate as Gregg's men. A fearless fighter,· Benning fell wounded during his attack. Richard Lewis of the 4th North Carolina watched the troops come back from Gregg's and Benning's assaults. "What a chill and horror to us—enough to unnerve and unman us! The groans and shrieks of the men lying by the side of the road; and the huzzah of the Yankees; the rattle of musketry and then here comes the wounded of the Texas and Benning's brigades, of our division, and two men on each side of a horse carrying Benning to the rear."

Field's final command, Law's Brigade under Perry, was to enjoy much more success. These Confederates, led by a former teacher and college president, advanced on the extreme left of the forming Confederate line. A force of troops belonging to the *15th New York Heavy Artillery* acting as infantry appeared to the north threatening Perry's right. These 1,000 troops scattered when the 450 men of Colonel W.C. Oates' regiment of the 15th Alabama sortied out to meet them. Oates later told of the incident in which he only lost 2 killed and 11 wounded, "I never did understand how I lost so few. I always attributed it to two things: first, that the troops were not veterans—they were unused to battle; and secondly, the rapidity and boldness of my movement, and the accuracy

# The Telegraph

The first message to be sent over Samuel Morse's electric telegraph was "What hath God wrought?" What Morse had wrought with his device was an information revolution. The telegraph helped railroads control traffic, speeded business messages from place to place and provided the press with better access to news. Telegraph wires extended from town to town linking areas by minutes when it used to take hours, days and even weeks to receive information. In 1853 there were almost 23,000 miles of telegraph wire in the United States. Seven years later this figure had more than doubled and a line connected the east and west coasts.

Like the railroad, existing telegraph lines immediately served a military purpose when the Civil War broke out. Armies in the field could be directly controlled from either Richmond, Washington, or many miles away from where military action was taking place. Strategically, the telegraph made an important contribution to the military during the first battle of the war. Wires were used to communicate orders to Confederate Briga-

dier General Joseph E. Johnston at Winchester and to reinforce Brigadier General P.G.T. Beauregard at Manassas Junction. These troops proved instrumental in defeating Brigadier General Irvin McDowell at the first battle of Bull Run on 21 July 1861. Sherman himself noted the importance of the telegraph in Grant's military campaigns of 1864 and 1865, "...the value of the magnetic telegraph in war cannot be exaggerated, as was illustrated by the perfect concert of action between the armies in Virginia and Georgia during 1864. Hardly a day intervened when General Grant did not know the exact state of facts with me more than fifteen hundred miles away as the wires ran."

Both sides had a department to handle the military use of the telegraph. In the North the *United States Military Telegraph Corps* handled communications behind the lines of combat and used civilian operators. The South had a separate Signal Corps to oversee telegraph communications also run by civilians. This arrangement was organized by E.P. Alexander who went on to become an artillery officer.

---

of the fire of my men." Most of Perry's men then took on the Federals belonging to Wadsworth to the east head on only to get stuck in the quagmire of a swamp while suffering severe casualties. Men were beginning to leave the ranks in search of cover from the heavy fire. Just when the brigade seemed ready to collapse, Colonel Oates' ubiquitous 15th Alabama

The Union also experimented with tactical telegraphs to be used in the field. A real success in these endeavors might have proven to be a dramatic advantage by offering a commander a way to break through much of the confusion of battle. During a fight the smoke of battle, mists and difficult terrain could obscure the usual method of transmitting messages by flags called the wig-wag. Communication more frequently relied on couriers who could become lost or casualties during the heat of battle. In the Wilderness communication was all the more difficult because of the harsh terrain. There, one message from Meade to Hancock on the first day of the battle of the Wilderness took nearly three hours to go just a few miles.

The Union made important headway in the development of the field telegraph, but the success was not dramatic and not without controversy. Under the stewardship of Albert James Myer, the Beardslee Patent Magneto Electric Field Telegraph Machine found its way on to numerous battlefields. This curious device required two wagons, one for the telegraph and another for a magneto to power the set. Five miles of wire with 200 poles from

15 feet to 18 feet in length to hold the wire accompanied the telegraph to connect communications with the field. The machine proved an immense boon to the Union forces during the battle of Fredericksburg where heavy mists prevented the use of signal flags. This success was short lived as the Beardslee device was somewhat faulty and proved utterly ineffective at the battle of Chancellorsville. After that battle the *Military Telegraph Corps* adopted the Morse key which used a battery with more power than the magneto of the Beardslee set. The telegraph was used extensively in the field throughout the rest of the war. When Grant went into the Wilderness, the brigades of the *Army of the Potomac* each had a mule with equipment to lay wire and Hancock had a line to Meade's headquarters by the second day of the battle. Due to limited resources, the South was unable to develop a field telegraph system to match that employed by the Union.

Despite the potential gifts of the telegraph, it never took the place of more conventional forms of communication such as the courier and the wigwag. Still, the device did herald the use of radio communications of great importance in later wars.

managed to get on the Federal right, delivering stunning volleys on the enemy flank. At the same time, Perry rallied the rest of his forces and advanced with a heavy attack. Wadsworth's Federals fled the field under the terrible pressure around 0740. As Perry recalled after the combined attack with Oates, "The enemy instantly disappeared...."

All at once Hancock's mighty offensive was successfully repulsed by the timely arrival of Longstreet's divisions. Given the half-hour delay Grant reluctantly accepted due to his corps commanders' insistence, historians have long wondered what might have occurred if Hancock's attack had gotten under way at 0430 as Grant had intended. Now it was Lee's and Longstreet's turn to take the offensive.

*A field telegraph wagon. The Union experimented with operating telegraphic communications between headquarters and commands with some success. Still, the main form of communication remained the courier and the wig-wag flagging system.*

CHAPTER IX

# Confederate Offensive

While Longstreet's timely counterattack began to wreck the Federal attack down the Plank Road, the Federal leadership desperately attempted to keep their offensive going. A flurry of messages went from Meade's headquarters to his corps commanders promising them troops and pressing them to attack. Hancock himself received news that Brigadier General Thomas G. Stevenson's *1st Division* of the *IX Corps* in reserve would be available to him if absolutely necessary in an 0700 dispatch from Humphreys:

> Your dispatch is received informing the major general commanding of the presence of Longstreet's force. I am directed to say that the only reserve force of the army (one division of the Ninth Corps) is here, and will be ordered to your support, should it become absolutely necessary. Call for it, therefore, only in case of the last necessity.

As on the day before, Meade pressed Warren to attack concomitantly with Hancock only to have his subordinate demur. At 0715 this desperate message was dispatched from Humphreys to Warren:

> General Hancock has taken rifle-pits and two flags. Longstreet has come up on his left. The major general commanding considers it of the utmost importance that your attack be pressed with the utmost vigor. Spare ammunition and use the bayonet.

At 0800, Hancock received this message from Meade himself:

> General Wadsworth with 5,000 on Birney's right is directed to take your orders. Two of Burnside's divisions have advanced nearly to Parker's Store, and are ordered to attack their left,

which will be your front. They ought to be engaged now, and will relieve you. Our only reserve is Burnside's third division, yet here, and I don't want to send it if possible.

This word proved to be of small consolation to Hancock as Wadsworth's division was being routed by the enemy and Burnside was nowhere near being in a position to assist the *II Corps*.

With Longstreet now on the field, the Federals desperately needed to employ Burnside's command in the fray. Two *IX Corps* divisions finally arrived on the actual field of battle around 0700, aiming for the gap between Ewell and Hill. While Hancock engaged the Confederates, Brigadier General Robert B. Potter's *2nd Division* and Brigadier General Orlando B. Willcox's *3rd Division* of the corps had finished its march to the Wilderness Tavern. From there, Potter, followed by Willcox's force, tromped onto the Orange Turnpike veering south over the Lacy farm taking a road in the direction of the Chewning Plateau. Potter's troops ran into enemy skirmishers near the Jones farm just south of the Lacy farm. Ewell had been concerned about the threat Burnside posed to his open right flank and to deter the threat he sent Ramseur's Brigade to block the advance of an entire corps. This action forced Potter to deploy his troops to drive off the annoyance while Willcox came up to join the fray. Potter was all ready to launch an attack against the Confederate forces in his front when sometime between 0800 and 0900, Grant's aide de camp, Lieutenant Colonel Cyrus Comstock, appeared at Burnside's headquarters to inform the corps commander of orders to aid the *II Corps* by taking position on its right. Instead of attacking, the *IX Corps* was back in motion towards the Orange Plank Road. Despite the necessity for haste, Burnside's advance to aid the *II Corps* was frustratingly slow. Meanwhile, the *Provisional Brigade*'s position near the river was taken by Ferrero's division of African-American troops so that the former could become Sedgwick's reserve.

Hancock now struggled to keep the initiative by launching his attack and brought up his reserve of Webb's brigade and Colonel Sumner Carruth's *IX Corps* brigade of Stevenson's division for the action. At 0840 Hancock issued orders for his continuation of the offensive and soon after Webb and Carruth, along with Colonel Paul Frank's brigade of Gibbon's division, all advanced, but failed to achieve anything in the way of gains. Webb's brigade advanced forth only to find the enemy on both its flanks. Though assistance was rendered by Carruth's brigade which managed to arrive on the scene, any significant penetration was found to be impossible. The troops of Webb's command fell back, their morale broken by the useless nature of their attack.

Hancock was still willing to do almost anything to attack, including the gamble of having Gibbon relinquish his guard on the Federal left to launch an attack to the west. Gibbon, however, was too concerned that the Rebels were active to the south and refused to budge. The Federals had been concerned about their left flank throughout the battle since it was fully expected that Longstreet might appear there when he finally made it to the field. Now that the missing enemy corps had made its presence felt, the Yankees were plagued by the existence of a phantom Confederate division. So far the Yankees knew they had encountered Field's and Kershaw's Divisions of Longstreet's Corps. Though Pickett's Division was far away to the south near Richmond, Hancock and his subordinates feared it was on the field that day, ready to attack where it could do the most damage. When cavalry skirmishing broke out to the south, Hancock dispatched reinforcements to the left to guard against a possible flank attack, diverting troops from his planned assault to renew the offensive down the Plank Road. Even a confused group of convalescents managed to give the Yankees a scare when it was mistaken for an enemy force. Making matters worse, the *II Corps* Federals were to be concerned about a flank attack around their right, for at 0930 Meade sent word to Hancock that the gap between the *II* and *V Corps* was being threatened. This caused two brigades to be sent there.

Despite a near disaster which almost wrecked most of Lee's Army in Northern Virginia in the Wilderness, the Confederates now hoped to completely turn the tide. Hancock was

*Wounded soldiers from the fighting in the Wilderness. Some are recent amputees.*

significantly trounced and stymied for the time being and the initiative, at least on the southern frontier of the battlefield, was solidly in Confederate hands. However, an offensive could not be the first order of business, for a dangerous gap still existed in Lee's line. If left uncovered the Federals could exploit it and salvage some victory for that day. Hill's Corps, which had been torn and battered throughout the battle on the sixth, was given the task. Heth's troops were to be left in support of Poague's guns at the Tapp farm while Wilcox's Division was reorganized and sent back to the Chewning Plateau. Richard Anderson's division which had followed the arrival of Longstreet's men added to the number of troops on the front line.

The confused terrain of the Wilderness again placed a

Confederate general close to capture. A.P. Hill was in front of his troops, leading them to the Chewning Plateau, when he paused at a deserted farm house. He and his staff dismounted, only to be dismayed by the sound of breaking wood. It turned out to be Federal soldiers tearing down a fence to make way for the advance of their comrades. The imperturbable Hill gave orders to his officers to walk away and not look back. Despite unbearable tension, the general and his men made it to safety without incident.

Meanwhile to the south, Longstreet was pressing his divisions to turn the enemy left. "Old Pete" had discovered an instrument for his enemy's destruction: an unfinished railway bed known to pass through the area. If the Federals were unaware of it, the track could prove an avenue for a fatal attack. Lee's chief engineer Martin L. Smith was dispatched to investigate the path's potential. Smith discovered that it veered around the left of the Federal forces on the Plank Road that had been whipped by Longstreet's counterattack. Better still, the path seemed to be well suited for a large movement and no Federals appeared to be on hand to obstruct it. Smith reported his findings to Longstreet around 1000. As the engineer had not gone far enough to see if Gibbon's troops on the extreme Federal left could be flanked as well, he was sent back to the track to explore the possibility of getting around those forces too.

While Smith returned to the path, Longstreet assembled an attacking force. The man he picked to lead it was G. M. Sorrel, a strange choice indeed for such an important mission. Sorrel had been a bank clerk before the war and his only military experience was as a private in a Georgia militia company. The 26-year-old colonel saw almost all of the Civil War up to that point as a staff officer to Longstreet and had never before commanded troops in combat. Still, his commander saw fit to give him an attacking force with this bit of counsel, "Hit hard when you start, but don't start until you have everything ready." Sorrel would command three brigades, G.T. Anderson's and William T. Wofford's of Longstreet's Corps along with William Mahone's of Hill's Corps, most of which had not seen any real action thus far. He would also get three regiments of Mississippi men from Davis' Brigade under Colonel Stone, which had joined the assault under their own initiative. While Sorrel led a flank attack, Kershaw's, Jenkins' and Anderson's Divisions would advance against the enemy front.

The Confederates attack was under way about 1100. Sorrel got his forces on Birney's flank and then set off to the north against the unsuspecting Federals. Mott's dangling left was the first target. A Union officer spotted the Rebel threat and attempted to report the danger to Mott, but he was too late, for, before an effective warning could be delivered, the woods swelled with musketry and gunsmoke. Through the trees broke a multitude of men in butternut raising the triumphant Rebel yell with Sorrel urging his troops on calling out, "Come on, Virginians!" The enthusiastic novice officer even attempted to grab the flag of the 12th Virginia in the triumphant advance, only to have the color bearer Benjamin May refuse to give them up.

Mott's men never stood a chance. McAllister's brigade on the Federal left desperately attempted to meet the attack, only to collapse from unbearable enemy fire. The rest of the Federal brigades south of the Plank Road fell like dominoes. Major L.B. Duff on Birney's staff told of the disheartening effect of Longstreet's flank attack: "Suddenly a heavy fire broke out on our left...and soon our line there gave way and got into one of those unaccountable panics which happen to the best of armies, and began to fall back rapidly. The infection spread to the rest of our line, and the whole advance line fell back pell-mell to the Brock Turnpike." Another soldier saw Yankee officers with drawn sabers attempting to rally their commands, but, in his words, "They might as well have appealed to the winds." Henry George of the *139th Pennsylvania* recalled that the situation on the Union left called for every man for himself and the Rebels take the hindmost. When the flank attack occurred, Corporal John H. Billson of the *14th Connecticut* had been detailed to help to the rear Private Charles H. House, who was wounded in the foot.

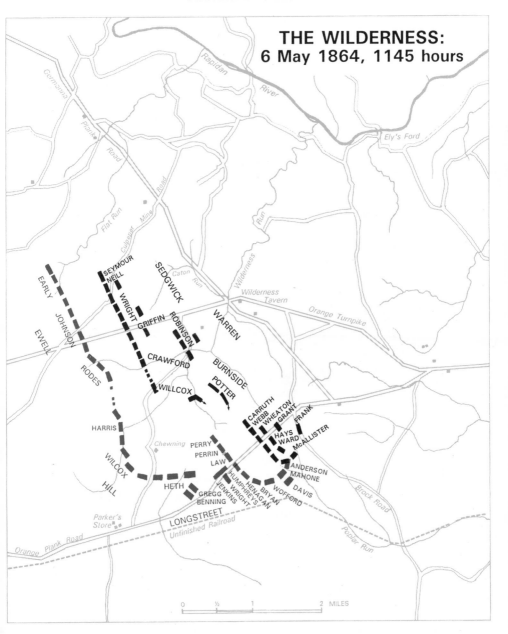

# THE WILDERNESS:
## 6 May 1864, 1145 hours

*Longstreet's choice to lead the flank attack on the Federal left, G. Moxley Sorrel.*

Billson was carrying House on his back as the enemy charge crashed on the Federal line. It cause the injured private to jump off Billson's back and in the corporal's words he "...beat a hasty retreat, running much faster with his wounded foot than I was able to do with two well ones."

The Federals didn't suffer a total panic. It seemed as though many of the Federals calmly and rationally accepted the danger posed to their line and headed to the rear. Many of the men retreating were heading east at an unhurried pace, their rifles leaning on their shoulders as they went. To the north of the collapsing Union formations, Colonel H.C. Barnes of the *Philadelphia Brigade* with Wadsworth's command watched the strange spectacle with awe. He later wrote,

Without any apparent cause that could be seen the troops on our left began to give way falling back to the Brock road. Those pressing past the left flank of the second division did not seem demoralized in any manner, nor did they present the appearance of soldiers moving under orders, but rather of a throng of armed men who were returning dissatisfied from a muster. Occasionally some fellow terror stricken, would rush past as if his life depended on speed, but by far the larger number acted with the utmost deliberation in their movements. In vain were efforts to stop this retrograde movement; the men were alike indifferent to commands or entreaties.

Lyman saw the masses in retreat as well:

They were not running, nor pale, nor scared, nor had they thrown away their guns....They had fought all they meant to fight for the present, and there was the end of it! If there is anything that will make your heart sink and take all the back bone out of you, it is to see men in this condition! The provost marshall attempted to round up these men and get them back into the fight as quickly as possible.

Though Mott's division and others south of the Plank Road had fled the field, Wadsworth's troops to the north tenaciously held on to their positions for as long as possible. Kershaw and Anderson pressed forth attempting to continue their success north of the Orange Plank Road, but found their advance halted by a counterattack. Mahone's troops came in to help, only to find they could make no real headway either.

Wadsworth displayed epic courage as he rode down the line attempting to maintain his position and launch an assault of his own. When the general unsuccessfully attempted to find Webb whose brigade was in reserve, he ordered Lieutenant Colonel Macy of the *20th Massachusetts* to have his lone regiment charge west down the Plank Road. Macy protested this move was a reckless one which would entail heavy casualties. To this Wadsworth challenged that if the colonel did not know how to attack, he would show him how and then galloped off to the fighting. A member of the *17th Maine* saw the general ride by:

...a mounted officer rode rapidly in from our right rear, through our right company, to our front; he was waving his sword over his head, his silvery hair shining like a meteor's glory. Without

*Struggling to fight back Longstreet's flank attack, Brigadier General James Wadsworth was mortally wounded when his horse bolted towards the enemy's line. He died on 8 May.*

halting, without asking who we were, or informing us of him-self—a stranger assuredly—yet with the fury of battle in his eyes, he half turned and shouted: 'Forward! Forward!' and rode out beyond the woods into the open field still brandishing his sword and shouting 'forward!' It fairly took away our breaths, and consternation rooted us to the ground. Where were the troops he was thus urging on?

The general's horse bolted in the conflagration of combat and broke towards enemy lines. An aide grabbed hold of the steed's reins to bring it back towards friendly ground. It was too late, the general fell unceremoniously to the ground, mortally wounded when a bullet struck him in the back of the head.

The Confederates continued to keep up the pressure on the unfortunates of Wadsworth's division until there was only one unavoidable conclusion to the fray. The Federal command slowly began to disintegrate, with troops breaking for the rear and safety as their comrades to the south had done earlier. Grant's crack Vermonters fell back as well. The com-

*Soldiers attempt to rescue wounded comrades from being consumed in flames. During the battle, some unfortunate soldiers suffered the awful fate of being burned alive when underbrush caught fire.*

mander of the *Vermont Brigade* remembered of the event, "Perceiving it was worse than useless to attempt further resistance there, I ordered the regiments to rally behind the breast-works on the Brock road at which point we had been ordered to rally in case of disaster. Our entire lines at this part of the army went back in disorder. All organization and control seemed to have been lost." Webb's brigade was in danger of having Rebel troops storm into its rear. Fortunately, the *19th Maine* came on the scene, forming on the southern flank of Wadsworth's division and protecting Webb's left. The colonel of the regiment suffered for his bravery when he was struck with a wound in the leg and had to be carried to the rear. The men of the *19th Maine* stayed on the field until Webb gave them the go-ahead to break "like partridges" for safety.

Brigade commander James C. Rice had tried to take control of the situation by stepping into Wadsworth's recently vacated command. He attempted to get his own brigade to face the south, but only managed to have it suffer severely from enemy fire on both flanks. The entire command collapsed as its troops joined the rout, leaving some of their unfortunate wounded comrades behind to burn to death in the fires set off by the intense fusillades. With Wadsworth's command in full retreat, Hancock's only task now was to rescue a salvageable line from the terrible destruction wreaked upon his troops. He rallied the retreating forces on the entrenched Brock Road line where they would await the next Confederate move.

After the success in flanking Hancock's advance force under Birney, Longstreet turned his attentions to continuing the momentum of his offensive against the enemy forces rallying on the Brock Road. Engineer Smith returned from his further reconnaissance to tell Longstreet that the railroad bed did indeed lead past Gibbon's left and the Confederate could use the road to attack the Federal flank. Old Pete then ordered Smith to gather the four brigades which had made the attack against Birney's troops and have them prepare for an assault on the Union left while Field and Kershaw pressed forward against the front of the battered troops. The plan became one of the great might-have-beens of the war as it and Longstreet both fell victim to the fortunes of chance of the battlefield.

At 1250, the victorious general headed down the Orange Plank Road with his staff discussing the coming operation. Micah Jenkins, a brigade commander in Field's Division, jubilantly proclaimed to his comrades, "I have felt despair for the cause for some months, but am relieved, and feel assured that we will put the enemy across the Rapidan before night." As Longstreet and his entourage continued forward, the 12th Virginia regiment started across the road moving south. In the confused interlude of the battle with stragglers and stray

*Brigadier General Micah Jenkins was mortally wounded by friendly fire in the confusion following Longstreet's flank attack. Moments before he was hit he expressed hope that Grant would be forced to retreat.*

shots going off, troops of Mahone's Brigade mistook the Virginians for the enemy and opened fire, catching the unsuspecting officers in the fusillade. While some hit the ground for safety, Kershaw quickly rode over to troops readying to empty their muskets as well, "I dashed my horse into their ranks crying, 'They are friends!,' as they instantaneously realized the position of things and fell on their faces where they stood." After the friendly fire was brought to a halt, the irreparable damage was assessed. Jenkins was mortally wounded, just as he saw Confederate victory in sight, and a captain and an orderly near him were killed. Longstreet was severely wounded; a bullet had struck his throat and passed on through his right shoulder (it was almost a year before that Stonewall Jackson was mortally wounded under eerily similar circumstances in almost the same location). The general was taken to the side of the road and leaned up against a tree where he attempted to convey his plans to his generals. Then he was placed on a stretcher to be carried from the field, his hat covering his face to protect it from the sun. He would not return to active service until November.

Command of the First Corps then devolved to division

*Federals desperately attempt to strengthen their fortifications on the Brock Road. After being routed by Longstreet's command, the Federals held behind these defenses.*

commander Major General Charles W. Field. Though Field had commanded a brigade in A.P. Hill's Light Divison from the Seven Days to Second Bull Run, a severe wound in the latter battle had left him out of combat command throughout the rest of 1862 and 1863 while he convalesced. He had returned to the Army of Northern Virginia with a promotion to major general in February of 1864 to take the leadership of John Bell Hood's old division. Though Field was to prove himself an admirable fighting general, his abilities were as yet unproven and there was doubt that the command of an entire corps was within his abilities. Indeed, Longstreet had been openly against Field's promotion to division command, for which he received a remonstrance from President Davis.

At any rate, Field was unsure about the wisdom behind continuing the attack. The command he had inherited was disorganized by its victorious advance, part of the troops being perpendicular to the Orange Plank Road and those brigades which had engaged in the turning movement parallel to it. Before any attack could take place, these troops would have to be tediously reorganized so that all were facing east, a difficult and dangerous maneuver that would take precious time. Worst still, while Longstreet's Confederates reorganized, the large Federal host would be strengthening their position in anticipation of the attack.

When Lee received the disturbing news of Longstreet's incapacitation, he too was not confident in an immediate renewed assault by his right, especially Longstreet's difficult flanking maneuver. The confusion of the First Corps and Field's short experience at divisional command plagued his mind as he pondered his next moves. Lee was not one to give up the initiative very easily; whatever his qualms, he was disposed to attack. Field's troops were to be reorganized and then set in motion, but instead of maneuvering around the Federal left, the attacking force would be engaged in all-out frontal assault.

Around 1200, the Federal high command convulsed in a panic over the collapsing situation on the right. As time passed though, and a continuation of the Confederate attack did not appear imminent, the situation became more relaxed and order was restored. Hancock's troops were settled in behind earthworks on the Brock Road, constructed of earth and timber, the sum of Federal efforts at fortifications for the past two days. The battered commands which had participated in Birney's assault and repulse had since been rallied, readied and resupplied with ammunition. On the extreme left of the line was Barlow's division followed by Gibbon's, Mott's, Birney's and Getty's divisions set up along the road.

Concern about the desperate situation on the right, caused more reinforcements to be sent to strengthen the lines there. To do this the Federal high command made a conscious decision to give up the initiative and concentrate on fielding a strong defense. Since Warren could not or would not engage in any substantial attempt to shake the enemy lines with a substantial offensive, troops from his command were to be funneled south. There was no more heard of such orders as, "Spare ammunition and use the bayonet." The *V Corps* was to dig in and hold fortifications with the minimum amount of troops necessary. At 1100, Warren informed Humphreys that he had ordered up entrenching tools. Once he was firmly ensconced, he claimed he would have 7,000 troops to dispatch to Hancock:

> I will go at once in person to consult with General Sedgwick, and have ordered up my tools. I will let the regular engineer officers take charge of the line, if you have no objection. I will then have comparatively fresh, two brigades of Pennsylvania Reserves, say about 2,200; two brigades of General Robinson, 2,000; two brigades of General Griffin, 2,000; engineer troops, 1,500; total about 7,700. Perhaps the remainder, heavy artillery and Wadsworth's division will hold my line entrenched.

In reality, he would only send about 2,000 men: Hancock received one brigade of Robinson's division at 1400 while the other still on its way. He also received 2 heavy artillery regiments of the *Provisional Brigade* of the *IX Corps*.

Further precautions were taken as the day progressed including efforts to protect the huge wagon train. Around 1300, Sheridan was informed of Hancock's rude handling by the Confederates and was advised to send elements of his cavalry command to guard the wagon train.

As the tides of disaster and victory ebbed and flowed through the woodland, Ambrose Everett Burnside's *IX Corps* inched towards the fighting at a snail's pace. When he finally went on the attack it was only a token contribution to the day's bloody work after noon had passed. At Jones Field, Burnside had been only two miles away from the fighting going on to the south around 0700. At 1050, Grant received a message from Comstock that Burnside's troops had marched only one and a half miles in roughly two hours to connect with Wadsworth's right, a mile away from the fighting. Grant was becoming anxious about Burnside's lack of belligerence and to impress upon the *IX Corps* commander the necessity of speed, the general in chief had his adjutant general Rawlins send a dispatch to Burnside to attack immediately:

> Push in with all vigor so as to drive the enemy from General Hancock's front, and get on the Orange and Fredericksburg plank road at the earliest possible moment. Hancock has been

expecting you for the last three hours, and has been making his attack and dispositions with a view to your assistance.

While anxiously waiting for Burnside to attack, Grant said, "The only time I ever feel impatient is when I give an order for an important movement of troops in the presence of the enemy, and am waiting for them to reach their destination. Then the minutes seem like hours."

Despite these measures, Burnside was finally ready to attack south on the left flank of the Confederate First Corps north of the Plank Road around the belated hour 1400. His troops weren't set up for a very aggressive assault. With most of his men set up on guard duty and supporting roles, Burnside only committed three brigades, one from Willcox's division and two from Potter's, both primarily composed of rookie troops. The attack touched the left flank of Field's Division where Brigadier General Edward A. Perry's Alabamians were stationed. One Yankee of the *45th Pennsylvania* recalled, "The musketry on both sides was most terrific and the rebel bullets whistled around me like hail, cutting leaves and branches." Captain Campbell of the same regiment urged his men on even though he was slowly dying from a mortal wound. The Federals caused some consternation when the force of their assault pressed the Confederates back. The effort was countered by reinforcements from Perry's Brigade of Floridians and Brigadier General Abner Perrin's Alabamians who rushed up to throw back the enemy in a countercharge. The *45th Pennsylvania* had gotten close enough to plant its colors on the enemy's defensive works, but it was thrown back in disorder. In the confusion of the smoke, burning leaves and musket fire, Captain R.C. Richards rallied his men to the colors by singing the "Battle Cry of Freedom" at the top of his lungs. With this brief sortie, Burnside's troops timidly settled down to entrench.

As the day continued on, the Federal command began to regain some of its nerve. By 1415, Meade informed Hancock that he was interested in having the forces under his command attack in conjunction with Burnside's corps at 1800:

I have been expecting to hear from Lyman as to the morale of your command. Should Burnside not require any assistance and the enemy leave you undisturbed, I would let the men rest till 6 p.m., at which time a vigorous attack made by you, in conjunction with Burnside, will, I think, overthrow the enemy. I wish this done.

At 1500, Hancock issued his reply that he would try, but such a forceful move with his tired and beaten forces would be risky.

> The present disabled condition of this command renders it extremely difficult to obtain a sufficiently reliable body to make a really powerful attack. I will, however, do my best and make an attack at that hour in conjunction with General Burnside. What development do you desire? Will you indicate a front?

An hour later, Hancock informed Meade's adjutant general, Seth Williams, that the woods to his left were on fire making it impossible to engage in the proposed attack. He did promise to support Burnside however.

At 1615, the tempest of musketry and bloodshed was renewed as Lee finally got his attack under way and threw as many as 13 brigades on his right against the Federal line on the Brock Road. Lee took direct control of Longstreet's and Hill's Corps for the assault, leaving a detachment connect the left with Ewell. The advancing Confederates clambered across abatis in the attempt to make their way to the enemy line. For the better part of 30 minutes both sides levelled their muskets and blasted away at each other. One witness recalled of the battle, "It was like one continuous roll of thunder, long and deep and heavy, grand yet fearful to listen to. It was music to enliven and electrify a soldier, and cheer after cheer went up from the Union lines, while out in the tangled jungle was heard the...'ki yi' of Longstreet's men." Sergeant Edwin G. Owen of the *141st Pennsylvania* wrote of the musketry, "Steadily it advanced up to us in one continuous roar, until they came in sight on our front, when it was our turn to begin. I had just discharged the third shot when a ball struck me over the right eye. I think I never heard such musketry as there was for about twenty minutes." Each Confederate assault against the main line met with a repulse. However, fortune granted assistance to the Confederates when part of the Union breast-

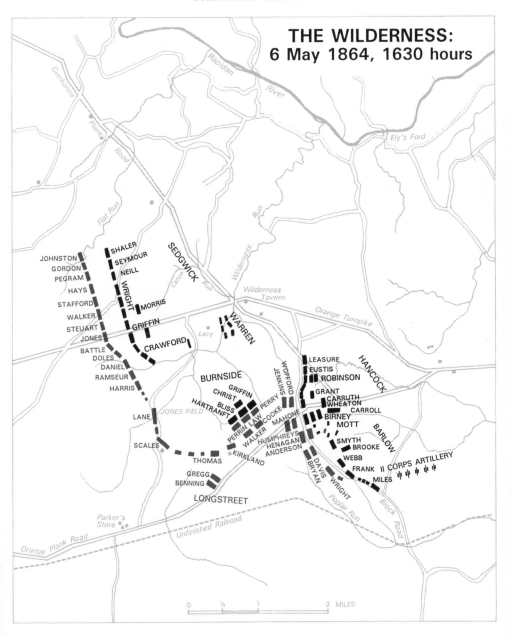

# THE WILDERNESS:
## 6 May 1864, 1630 hours

*Mott's division crumbles after its breastworks on the Brock Road take fire. The Confederates were only briefly able to take advantage of the confusion by pushing through the resulting gap in the enemy line. Muskets and canister forced them back.*

works caught fire. The blaze and its resulting choking smoke forced some troops from Mott's division to fall back. This allowed G.T. Anderson's men to move forward into the breach, an action which caused Mott's formation to once again fall apart (this division would later be combined with Birney's as corps commander Hancock believed Mott could not control his troops). All of a sudden, the Federal line was in jeopardy, as supporting units were forced into retreat as well and part of Birney's line began to come undone. Jenkins' Brigade enjoyed some success when it forced Owen's Union brigade back. As a stream of Yankees flowed to the rear past the Chancellorsville house where Federal supply wagons were placed, the wagoners became concerned that another rout might be imminent and began to put their vehicles in motion towards Ely's Ford.

While there was some concern about the ability of Hancock's line to hold, the rest of the Yankees managed to stay on the front. These men were assisted by the guns of the *6th Maine Artillery* which tortured the Confederates with grapeshot and canister. The men of the battery stood by their guns even as flames set off ammunition stacked nearby. The Confederates who broke through proved to be a more immediate concern as they moved forward despite the blasts of iron to take the firing cannons. Birney met the threat by sending in Carroll's brigade to force the enemy back. These troops fixed bayonets and ran at the Rebels forcing them to halt, waver and then fall back in retreat over the burning timber and abatis. With the assistance of a detachment of Brooke's brigade sent by Gibbon, Carroll's men restored the line bolstered by some of Mott's men who returned to the fray. The Confederate counteroffensive which had begun with Longstreet's arrival had run out of steam.

At 1725, Hancock informed Meade that he had handsomely repulsed the enemy assault, but advised against launching an offensive with the battered Federal left. At 1730, Hancock sent another message lobbying against the 1800 attack.

> Owing to the fact that I cannot supply my command with ammunition, my wagons being so far to the rear, having been sent father back on account of the enemy's assault this morning, I do not think it advisable to attack this evening, as the troops I would select are the ones whose ammunition is exhausted, and I would have no time to prepare a formidable attack, the troops are so mixed up, owing to the occurrences of to-day. Still if I get the order, I will send some in on my right, where I find considerable want of order, which I would wish to correct. Therefore, my opinion is adverse, but I await your order.

Meade came to agree with Hancock's criticism of the attack and informed Grant of his opinion. Grant acquiesced by giving orders for his troops to stay on the defensive, though Burnside was to come to Hancock's aid if he was attacked again. Burnside himself took to the offensive around 1730

187

with an attack that failed to accomplish much but the wounding of Confederate Brigadier General E.A. Perry.

Both sides had been taxed to the limit in the charge and countercharge operations on the Plank Road. Both Grant and Lee had exhausted their opportunities there, though the Federal general suffered from the timorous activities of Ambrose Burnside who had yet to exercise any ambitious initiative. As the battle sputtered out to the south, it was renewed with intensity on the northern portion of the lines of both armies.

# Elite Units of the Wilderness Campaign

During the Civil War, several units won distinction for their fighting prowess, courage and elan. Many such units took part in the Wilderness campaign.

## The Vermont Brigade

This brigade was composed of Vermont regiments throughout the entire war. In its original incarnation, the brigade consisted of the *2nd* and *3rd Vermont Regiments* in August of 1861, but was later merged with the *4th, 5th* and *6th Vermont Regiments*.

At Lee's Mill on 16 April, the Vermonters suprised a regiment of North Carolinians but were driven back by the arrival of another brigade. At Savage Station the brigade broke through two lines of Confederate infantry during which the *5th Vermont* lost 109 out of 420 men. This was the highest battle loss of any Vermont regiment during the war. The Vermonters participated in the Union defeat at Chancellorsville, but failed to get into any major action at Gettysburg. They left the *Army of the Potomac* and kept order in New York after the destructive riots there in July of 1863.

The brigade fought with distinction at the Wilderness fighting on 5-6 May on the Orange Plank Road. Reinforced by the *1st Vermont Heavy Artillery*, the force was then involved in the terrible fighting at the Angle during the battle of Spotsylvania on 12 May. There the

troops fought nearly face to face with their enemies. The *Vermont Brigade* participated in several battles as Grant continued to force his way South, but went with the *VI Corps* to defend Washington against Early's raid against the Federal capital. The command then participated in Sheridan's campaign down the Shenandoah Valley before rejoining the *Army of the Potomac* for the final campaigns of the war.

## The Philadelphia Brigade

The *Philadelphia Brigade* had a singularly ironic and unique history. It was initially composed of the *1st, 2nd, 3rd* and *5th California* regiments all of which were manned by Pennsylvania troops from Philadelphia. The reason for this aberration was the desire by a senator from California, James A. McDougall, and a senator from Oregon, Edward Baker, to raise a contingent to fight for California. Since the state was too far way to send troops, Baker, a good friend of President Lincoln, raised the regiment in Philadelphia only to lead it to disaster at Ball's Bluff. The regiments of the brigade then attained designations as Pennsylvania regiments with the *1st California* becoming the *71st Pennsylvania*, the *2nd California* becoming the *72nd Pennsylvania*, the *3rd California* becoming the *69th Pennsylvania* (being a regiment of soldiers of Irish descent, the men wanted the same unit number as the all-Irish *69th New York*), and the *5th California* becoming the *106th Pennsylvania*.

The brigade fought throughout the Peninsula campaign in the *II Corps* under Brigadier General William Burns who was wounded in the face leading the repulse of a Confederate charge. Oliver O. Howard took over the brigade and led in the battle of Antietam. There it was caught in a destructive cross fire in the West Woods along with Sedgwick's division. The force suffered some 550 casualties in roughly 10 minutes.

After resting for a time at Harper's Ferry, the *Philadelphia Brigade* found itself in another desperate fix when it fought at Marye's Heights at Fredericksburg on 13 December 1862. It was at Gettysburg that the brigade would win its greatest distinction fighting on the second day of the battle on 2 July 1863 and repelling Pickett's Charge the next day. There the Philadelphians were in the thick of things as Armistead's Brigade tried to break through the Union line. While the *71st Pennsylvania* broke and had to be rallied by commanders at sword point and the *72nd Pennsylvania* refused to advance to the front line, the *69th Pennsylvania* held on against the assault with assistance from the *106th Pennsylvania*. Around 490 Philadelphians were casualties at Gettysburg, but the force managed to capture 750 prisoners.

Like many other brigades, depleted by casualties it lost its distinctiveness as other units joined

the command and others were mustered out. The *152nd New York* joined the *Philadelphia Brigade* for the campaign in the Wilderness where it fought on the Orange Plank Road on the 5-6 of May 1864. After the *Army of the Potomac* had advanced south past Spotsylvania and Cold Harbor to besiege the Confederates at Petersburg, the depleted ranks of the *Philadelphia Brigade* were broken up and its remaining strength was funneled into other units.

## The Iron Brigade

One of the toughest Federal brigades, and arguably the most famous, was a unit comprised of men from mid-western states called the *Blackhat Brigade* or the *Iron Brigade*. The unit was organized on 15 October 1861 and comprised the *2nd, 6th* and *7th Wisconsin* and the *19th Indiana*. Its first commander was Rufus King who went on to ignominiously command a division leaving the brigade to the capable John Gibbon. A North Carolina Regular Army officer, Gibbon was a harsh taskmaster who disciplined his men into fine soldiers. He also made them wear distinctive uniforms including a long blue frock coat with turned up light blue color, light blue trousers, white gaiters and a black hardee hat. Later in the war, Gibbon's troops abandoned the gaiters and the coat for the regular government issue, but kept their distinctive hats which became the trademark of the brigade.

The first real battle of the *Iron*

*Brigade* was at Groveton on 28 August 1862. There it performed admirably in the face of a large contingent of Stonewall Jackson's veterans. The western regiments suffered severely loosing 731 men in the fight, 33 percent of its strength. Bloodier battles awaited on the horizon including Second Manassas on 29-30 August where the brigade kept its cool in the chaotic battle which resulted in a Federal disaster. On 14 September 1862, it went into action at South Mountain where it lost 318 men. The westerners went into action at Antietam three days later where they distinguished themselves further. Supposedly, the commander of the *Army of the Potomac* Major General George B. McClellan mused upon watching the blackhats fight at South Mountain, "They must be made of iron." Perhaps this story is apocryphal, but somehow the westerners attained the title of the *Iron Brigade* and the name stuck. After Antietam its ranks were reinforced by the arrival of another western regiment, the *24th Michigan*.

While the entire force was not fiercely engaged at Fredericksburg or Chancellorsville, the *Iron Brigade* faced its greatest challenge at Gettysburg. While going into the fray on the first day of the battle on 1 July 1863, the opposing Confederates were heard to exclaim, "Here are those damned black hatted fellers again." The westerners completely crushed Confederate Brigadier General J.J. Archer's bri-

gade capturing its commander and 75 men. It also assisted in the destruction of Brigadier General Joseph R. Davis' Brigade which included the capture of an entire regiment. When forced to give ground under terrible pressure, the blackhats did so grudgingly, making the enemy pay for every step gained. The *Iron Brigade* suffered an incredible price for its valor. Though not engaged for the next two days of the battle, 1,900 men had been lost, 65 percent of the command's strength.

After Gettysburg, the shattered *Iron Brigade* lost its distinctive character. Easterners, substitutes and conscripts were added to the rolls, men poorly received by the proud western veterans. The brigade participated in the Wilderness campaign where it was routed from the field on the first day of the fighting. For the rest of the war, it remained, but a pale shadow of its former glory.

## Hood's Texas Brigade

One of the most famous fighting units in the Confederate army was a brigade of Texans initially under the command of John Bell Hood. Composed of the 1st, 2nd, 4th and 5th Texas, these soldiers of the Lone Star State resisted any attempt to submit them to military discipline. After First Bull Run, members of the 1st Texas slipped across the Potomac River to give Federals in the Washington capital a good natured scare. Later joined by the 18th Georgia and 3rd Arkansas, the brigade's first real engagement took place at Eltham's Landing during the Peninsula campaign. Serving in the Seven Days and at Second Bull Run, the Texans won a fearsome reputation amongst the Yankees for their destructive charges. At Antietam the brigade shattered the offensive of Major General Joseph Hooker's drive on the Confederate left. The cost was two-thirds of the command as casualties. The 1st Texas lost a total of 82 percent of its men in the battle.

After participating in the Fredericksburg and Chancellorsville battles, the brigade was involved in the desperate fight for Little Round Top on the second day of the battle of Gettysburg. The force then went West with the rest of Longstreet's First Corps of the Army of Northern Virginia to help out Bragg's men. At the battle of Chickamauga on 20 September of 1863, the brigade participated in the breaking a hole in the line of the Union *Army of the Cumberland*. The Texas Brigade returned to Lee's army to participate in the attempt to stop the *Army of the Potomac*'s offensive on Richmond. At the Wilderness, the unit played a role in fighting back the Union offensive after Hill's Corp broke on the Plank Road on 6 May 1864. General Lee appeared willing to go into the fray with the troops, but the Texans refused to fight until their beloved commander went to the rear and safety.

The Texas Brigade continued in the war until the surrender at Appo-

mattox. By then, only 600 of the 5,300 that had served under the standard of the illustrious unit remained to surrender.

## The Louisiana Tigers

The original Louisiana Tigers were the men of a company called the Tiger Rifles raised in New Orleans by Captain Alex White after the outbreak of the Civil War. The name was soon adopted by the unit White's command joined, the 1st Louisiana Special Battalion commanded by adventurer Chatham "Rob" Wheat, a filibuster and veteran of the Italian Revolution. Early on the Tigers won the reputation as an outfit of unruly cutthroats and brigands who spurned authority and discipline. They also had the reputation for being best dressed troops in the Confederate army. The costume, styled on that used by the famed French zouaves, contained a tasseled cap, brown jacket, red shirt, baggy white trousers with blue stripes and white gaiters. Some wore straw hats with a small banner containing a belligerent phrase such as "Tiger Looking for Old Abe." In an act of superlative irony, they carried a battle flag which had a lamb with an inscription, "As gentle as."

The Tigers proved their fighting merit at First Bull Run, supposedly engaging the Federals with Bowie knives. They were later brigaded with several other regiments from their native state including 6th, 7th, 8th and 9th Louisiana. The truculence of the Tigers led to a showdown with the brigade's commander Brigadier General Richard Taylor, son of former President Zachary Taylor and brother-in-law to Jefferson Davis. Taylor managed to bring the Tigers under control through strict discipline including the execution of two soldiers. The fighting spirit of the battalion and the entire brigade was not daunted by the experience and the command proved to be one of the best such units in the Confederate army. It wasn't long before the entire brigade adopted the name of Tigers which aptly described their fighting prowess.

The Tigers demonstrated their ability and won the praise of even Stonewall Jackson himself. While serving in Richard Ewell's division during Jackson's Shenandoah Valley campaign of May-June 1862, they were constantly thrown into desperate situations. At Winchester, Front Royal and Port Republic they helped win the day for the Confederacy. Tragedy awaited when the force rejoined Lee's army as Rob Wheat fell mortally wounded on the field at Gaines' Mill. Command of the force fell to Brigadier Harry T. Hays who led the force through many of the harshest battles of the war. At Antietam the brigade was cut up in a severe fire from the enemy as it charged through the Cornfield. Though it lost nearly half of its men in that battle, it fought again at Fredericksburg and Chancellorsville. At Gettysburg, it managed to seize a position on Cemetery Ridge for a short while before it was forced to retire due to the coming darkness and lack of support.

The rest of the war proved ill for the stalwart Louisianians. On 7 November 1863, the force was routed at Rappahannock Station with heavy losses. Hays' troops helped stymie Federal efforts against Lee's extreme left throughout the battle of Wilderness on 5-6 May 1864. At the battle of Spotsylvania on 12 May the Louisianians suffered heavy casualties including Hays who fell wounded there. The brigade was then merged with the Second Louisiana Brigade which included the 1st, 2nd, 9th, 10th, 14th, and 15th regiments. This understrength unit continued to use the name Tigers as it fought during the waning days of the Confederacy.

## The Stonewall Brigade

Perhaps the foremost brigade in the Confederate army if not the entire Civil War was the Stonewall Brigade, comprised of the 2nd, 4th, 5th, 27th, and 33rd Virginia. All of these regiments were raised from the Shenandoah Valley. The legendary Thomas J. Jackson took command of this force in May of 1861 and through strict discipline and drill, turned the novice troops into crack fighters. The brigade won distinction in the first great battle of the Civil War at First Manassas on 21 July 1862. There the brigade held the left of the Confederate line in the face of a terrific onslaught from Union forces under Brigadier General Irvin McDowell. While troops from other commands were fleeing the field, Jackson's brigade held its position on Henry House Hill prompting one general, Bernard Bee, to utter the immortal words, "Look at Jackson's Brigade, it stands there like a stone wall! Rally behind the Virginians!" The battle was won for the Confederate cause, and the brigade and its commander had a name they would carry throughout history. The Confederate Congress validated matters by confirming the name of the Stonewall Brigade on 30 May 1862.

Jackson went on to higher command, but he never lost his affection for his old brigade. It served him well during the general's famous campaign in the Shenandoah Valley during May through June of 1862. However, Jackson was not as enthused with the man who replaced him, Richard B. Garnett, and removed him in favor of Charles Winder. The brigade won further distinction at Gaines' Mill where it smashed through a Union line to attain victory. At Cedar Mountain on 9 August 1862, Winder was killed when an artillery shell mangled his body and the brigade collapsed in the face of an enemy charge. However, the Virginia troops performed well at Second Bull Run, where Winder's successor Colonel W.H.S. Baylor was killed, and at Antietam and Fredericksburg. At Chancellorsville on 1-4 May, the brigade participated in Jackson's successful flank attack on the Union lines, but lost another commander, Colonel Elisha F. Paxton. At Gettysburg, the Stonewall Brigade engaged in the fight at Culp's Hill while grander events transpired elsewhere on that awful field. It fought well on the Orange Turnpike with Major General Edward Johnson's division at the Wilderness on 5-6 May 1864, but the brigade would suffer a calamitous tragedy almost a week later. At Spotsylvania on 12 May, the force was overrun with much of Johnson's Division at the Angle and many of its troops were killed or captured during the battle. Only 200 men were left after the fight and the commander Colonel James A. Walker was wounded and captured. The force was then consolidated into a single regiment and fought in many of the great battles during the final stages of the war.

# CHAPTER X

# Crisis on the Federal Right

$A$s Longstreet exploited the avenue of opportunity which allowed him to get around the advance positions on the Union left, Brigadier General John B. Gordon was investigating the possibilities to get around the enemy right. Gordon was one of those individuals in the war with little if any prior military experience who displayed a sudden aptitude for leadership on the field of battle. Before the war he had been a lawyer and had engaged in a mining business. After the guns of Sumter sounded, Gordon consistently demonstrated his significant ability in commanding troops throughout the conflict and during the campaigns of 1864 his star was on the rise. By Appomattox nearly a year later he would command a corps in the Army of Northern Virginia. On the fifth, Gordon was instrumental in turning back Warren's attack on the Confederate left flank. On the sixth he would also play a major role in events there. After the Confederate repulse of Seymour's assault earlier in the day, Brigadier Gordon discovered his position overlapped the Federal right. During the morning, he even managed to send scouting parties about one to two miles behind enemy lines where they encountered few pickets to block them. Since the Federals were preoccupied with their assault and the ensuing disaster on the Plank Road, Gordon realized an attack against the exposed right could yield significant gains. It might even crack the *Army of the Potomac* open and send it reeling in defeat.

An enthusiastic Gordon rode off to discuss the matter with division commander Jubal Early. Since Early was away con-

*Mastermind behind the Confederate attack that jeopardized the Union right, Brigadier General John B. Gordon.*

ferring with R.D. Johnston, whose brigade had just finished its march from Hanover Junction, the general went off in search of his corps commander Richard Ewell. Ewell was intrigued by Gordon's proposition, but was unwilling to make any commitment without consultation with his chief advisor Early, an imperturbable commander who had proven himself on many a field of battle. When Early arrived to meet with Gordon and Ewell, he was critical of the proposed attack, arguing that Grant had substantial reinforcements in the form of Burnside's *IX Corps*, which as yet had seen relatively little action. All Ewell could rely on were the exhausted troops of R.D. Johnston's brigade. Ewell was swayed by these arguments, but still did not rule out the possibility of an attack until he investigated the situation on the Federal right himself.

Somehow, the Confederate leadership came to the decision

# John Brown Gordon

John Brown Gordon (1832-1904) had no prior military experience when the Civil War broke out. However, he would end the war as one of the South's best commanders and a major general in command of the Second Corps. Born in Upson City, Georgia, Gordon led an undistinguished academic career, dropping out of the University of Georgia. He then decided to start a career in law, but attained his greatest success in a mining business.

When the war broke out, Gordon began his service as a captain of a company with the rustic name Raccoon Roughs. He distinguished himself as a regimental commander of the 6th Alabama during the Antietam campaign. During the battle of Antietam, Gordon was severely wounded while defending the Sunken Road against heavy Union assaults. After suffering several wounds, he was hit in the head and fell to the ground with his face in his cap. Rendered unconscious from the hit, he might very well have drowned in his blood which leaked from his body into his headware. Fortunately, an enemy bullet had pierced the cap. Gordon was saved from capture and managed to fully recover from his wounds.

Promoted to brigadier general, Gordon led a brigade during the Chancellorsville and Gettysburg campaigns. He was superb at the Wilderness where he broke up the attack of Griffin's and Wadsworth's divisions on 5 May 1864. The next day, he led a flanking maneuver which threatened the *Army of the Potomac*'s right, led to the capture of hundreds of prisoners and gave the Union high command a good scare. He was made a major general almost a week later and given a division. Fighting in many of the final battles of the war, he eventually rose to command the Second Corps, Stonewall Jackson's old command. Gordon held the Petersburg trenches with his men as the rest of Lee's army retreated on the last campaign of the war, a path that would take his army to Appomattox and final surrender. Gordon was next engaged at Sayler's Creek and his weary and outnumbered command suffered severely though it managed to escape to surrender at Appomattox with the rest of the Army of Northern Virginia.

Following the war, Gordon pursued a successful profession in politics. He was elected to the U.S. Senate three times from his native state. His memoirs *Reminiscences of the Civil War* are overly romantic, but informative and fun to read.

to seize the opportunity discovered by Gordon. How they did so is open to some debate. Both Ewell and Early claim that they agreed on the move after a reconnaissance and when Burnside's command was sent south towards the fighting on the Plank Road. On the other hand, Gordon, in his wonderfully romantic and self-glorifying memoirs, claimed that the matter was settled when he put the plan before General Lee. The commanding general arrived at Ewell's headquarters around 1730 to explore the possibility of an attack on the Federal right after the battle against the enemy left sputtered to its conclusion. According to Gordon, he advanced his idea for a flank attack when Lee was discussing his options with Ewell and Early. Early then gave his objections to the move on the grounds that an unspecified Federal force was in the area of the planned attack, along with the claim that he had no large force of reserves on hand to block any enemy counterattacks. However, Lee proved willing to risk the danger for the reward of possible victory.

Whatever actions were behind the go-ahead for Gordon's attack, the brigade commander moved his command to the north of the enemy position before 1800. There his forces faced south ready to eagerly descend on the unsuspecting Federal flank with R.D. Johnston's brigade in support. The rest of Early's brigades were to assist the attack with an en echelon assault against the enemy front, each brigade going into the fight one after the other from north to south.

Truman Seymour's *2nd Brigade* of the *3rd Division* of the *VI Corps* occupied the Federal extreme right for the morning of the sixth. Around 1200, Brigadier General Shaler's bantam *4th Brigade* of Wright's division was placed on Seymour's right. Throughout the day, events and policies conspired to enfeeble Shaler's already weak position. The entire Union left was not in the best defensive shape, since many of the costly attacks against Ewell's line during the fifth and sixth and the dispatch of reinforcements to the south had forced the Federals to contract their lines. Shaler's flank was in the air lacking any defensible area on the right to anchor and defend against the maneuver Gordon was planning to undertake. Entrenching tools that might have helped Shaler's troops dig in were slow in coming since such equipment had been given out first to troops on the left of the *V Corps* and were being passed northwards as each brigade finished making their defenses.

Thus, the brigade in the most imminent danger would receive the picks and shovels needed to strengthen their position last. Unnerved by the danger of his situation, Shaler complained to Seymour that he needed 4,000 to 5,000 men (a good sized division in 1864) to guard the position he held. Seymour couldn't spare any troops so he ignored the pleas coming from his right for more strength, nor was there any reserve for Shaler to draw upon in case a heavy attack did come. Worse still, the Federals on the extreme right were maintaining a careless vigilance, with many troops relaxing unaware of the harsh storm that was preparing to burst upon them. Soldiers had their guns stacked, and some were even resting on their rolled out blankets. With Shaler's men in a complete state of unreadiness, the enemy was able to get within 100 yards of the unsuspecting Federal line before being spotted.

All of a sudden, the Rebel yell broke forth on the field of battle once more as a tumultuous firestorm of fusillades enveloped Shaler's left sometime before 1900. As one Federal remembered, "Cheer after cheer arose from the rebel ranks, and, in fifteen minutes after, their yells were mingled with terrific volleys of musketry as they poured in overwhelming numbers on our ranks." Not only did the Federals have to deal with Gordon on their immediate right, but R.D. Johnston's brigade managed to swarm into their rear while Pegram's troops advanced to strike their front. One witness wrote of the attack, "The scene was instantly a very pandemonium of sights and sounds. The crashing of the timber under artillery fire, the rolling volleys, the rattling rifle fire, the commands, the cheers of our people and the fierce Rebel yell filled the air with sounds...." Shaler found the attack almost completely enveloping his command in fire giving his panicked troops no other option but to break for the rear or surrender. Seymour's troops next in line dropped their picks to grab muskets in order to meet the attack, but these too could not hold.

Next to undergo the attack was Neill's brigade under Colonel Daniel Bidwell, in two lines with the one in front beating off the Confederate frontal assault while the other in

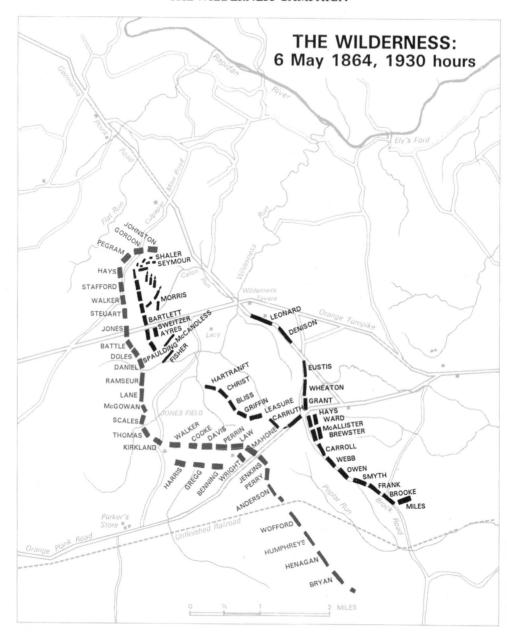

# THE WILDERNESS:
## 6 May 1864, 1930 hours

the rear faced towards the disorganized rout. Seymour and Shaler attempted to rally their men on Bidwell's right, but their efforts resulted in both officers being captured as the Confederate tide attempted to sweep on.

However, the success of the Confederate attack was waning. Neill's brigade under Bidwell managed to hold despite the enemy creeping around their right. At the same time R.D. Johnston's brigade managed to veer off harmlessly to the east while Gordon continued to attempt to sweep up the enemy. Ewell's attempt to use Pegram's Brigade in a supporting attack came to naught when it moved off to the right, running into the front of entrenched Union lines. While their attack was suddenly succumbing to this debilitating confusion, the Rebels did manage to bag an interesting prize, a group of mortified Yankee newspaper correspondents who were later freed.

At the same time, the Federals were quick to react by sending reinforcements to the point of danger. Troops from two *VI Corps* brigades, Morris' and Upton's, dispatched to Hancock were quickly recalled. Warren was ordered to help as well by sending in Crawford's *Pennsylvania Reserves*, but these troops would not arrive in time to have any impact on the fight. Morris' regiments set up east of the main Federal line facing any Confederate troops that might continue south attempting to get farther into the Union rear. The brigade encountered difficulties in organizing this line due to a torrent of Yankees attempting to flee the chaos. Sedgwick then appeared on the scene to aid the defenses only to meet with an extremely close call. A Confederate officer rode up to the Federal corps commander with a revolver and shouted, "Surrender, you Yankee son of a bitch!" The belligerent Rebel was shot down before he could harm Sedgwick, but the Yankee general's horse was wounded in the fray and went bolting off for the rear. ("Uncle John" escaped death then, but he had an appointment with the reaper three days later at Spotsylvania.)

Upton sent two regiments of his brigade forward under Lieutenant Colonel James Duffy into the fray before bringing

*Major General John Sedgwick commanding the* **VI Corps** *helped block Gordon's assault from causing the* **Army** of the Potomac *any real concern. The Wilderness would be his last major battle; he was killed on 9 May 1864.*

the rest of his command. Duffy's troops were thrown into confusion by masses of retreating troops, forcing him to take position in rifle pits dug to protect Sedgwick's headquarters. Duffy was then pressed back by a large number of Confederates before his Yankees rallied upon the arrival of the rest of Upton's men.

As the fighting progressed, the imperturbable Grant spent time interrogating officers from the front and making dispositions to protect his right against further setbacks. One distressed officer arrived at headquarters telling of a panic in which Sedgwick was killed. Grant merely said, "I don't believe it" and Meade had the man arrested. Another officer arrived to say, "General Grant, this is a crisis that cannot be looked upon too seriously. I know General Lee well by my past experience; he will throw his whole army between us and the Rapidan, and cut us off completely from our communications." The lieutenant general heatedly replied, "Oh, I am heartily tired of hearing about what Lee is going to do. Some of you always seem to think he is suddenly going to turn a double somersault, and land in our rear and both of our flanks at the same time. Go back to your command, and try to think what we are going to do ourselves, instead of what Lee is going to do."

# John Sedgwick

One of the more beloved commanders in the *Army of the Potomac* was John Sedgwick (1813-1864), also known as "Uncle John." In 1837, Sedgwick graduated from West Point 24th in his class with the likes of Braxton Bragg, John Pemberton, and one of Sedgwick's future superiors, Joseph Hooker. Sedgwick's prewar service included fighting against the Seminoles and the removal of the Cherokees west of the Mississippi, the infamous "Trail of Tears." Sedgwick also won two brevets fighting in the Mexican War.

When the Civil War broke out, Sedgwick found himself in charge of the *2nd U.S. Cavalry*, Robert E. Lee's former command before he went to the South. Sedgwick quickly rose to brigadier general as inspector general of the defenses around Washington, D.C., and then as the commander of a brigade in the *Army of the Potomac*. By the Peninsula campaign, Sedgwick was leading a division. After being promoted to major general, he almost saw his command wrecked at Antie-

tam on 17 September 1862 when it was trapped in a pocket of enemy fire. The commander stayed with his men attempting to rescue the awful situation and was wounded three times.

Out of the war for about three months, Sedgwick was given corps command and eventually was handed the reins of the *VI Corps* which he would command until his death. Sedgwick fought with distinction at Chancellorsville, Gettysburg and the Wilderness. At Spotsylvania on 9 May 1863, he was assisting in the placement of cannons on the field. While the gunners were seeking cover from sniper fire, Sedgwick remained exposed and joked, "They couldn't hit an elephant at this distance." Shortly thereafter, the general was killed when struck in the head by a enemy sniper's bullet. Grant was stunned when he heard the news, twice asking, "Is he really dead?" He later remarked that the loss of Sedgwick was similar to losing an entire division of troops.

The fighting on the Federal right continued until darkness brought an end to the conflict. The Confederates had failed to reap great benefits from their flank attack, though they fell back to their entrenchments with some 600 Yankees as prisoners. Brigadier General Gordon was to claim that darkness was the only obstacle between him and victory on the sixth. Early disputed this appraisal of the fight, arguing instead that darkness saved the weakened Confederate forces involved from a destructive enemy counterattack. He wrote in his memoirs, "It was fortunate...that darkness came to close this

*A division of African-American soldiers accompanied Grant's offensive into the Wilderness. Though they were primarily used for guard details in the rear, such soldiers would prove their fighting mettle on other battlefields.*

affair, as the enemy, if he had been able to discover the disorder on our side, might have brought up fresh troops and availed himself of our position."

Grant made dispositions to correct his battered right flank by boldly refusing his line across the Germanna Plank Road. The exhausted troops formed the new position that night. This action effectively left him cut off from the Germanna Ford if the Rebels decided to take the crossing. The Federals were going to make no disposition to protect it. At 2130, Ferrero's African-American troops were ordered to advance from the ford to a position near the Wilderness Tavern and at 2300 Meade gave orders to pack up the pontoon there and move it downstream.

Once again men tried to find rest while the screams of the wounded, stray shots from nervous pickets and the deathly smell of burning flesh penetrated the dark woodland. Both sides had failed to crush and drive off the other despite the greatest exertion of both Yankee and Rebel. It remained to be seen if dawn would bring a renewal of the awful struggle in the Wilderness.

# Chapter XI

# "There Will Be No Turning Back"

$T$he next day, both armies felt out the enemy's line while scattered skirmishing broke out from time to time up and down the lines as Federal and Confederate cavalry troopers battled each other to the south. In the headquarters of both camps, generals were up early in the morning mist suffused with smoke to plot and plan their next moves. Between the opposing armies was the human wreckage and impedimenta of one of the hardest fought battles of the war.

The *Army of the Potomac* had encountered near disaster on 6 May, suffering thousands of casualties while achieving no perceptible gain. Indeed, the Federal campaign in the Wilderness had all but utterly failed; Grant had been unable to flank his adversary, his attacks in the woodland had all been severely repulsed, and both his flanks narrowly escaped collapse. The only source of consolation for the men and commanders, a very small one at that, was that they still remained on the field of battle.

Grant faced three options: he could either continue to battle it out in the Wilderness where his opponent would be at a supreme advantage, he could retreat, or he could advance further south to either attempt to flank Lee again or fight a battle on better ground. To attack again would be foolish, the previous two days demonstrated the folly of fighting an offensive battle in the Wilderness. As Meade's chief of staff Humphreys later explained, "On the morning of the 7th,

*Hancock's position on the Brock Road on 7 May.*

reconnaissances were made of the enemy's position, which was found to be well entrenched...artillery was placed not only where the ground was open, but at other portions of the line....To attack a position of such character, situated as this was, covered by a tangled forest that inevitably disordered the attacking forces as they advanced was not judicious; it promised no success." Retreat seemed, perhaps, the wisest course for Grant had fared no better than McClellan, Burnside or Hooker who all had fought great battles, been defeated and then retreated to take up the fight another day.

But for Grant, there was to be no such admission of defeat—the army would press forward. In summing up the situation that faced him on 7 May, the general said, "While it is in one sense a drawn battle, as neither side has gained or lost ground substantially since the fighting began, yet we remain in possession of the field, and the forces opposed to us have withdrawn to a distance from our front and taken up a defensive position. We cannot call the engagement a positive victory, but the enemy have only twice actually reached our lines in their many attacks, and have not gained a single advantage. This will enable me to carry out my intention of

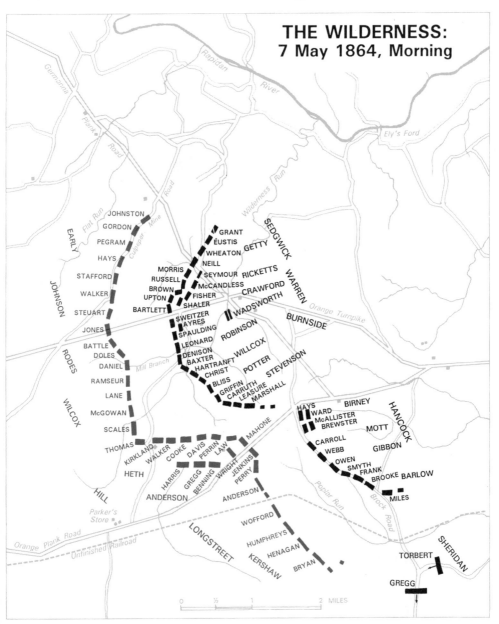

# THE WILDERNESS:
## 7 May 1864, Morning

*Federal forces near the Wilderness Tavern at 1400 on 7 May. Grant
had decided earlier in the day that he would abandon the fight in
the Wilderness to move south.*

moving to the left, and compelling the enemy to fight in more
open country outside of their breastworks."

Early in the day, at 0630, Grant had decided to advance his
army south to reach Spotsylvania Court House on the eighth
and then to move on to the North Anna River to fight another
battle with Lee. The nature of the movement would have the
*II Corps* stay in place on the Brock Road while the *V Corps*
followed that route south for Spotsylvania. The *VI Corps* was
to push east down the Orange Plank Road to Chancellorsville
and then move south for the court house. The *IX Corps* would
follow the *VI Corps* and *II Corps* would follow the *V Corps*. In
preparation for the move, Hancock was ordered at 1345 to
return the reinforcements he had received over the past two
days from other commands.

On the other side of the field, Lee faced a command change
as well as the quandary of divining his enemy's next move.
With the wounding of Longstreet, the First Corps needed an
adequate commander to lead the force in his absence. The
selection of experienced commanders limited him to three

*The burial of troops killed in the Wilderness. Some 2,246 Federal soldiers lost their lives in the fighting there. The true number of Confederate casualties is unknown.*

choices: Jubal Early, Edward A. Johnson, both of the Second Corps, and Richard Anderson, of the Third Corps. Lee thought enough to consult Longstreet's chief of staff, Colonel Sorrel, before he made a decision. While Sorrel tepidly admitted Early's and Johnson's fighting abilities, the former was difficult to deal with and the latter was unfamiliar to the troops of Longstreet's command. Instead, he argued in favor of the commander known by the men of the First Corps, Richard Anderson, who had led both a brigade and division under Longstreet during some of the great battles of the war. While Sorrel left the meeting holding the opinion that Early would receive the appointment, Anderson later rode into the camp to take command to the elation of the First Corps troops.

Giving thought to the moves of his enemy, Lee was of the belief that since Grant had not engaged in battle on the seventh, the *Army of the Potomac* would most likely leave the field. The question then was where would the enemy go? There were two paths the Federals would most likely take,

**The Army of the Potomac** *on the march out of the Wilderness. From the Wilderness to the beginning of the siege at Petersburg, Grant lost an average of 2,000 men per day.*

since the Rebels had discovered the removal of the enemy's pontoon bridges at Germanna Ford: east to Fredericksburg or south to Spotsylvania. Lee decided to hedge his bets by placing troops at Spotsylvania. If Grant was retreating to the east, a force there would be on the enemy's flank as he pulled back. If the enemy advanced to the south, the force would be in his way. Stuart's cavalry was sent out to probe the roads leading south for any Federal motion in that direction. The commander of the Reserve Artillery, Episcopalian preacher Brigadier General William Pendleton, was to have his troops hew a path through the Wilderness leading south for the move.

The Federals got under way after dark with Warren's troops taking the lead. Many Yankees believed that after a destructive battle in the Wilderness, they were now on the road to retreat at the end of another failed and futile campaign. In the growing darkness of night, they eventually learned the stirring news that they were not humbly falling back with their exertions all for naught, but advancing further into the state of Virginia for more battles and hopefully for eventual victory. When Grant, Meade and their staffs rode by, the troops of Hancock's *I Corps* let loose in an open display of adulation. Horace Porter recorded the event,

> Troops know but little about what is going on in a large army, except the occurrences which take place in their immediate vicinity; but this night ride of the general-in-chief told plainly the story of success, and gave each man to understand that the cry was "On to Richmond!" Soldiers weary and sleepy after their long battle, with stiffened limbs and smarting wounds, now sprang to their feet, forgetful of their pains, and rushed forward to the roadside. Wild cheers echoed through the forest, and glad shouts of triumph rent the air. Men swung their hats, tossed up their arms, and pressed forward to within touch of their chief, clapping their hands, and speaking to him with the familiarity of comrades....Instead of being elated by this significant ovation, the general, thoughtful only of the practical question of success of the movement, said: "This is most unfortunate. The sound will reveal our movement." By his direction, staff-officers rode forward and urged men to keep quiet so as not to attract enemy attention; but the demonstration did not really cease until the general was out of sight.

On 8 May Grant summed up his perception of the battle in the Wilderness in a dispatch to Halleck in which he claimed a slim victory, "The results of the three days at Old Wilderness was decidedly in our favor. The enemy having a strong entrenched position to fall back on when hard pressed, and the extensive train we had to cover, rendered it impossible to inflict the heavy blow on Lee's army I had hoped."

Lee's army was also on the move the night of 7-8 May towards Spotsylvania Court House. The First Corps under Anderson departed from the battlefield around 2300 to move down the rough road carved out of the thickets, wood and undergrowth by Pendleton's cannoneers. The next day the rest of both armies were in motion for Spotsylvania where another bloody fight awaited them. Behind on the ground of the Wilderness lay the dead of the battle. There was no time for the Federals to bury the bodies of those who fell; a few corpses had dirt unceremoniously thrown across them but most were left to rot on the ground where they fell.

Lieutenant General Richard Ewell wrote in his report, "The burial parties from two divisions reported interring over

1,100 of the enemy. The third and largest made no report. When we moved one-third or more were still unburied of those who were within reach of our lines." S.B. Sterling of the *11th New Jersey* remembered the sight of the field on 8 May. "In one place I counted twenty-four Confederate and Union soldiers lying close together. In another place I noticed a dead Confederate upon his knees, with his face bruised in the dirt. Still another I saw hanging dead upon the top of a rail fence, his feet on one side and his head on the other." Sterling's comrade Thomas Marbaker wrote, "In places the positions of the opposing forces were marked by two lines of dead, lying almost as thickly as lines of battle, and not over 20 yards apart."

Grant's army lost 17,666 casualties in the Wilderness: 2,246 killed, 12,037 wounded and 3,383 captured or missing. The first battle in the East of the general from the West proved to be one of the most costly battles for the Union. Figures for the Confederate casualties are incomplete. More than 7,750 troops may have been lost in the fight there.

Grant had been defeated at the Wilderness, a fight that he mismanaged tactically with assistance from Meade. For the most part forces had been thrown in piecemeal on the first day and attacks were never really coordinated between the right flank under the *V* and *VI Corps* and the *II Corps* on the left. Warren and Burnside added to the failure in command with the former's reluctance to go on a serious offensive after his attack on the first day and the latter's penchant for slowness. Another fault with the Union leadership was their glaring misuse of cavalry, relegating it for the most part to watching wagons and some reconnaissance. Wilson's failure to detect Hill's advance and his near loss of his own division was a serious blunder. Sheridan would show the Union leadership what cavalry could do if unleashed to raid and destroy when he was finally unbridled by Grant.

Lee, his lieutenants and his men once again displayed their superlative battlefield skills and provided a performance of masterful defense. Each enemy attempt to crack the Rebel line had met defeat or a counterattack that wiped out all potential

*Grant reconnoiters as his forces continue their march south. After Grant proclaimed there would be "no turning back" the fate of the Confederacy was sealed.*

gains. Still, success on the defensive did not translate into any major offensive victories. The tremendous attack of Longstreet and, to a smaller extent, that of Gordon on the 6th pressed back the Yankees in a panicky retreat. However, Longstreet's wounding led to the failure to pursue his offensive and Gordon's assault was hampered by lack of troops and darkness. When Lee engaged in his offensive against the

*II Corps* line on the afternoon of 6 May, he met with a short victory and a palpable repulse.

While the Confederates had managed to defeat their Yankee foe, the Wilderness did not become the same sort of defeat as the long litany of reverses recorded in the annals of the *Army of the Potomac* thus far. In advancing south, Grant's refusal to turn back signalled the end of the Confederacy. With his superior numbers along with his vast stockpiles of supplies he would gradually push Lee back to Richmond and eventual surrender. The road would be bloody, with thousands of Union casualties incurred at places like Spotsylvania, Cold Harbor and Petersburg. But Grant was now in control and his ceaseless pressure would keep Lee on the defensive. No longer would the Rebel "Gray Fox" be able to befuddle and throw back the enemy with the brilliant stratagems he had conceived in the battles before his defeat at Gettysburg. Along with Sherman's moves in the West, Grant's battle in the Wilderness campaign was the first step in an operation that would eventually subdue the South and bring about the demise of the Confederacy.

# The Amazing Adventure of Henry Wing

Hundreds of reporters covered the Civil War for a variety of newspapers. Many more intrepid souls risked life and limb to get a scoop for their employers. One such individual was Henry E. Wing. Wing was a native of Connecticut who had enlisted in the volunteers to serve in the war for the Union. His patriotism was rewarded with a serious wounding at Fredericksburg where he was hit in the leg and lost two of his fingers. Out of the war as a soldier, he turned to reporting and wrote for the *Bulletin* in Norwich, Connecticut. His abilities then won him a more prominent post at the *New York Tribune's* office in Washington D.C in 1864. But Wing yearned to follow the fighting and soon took a position as a messenger for the *Tribune's* reporters following the *Army of the Potomac's* new campaign that spring. Despite orders from Secretary of War Edwin M. Stanton forbidding the issuance of passes, Wing managed to sneak into the camp of the *Army of the Potomac* before it began its march south. Once in the field, the company of *Tribune* reporters proved insufficient to cover the large Union force. This proved to be beneficial to Wing who secured a field promotion to reporter assigned to cover the *VI Corps*.

The reporters were busy early in the campaign as Grant and the *Army of the Potomac* engaged Lee's Army of Northern Virginia in the Wilderness. After the first day's bat-

tle on 5 May, the *Tribune* reporters wanted to get word to their paper that the new general in chief was fighting and would continue to press the enemy. Such a mission would prove a dangerous one. The Union rear remained a fluid situation with groups of Confederate cavalry and partisans as well as Southern sympathizers roaming about who might waylay a vulnerable Yankee if given the chance. Despite the danger, Wing volunteered. The reporter visited with Grant informing him of his journey and asked him if there was any message that he might want to give the nation. Grant replied, "You may tell the people that things are going swimingly down here." The general also saw fit to give the reporter a special message to the President.

Wing left early on the sixth making his way to the house of a Virginian favorable to the Union cause whom he wanted as a guide. The man refused but provided Wing with some shabby clothes to act as a disguise and a cover story that he was a Confederate courier heading to Washington to give Southern sympathizers news of a victory Lee had attained in the Wilderness. Wing took off for the North only to run into some of the partisans belonging to the infamous John Singleton Mosby. The irregular Confederates believed Wing's story and offered to escort him to Kelly's Ford, a crossing on the Rappahannock River. The reporter became

215

worried for he had passed through Kelly's Ford with the *Army of the Potomac* and someone there might recognize him. Indeed, when he reached the ford, someone spotted Wing and alarm was given, but the reporter made his escape on his swift steed while under fire from his former protectors.

Wing abandoned his horse to evade possible recognition and walked to Warrenton Junction. He went on to Cedar Run where he found rest and food at a camp of Federal soldiers. When he continued his journey, he had soldiers fire on him as he pretended to escape in order to fool any enemy that might be watching. On the afternoon of his journey he was captured and detained by a contingent of Confederate cavalry at Manassas Junction. Fortunately, his guards did not maintain much vigilance and he was able to escape by dusk.

Finally, the exhausted Wing arrived at a Federal camp at Union Mills. To his consternation he found no transportation available to take him to Washington. Wing had much reason to be concerned. It was Friday evening and if his information did not get to the *Tribune* soon his story would have to wait until Monday since there was no Sunday edition for his newspaper. By then his information would be too old and all his adventures would have been for nothing. Since the telegraph was only to be used for military purposes, he decided to telegraph Assistant Secretary of War Charles A. Dana telling him that he had left Grant and wanted

to get information to his paper. A message came back over the wire from Secretary of War Stanton who demanded Wing's news of Grant. (Washington had heard little from the *Army of the Potomac* since it went into its engagement in the Wilderness.) Wing replied in a message that he would tell Stanton everything if he could send some information to the *Tribune* first. When Stanton pressed the reporter for his news first, Wing maintained his loyalty to his employer over his government. Stanton then had Wing put under arrest as a spy. Wing fumed afterwards, "I would not have told him one little word to save my life." Another message came over the wire, this time from the President himself who asked if Wing might tell him the news of Grant. Wing once again asked for permission to get news to his paper, which the President granted though he had Wing agree to sharing his story with the Associated Press. Wing told what he knew and then went to get a well deserved rest. However, he was awakened shortly afterwards and hustled to Washington on a special train. Lincoln wanted the full story from the reporter and received him at 0200 on 7 May. The reporter recounted his tale and then told the President he had a special message from the general in chief, "whatever happens, there will be no turning back." Lincoln beamed at the news and was so elated that he kissed the reporter. Wing later recounted his adventures in an essay entitled "When Lincoln Kissed Me."

# Guide for the Interested Reader

$B$y far the best book on Grant's offensive into the Wilderness is Edward Steere's *The Wilderness Campaign* (Harrisburg, 1960), a thoughtful military history which investigates what really happened in the dense woodland, a difficult task indeed. Steere's work was instrumental in this author's study of the campaign. Noah A. Trudeau gives a stirring and horrifying picture of combat from the Wilderness to Cold Harbor in his *Bloody Roads South* (Boston, 1989). *No Turning Back* (New York, 1991) by Don Lowry places the Wilderness fighting in a day by day context with other events occurring in different theaters at the same time. *Into the Wilderness with the Army of the Potomac* (Bloomington, 1985) by Robert G. Scott is also a fascinating work to read. *The Official Records of the Union and Confederate Armies* is invaluable to any investigation of the Civil War. There is an abundance of dispatches and reports for the Union forces in the Wilderness campaign, but Confederate records for the same period are sadly incomplete.

There are many first hand accounts of the campaign on the Union side. Grant's *Personal Memoirs* offer an illuminating look at that general's theory and practice of war. The study of the Wilderness campaign also benefits from several personal reminiscences by individuals serving on Grant's staff. The most lively is by Horace Porter, Grant's aide-de-camp, who wrote *Campaigning with Grant* (New York, 1897). Theodore

Lyman was an aide-de-camp to Meade and had his views recorded in a collection of vivid letters entitled *Meade's Headquarters, 1863-1865* (New York, 1922). Meade's chief of staff Major General Andrew A. Humphreys wrote the dry, but important *The Virginia Campaign of 1864 and 1865* (New York, 1883). More primary sources can be found in *Battles and Leaders of the Civil War* (New York, 1884-1888).

Interesting studies of Grant's leadership include Adam Badeau's, *Military History of U.S. Grant* (New York, 1881), J.F.C. Fuller's *The Generalship of U.S. Grant* (Bloomington, IN, 1958), Albert D. Richardson's *Personal History of U.S. Grant* (Hartford, 1898) and William S. McFeely's *Grant* (New York, 1981). Books on other prominent Union generals active in the Wilderness campaign are Glenn Tucker's *Hancock the Superb* (Indianapolis, 1960) and Emerson G. Taylor's *Gouverneur Kemble Warren: The Life and Letters of an American Soldier* (Boston, 1932).

Confederate primary source material contains some interesting writings such as *Recollections and Letters of General Robert E. Lee* (New York, 1904) a compilation of some of Lee's private letters. Among the autobiographies of Confederate generals, James Longstreet's *From Manassas to Appomattox* (Philadelphia, 1903), Jubal A. Early's *Autobiographical Sketch and Narrative of the War Between the States* (Philadelphia, 1912) and John Brown Gordon's florid *Reminiscences of the Civil War* (New York, 1904) are the most fascinating reads. *The Papers of the Southern Historical Society* offers an unmatched wealth of Confederate sources.

As for writings on Confederate generals, the great historian Douglas Southall Freeman gave an incomparable look into the leadership of the Army of Northern Virginia in his four volume *Robert E. Lee: A Biography* and *Lee's Lieutenants*. Two particularly helpful biographies on individual Southern Generals include *James Longstreet* by Bryan Conrad (Chapel Hill, N.C. 1936) and *A.P. Hill* (New York, 1987) by James I. Robertsons Jr.

For more information on the use of the signal telegraph during the Civil war consult these articles from *Civil War*

*Times Illustrated*: "Don't Cut—Signal Telegraph" by Raymond Smith (May, 1976 and "The Military Telegraph Became the Signals Workhorse (June, 1964)."

Henry Wing's account of his adventures can be found in his work *When Lincoln Kissed Me* or in the *Civil War Times Illustrated* article, "Henry Wing's Wilderness Adventure." Books that offer more on reporters during the war include, *The North Reports the War* and *The Bohemian Brigade* (New York, 1954).

Good general approaches to the war include *How the North Won* (Urbanna, Il., 1983) by Herman Hattaway and Archer Jones, James M. McPherson's superlative *Battle Cry of Freedom* (New York, 1988), *Civil War Command and Strategy* by Archer Jones (New York, 1992), *Why the South Lost the Civil War* by Richard E. Beringer, Herman Hattaway, Archer Jones and William N. Still, Jr. and T. Harry Williams' *Lincoln and His Generals* (New York, 1952). Paddy Griffith's *Battle Tactics of the Civil War* (New Haven, 1989) is a controversial look at the war from the viewpoint of a British officer and military historian. *Battle Tactics* has either been lauded as provocative and intelligent or criticized for its erroneous assumptions. Albert A. Nofi's *The Civil War Treasury* (Conshohocken, Pa, 1992) is a novel treasure trove of information. David Martin's *The Chancellorsville Campaign* (Conshohocken, PA., 1991) and *The Peninsula Campaign* (Conshohocken, PA., 1992) and Albert Nofi's *The Gettysburg Campaign* which will be reprinted in 1993, all provide illuminating studies of other important operations, battles and details of the Civil War. For an inside look at the life of the Southern solider and his religion, please see Bell Wiley's *The Life of Johnny Reb*. One of the most valuable resources available to the Civil War scholar is the *Historical Times Illustrated Encyclopedia of the Civil War*.

To really understand the war, it is of course necessary to turn away from the pedantic writings of today's historians and read the multitude of reminiscences, autobiographies and letters of the soldiers who fought in the war. Books that include eyewitness accounts of the Wilderness campaign include:

Adams, Captain John B., *Reminiscences of the 19th Massachusetts Regiment* (Boston, 1899).

Bidwell, Frederick D., *History of the 49th New York Volunteers* (Albany, NY, 1916).

Birdsong, James C., *Brief Sketches of North Carolina Troops* (Raleigh, NC, 1894).

Brainard, Mary G.G., *Campaigns of the 146th Regiment, New York State Volunteers* (New York).

Caldwell, J.F.J., *The History of a Brigade of South Carolinians Known as "Gregg's" and Subsequently as McGowan's Brigade* (Philadelphia, 1866).

Casler, John O., *Four Years in the Stonewall Brigade* (Guthrie, OK, 1893).

Clark, Walter, Ed., *Histories of Several Regiments and Battalions from North Carolina* (Goldsboro, NC, 1901).

Cogswell, Leander W., *A History of the Eighth New Hampshire Regiment* (Concord, NH, 1891).

Corby, William, *Memoirs of Chaplain Life* (Notre Dame, IN, 1899).

Dame, William Meade, *From the Rapidan to Richmond* (Baltimore, 1920).

Dickert, D. Augustus, *History of Kershaw's Brigade* (Newbury, SC, 1899).

Haines, William P., *History of the Men of Company F* (N.J., 1897).

Howard, McHenry, *Recollections of a Maryland Soldier and Staff Officer Under Johnston, Jackson, and Lee* (Baltimore, 1914).

Hutchinson, Nelson V., *History of the 7th Volunteer Infantry in the War of the Rebellion Against Constitutional Authority.* (1890).

Isham, Asa B., *Through the Wilderness to Richmond* (Cincinnati, 1884).

Jones, Evan, *Four Years in the Army of the Potomac* (London, 1881).

Lewis, Richard, *Camp Life of a Confederate Boy* (Charleston, SC, 1883).

Lyman, Jackman, *History of the 6th New Hampshire Regiment in the War for the Union* (Concord, NH, 1891).

Marbaker, Thomas D., *History of the 11th New Jersey Volunteers* (Trenton, N.J., 1898).

Melcher, Holman, *An Experience in the Battle of the Wilderness* (Portland, 1898).

Nash, Eugene, *A History of the 44th Regiment New York Volunteer Infantry* (Chicago, 1911).

Nichols, G.W., *A Soldier's Story of His Regiment* (1898).

Page, Charles D., *History of the 14th Regiment Connecticut Volunteer Infantry* (Meriden, CT, 1906).

Roback, Henry, *The Veteran Volunteers of Herkimer and Ostege Counties* (Utica, NY, 1888).

Roe, Alfred S., *The 10th Massachusetts Volunteer Infantry* (Springfield, Ma., 1904).

Sorrel, Moxley G., *Recollections of a Confederate Staff Officer* (New York, 1905).

Stevens, George T., *Three Years in the VI Corps* (Albany, 1866).

Toney, Marcus B., *The Privations of a Private* (Nashville, 1905).

Tyler, Mason W., *Recollections of the Civil War* (New York, 1912).

Vauntier, John D., *The 88th Pennsylvania in the War for Union* (Philadelphia, 1894).

Verrill, George W., *The Seventeenth Maine at Gettysburg and in the Wilderness* (Portland, 1898).

# Order of Battle

## Union Army

Lt Gen. Ulysses S. Grant

*Escort: B, F, K, 5th U.S. Cav.*, Capt Julius W. Mason

## *Army of the Potomac*

Maj. Gen. George G. Meade
*Provost Guard,* **Brig. Gen. Marsena R. Patrick:**
*C and D, 1st Mass. Cav.,* Captain Edward A. Flint
*80th N.Y. Inf. (20th Militia),* Col. Theodore B. Gates

*3rd Pa. Cav.,* Maj. James W. Walsh
*68th Pa. Inf.,* Lt. Col. Robert E. Winslow
*114th Pa. Inf.,* Col Charles H.T. Collis

## *II Army Corps,* Maj. Gen. Winfield Scott Hancock

*Escort: M, 1st Vt. Cav.,* Capt Daniel P. Mann

**1st Division, Brig. Gen. Francis C. Barlow**
*1st Brigade,* Col. Nelson A. **Miles**
*26th Mich.,* Maj. Lemuel Saviers
*61st N.Y.,* Lt. Col. K. O. Broady
*81st Pa.,* Col. H. Boyd McKeen
*140th Pa.,* Col John Fraser
*183rd Pa.,* Col. George P. McLean

*2nd Brigade,* **Colonel Thomas A. Smyth**
*28th Mass.,* Lt. Col. George W. Cartwright
*63rd N.Y.,* Maj. Thomas Touhy
*69th N.Y.,* Capt. Richard Moroney
*88th N.Y.,* Capt Denis F. Burke
*116th Pa.,* Lt. Col. Richard C. Dale
*3rd Brigade,* **Col. Paul Frank**
*39th N.Y.,* Col. Augustus Funk
*52nd N.Y.* (detachment of *7th New York* attached), Maj. Henry M. Karples
*57th N.Y.,* Lt. Col. Alford B. Chapman

*111th N.Y.*, Capt. Aaron P. Seeley
*125th N.Y.*, Lt. Col. Alford B. Chapman
*126th N.Y.*, Capt. Winfield Scott

**4th Brigade, Col. John R. Brooke**
*2nd Del.*, Col. William P. Bailey
*64th N.Y.*, Maj. Leman W. Bradley
*66th N.Y.*, Lt. Col. John S. Hammell
*53rd Pa.*, Lt. Col. Richards McMichael
*145th Pa.*, Col. Hiram L. Brown
*148th Pa.*, Col. James A. Beaver

## 2nd Division, Brig. Gen. John Gibbon
**1st Brigade, Brig. Gen. Alexander S. Webb**
*19th Me.*, Col. Selden Connor
*1st Co. Andrew (Mass.) Sharpshooters*, Lt. Samuel G. Gilbreth
*15th Mass.*, Maj. I. Harris Hooper
*19th Mass.*, Maj. Edmund Rice
*20th Mass.*, Maj. Henry L. Abbott
*7th Mich.*, Maj. Sylvanus W. Curtis
*42nd N.Y.*, Maj. Patrick J. Downing
*59th N.Y.*, Capt. William McFadden
*82nd N.Y. (2nd Militia)*, Col. Henry W. Hudson

**2nd Brigade, Brig. Gen. Joshua T. Owen**
*152nd N.Y.*, Lt. Col. George W. Thompson
*69th Pa.*, Maj. William Davis
*71st Pa.*, Lt. Col. Charles Kochersperger
*72nd Pa.*, Col. De Witt C. Baxter
*106th Pa.*, Capt. Robert H. Ford

**3rd Brigade, Col. Samuel S. Carroll**
*14th Conn.*, Col Theodore G. Ellis
*1st Del.*, Lt. Col. Daniel Woodall
*14th Ind.*, Col. John Coons

*12th N.J.*, Lt. Col. Thomas H. Davis
*10th N.Y. (Battalion)*, Capt. George Dewey
*108th N.Y.*, Col. Charles J. Powers
*4th Ohio*, Lt Col. Leonard W. Carpenter
*8th Ohio*, Lt. Col. Franklin Sawyer
*7th W.Va.*, Lt. Col. J.H. Lockwood

## 3rd Division, Brig. Gen. David B. Birney
**1st Brigade, Brig. Gen. J.H.H. Ward**
*20th Ind.*, Col W.C.L. Taylor
*3rd Me.*, Col. Moses B. Lakeman
*40th N.Y.*, Col Thomas W. Egan
*86th N.Y.*, Lt. Col Jacob H. Lansing
*124th N.Y.*, Col. Francis M. Cummins
*99th Pa.*, Lt. Col. Edwin R. Biles
*110th Pa.*, Lt. Col. Isaac Rogers
*141st Pa.*, Lt. Col. Guy H. Watkins
*2nd U.S. Sharpshooters*, Lt. Col. Homer R. Stoughton

**2nd Brigade, Brig. Gen. Alexander Hays (k), Col. John S. Crocker**
*4th Me.*, Col. Elijah Walker
*17th Me.*, Col. George W. West
*3rd Mich.*, Col. Byron R. Pierce
*5th Mich.*, Lt. Col. John Pulford
*93rd N.Y.*, Maj. Samuel McConihe
*57th Pa.*, Col. Peter Sides
*63rd Pa.*, Lt. Col. John A. Danks
*105th Pa.*, Col. Calvin A. Craig
*1st U.S. Sharpshooters*, Maj. Charles P. Mattocks

## 4th Division, Brig. Gen. Gershom Mott
**1st Brigade, Col. Robert McAllister**
*1st Mass.*, Col N.B. McLaughlen
*16th Mass.*, Lt. Col. Waldo Merriam

5th N.J., Col. William J. Sewell
6th N.J., Lt. Col. Stephen R. Gikyson
7th N.J., Maj. Frederick Cooper
8th N.J., Col. John Ramsey
11th N.J., Lt. Col. John Schoonover
26th Pa., Maj. Samuel G. Moffett
115th Pa., Maj. William A. Reilly

**2nd Brigade, Col. William R. Brewster**
11th Mass., Col. William Blaisdell
70th N.Y., Capt. William H. Hugo
71st N.Y., Lt. Col. Thomas Rafferty
72nd N.Y., Lt. Col. John Leonard
73rd N.Y., Lt. Col. Michael W. Burns
74th N.Y., Lt. Col. Thomas Holt
120th N.Y., Capt. Abram L. Lockwood
84th Pa., Lt. Col. Milton Opp

**Artillery Brigade, Col. John C. Tidball**
6th Me., Capt. Edwin B. Dow
10th Mass., Capt. J. Henry Sleeper
1st N.H., Capt. Frederick M. Edgell
1st N.Y., Bat. G, Capt. Nelson Ames
4th N.Y. Heavy (Third Battalion), Lt. Col. Thomas R. Allcock
1st Pa., Bat. F, Capt. R. Bruce Ricketts
1st R.I., Bat. A, Capt William A. Arnold
1st R.I., Bat. B, Capt. T. Fred Brown
4th U.S., Bat. K, Lt. John W. Roder
5th U.S., Bat. C and I, Lt. James Gilliss

# V Army Corps, Maj. Gen. Gouverneur K. Warren

Provost Guard, 12th N.Y. Battalion, Maj. Henry W. Rider

## 1st Division, Brig. Gen. Charles Griffin

### 1st Brigade, Brig Gen. Roman C. Ayres
140th N.Y., Col. George Ryan
146th N.Y., Col. David T. Jenkins
91st Pa., Lt. Col. Joseph H. Sinex
155th Pa., Lt. Col. Alfred L. Pearson
2nd U.S., Cos. B, C, F, H, I, K, Capt. James W. Long
11th U.S., Cos. B, C, D, E, F, G, 1st Battalion, Capt. Francis M. Cooley
14th U.S., 1st Battalion, Cos. A, B, C, D, G, Capt. E McK. Hudson
17th U.S. 1st Battalion, Cos. A, C, D, G, H and 2nd Battalion Cos. A, B, C, Capt. James F. Grimes

### 2nd Brigade, Col Jacob B. Sweitzer
9th Mass., Col. Patrick R. Guiney
22nd Mass. (2nd Co. Mass. Sharpshooters Attached), Col. William S. Tilton
32nd Mass., Col. George L. Prescott
4th Mich., Lt. Col. George W. Lumbard
62nd Pa., Lt. Col. James C. Hull

### 3rd Brigade, Brig. Gen. Joseph J. Bartlett
20th Me., Maj. Ellis Spear
18th Mass., Col. Joseph Hayes
1st Mich., Lt. Col. William A. Throop
16th Mich., Maj. Robert T. Elliott
44th N.Y., Lt. Col. Freeman Conner
83rd Pa., Col. O.S. Woodward
118th Pa., Col. James Gwyn

## 2nd Division, Brig. Gen. John C. Robinson

**1st Brigade, Col. Samuel H. Leonard, Col. Peter Lyle**
*16th Me.*, Col. Charles W. Tilden
*13th Mass.*, Capt. Charles H. Hovey
*39th Mass.*, Col. Phineas S. Davis
*104th N.Y.*, Col. Gilbert G. Prey

**2nd Brigade, Brig. Gen. Henry Baxter (w), Col. Richard Coulter**
*12th Mass.*, James L. Bates
*83rd N.Y. (9th Militia)*, Col. Joseph A. Moesch
*97th N.Y.*, Col. Charles Wheelock
*11th Pa.*, Col. Richard Coulter
*88th Pa.*, Capt. George B. Rhoads
*90th Pa.*, Col. Peter Lyle

**3rd Brigade, Col. Andrew W. Denison**
*1st Md.*, Maj. Benjamin H. Schley
*4th Md.*, Col. Richard N. Bowman
*7th Md.*, Col. Charles E. Phelps
*8th Md.*, Lt. Col. John G. Johannes

## 3rd Division (Pennsylvania Reserves), Brig. Gen. Samuel W. Crawford

**1st Brigade, Col. William McCandless**
*1st Pa.*, William C. Talley
*2nd Pa.*, Lt. Col. Patrick McDonough
*6th Pa.*, Col. Wellington H. Ent
*7th Pa.*, Maj. LeGrand B. Speece
*11th Pa.*, Col. Samuel M. Jackson
*13th Pa. (1st Rifles)*, Maj. W.R. Hartshorn

**3rd Brigade, Col Joseph W. Fisher**
*5th Pa.*, Lt. Col. George Dare
*8th Pa.*, Col., Silas M. Baily
*10th Pa.*, Lt. Col., Ira Ayer, Jr.
*12th Pa.*, Lt. Col. Richard Gustin

## 4th Division, Brig. Gen. James S. Wadsworth (mw), Col. Richard Coulter

**1st Brigade, Brig. Gen. Lysander Cutler**
*7th Ind.*, Col. Ira G. Grover
*19th Ind.*, Col. Samuel J. Williams
*24th Mich.*, Col. Henry A. Morrow
*1st N.Y. Battalion Sharpshooters*, Capt. Volney J. Shipman
*2nd Wis.*, Lt. Col. John Mansfield
*6th Wis.*, Col. Edward S. Bragg
*7th Wis.*, Col. William W. Robinson

**2nd Brigade, Brig. Gen. James C. Rice**
*76th N.Y.*, Lt. Col. John E. Cook
*84th N.Y. (14th Milita)*, Col. Edward B. Fowler
*95th N.Y.*, Col. Edward Pye
*147th N.Y.*, Col. Francis C. Miller
*56th Pa.*, Col. J. Wm. Hoffmann

**3rd Brigade, Col. Roy Stone (w), Col. Edward S. Bragg**
*121st Pa.*, Capt. Samuel T. Lloyd
*142nd Pa.*, Maj. Horatio N. Warren
*143rd Pa.*, Col. Edmund L. Dana
*149th Pa.*, Lt. Col. John Irvin
*150th Pa.*, Capt. George W. Jones

## Artillery Brigade, Col. Charles S. Wainwright

*3rd Mass*, Capt. Augustus P. Martin
*5th Mass*, Capt. Charles A. Phillips
*1st N.Y., Bat. D*, Capt. George B. Winslow
*1st N.Y., Bat. E and L*, Lt. George Breck
*1st N.Y., Bat. H*, Capt. Charles E. Mink
*4th N.Y. Heavy, 2nd Battalion*, Maj. William Arthur

1st Pa., Bat. B, Capt James H. Cooper

4th U.S., Bat. B, Lt. James Stewart

5th U.S., Bat. D, Lt. B.F. Rittenhouse

# VI Army Corps, Maj. Gen. John Sedgwick

Escort, 8th Pa. Cav., Bat. A, Capt. Charles E. Fellows

## 1st Division, Brig. Gen. Horatio G. Wright

### 1st Brigade, Col. Henry W. Brown
1st N.J., Lt. Col. William Henry, Jr.
2nd N.J., Lt. Col. Charles Wiebecke
3rd N.J., Capt. Samuel T. Du Bois
4th N.J., Lt. Col. Charles Ewing
101st N.J., Col. Henry O. Ryerson
15th N.J., Col. William H. Penrose

### 2nd Brigade, Col. Emory Upton
5th Me., Col Clark S. Edwards
121st N.Y., Col. Egbert Olcott
95th Pa., Lt. Col. Edward Carroll
96th Pa., Lt. Col. William H. Lessig

### 3rd Brigade, Brig. Gen. David A. Russell
6th Me., Maj. George Fuller
49th Pa., Col. Thomas M. Hulings
119th Pa., Maj. Henry P. Truefitt, Jr.
5th Wis., Lt. Col. Theodore B. Catlin

### 4th Brigade, Brig. Gen. Alexander Shaler (c), Col. Nelson Cross
65th N.Y., Col. Joseph E. Hamblin
67th N.Y., Col. Nelson Cross
122nd N.Y., Lt. Col. Augustus W. Dwight
82nd Pa. (detachment)

## 2nd Division, Brig. Gen. George W. Getty (w), Brig. Gen. Frank Wheaton, Brig. Gen. Thomas Neill

### 1st Brigade, Brig Gen. Frank Wheaton
62nd N.Y., Col. David J. Nevin
93rd Pa., Lt. Col. John S. Long
98th Pa., Col. John F. Ballier
102nd Pa., Col. John W. Patterson
139th Pa., Col. William H. Moody

### 2nd Brigade, Col. Lewis A. Grant
2nd Vt., Col. Newton Stone
3rd Vt., Col. Thomas O. Seaver
4th Vt., Col. George P. Foster
5th Vt., Lt. Col. John R. Lewis
6th Vt., Col. Elisha L. Barney

### 3rd Brigade, Brig. Gen. Thomas H. Neill, Col. Daniel D. Bidwell
7th Me., Col. Edwin C. Mason
43rd N.Y., Lt. Col. John Wilson
49th N.Y., Col. Daniel D. Bidwell
77th N.Y., Maj. Nathan S. Babcock
61st Pa., Col. George F. Smith

### 4th Brigade, Brig. Gen. Henry L. Eustis
7th Mass., Col. Thomas D. Johns
10th Mass., Lt. Col. Joseph B. Parsons
37th Mass., Col. Oliver Edwards
2nd R.I., Lt. Col. S.B.M. Read

**3rd Division, Brig. Gen. James B. Ricketts**

*1st Brigade,* Brig. Gen. William H. Morris
14th N.J., Lt. Col. Caldwell K. Hall
106th N.Y., Lt. Col. Charles Townsend
151st N.Y., Lt. Col. Thomas M. Fay
87th Pa., Col. John W. Schall
10th Vt., Lt. Col. William W. Henry

*2nd Brigade,* Brig. Gen. Truman Seymour (c), Col. Benjamin F. Smith
6th Md., Col. John W. Horn
110th Ohio, Col. J. Warren Keifer
122nd Ohio, Col. William H. Ball
126th Ohio, Benjamin F. Smith
67th Pa. (detachment), Capt. George W. Guss

138th Pa., Col. Matthew R. McClennan

*Artillery Brigade,* **Col. Charles H. Tompkins**
4th Me., Lt. Melville C. Kimball
1st Mass., Capt. William H. McCartney
1st N.Y., Capt. Andrew Cowan
3rd N.Y., Captain William A. Harn
4th N.Y. Heavy (First Battalion), Maj. Thomas W. Sears
1st R.I., Bat. C, Capt. Richard Waterman
1st R.I., Bat. E, Capt. William B. Rhodes
1st R.I., Bat. G, Capt. George W. Adams
5th U.S., Bat. M, Capt. James McKnight

## IX *Army Corps,* Maj. Gen. Ambrose Burnside

*Provost Guard: 8th U.S.,* Capt. Milton Cogswell

**1st Division, Brig. Gen. Thomas G. Stephenson**

*1st Brigade,* **Col. Sumner Carruth**
35th Mass., Maj. Nathaniel Wales
56th Mass., Col. Charles E. Griswold
57th Mass., Col. William F. Bartlett
59th Mass., Col. J. Parker Gould
4th U.S., Capt. Charles H. Brightly
10th U.S. Maj. Samuel B. Hayman

*2nd Brigade,* **Col. Daniel Leasure**
3rd Md., Col. Joseph Sudsburg
21st Mass., Lt. Col. George P. Hawkes
100th Pa., Lt. Col. Matthew M. Dawson

*Artillery:*
2nd Me., Capt. Albert F. Thomas

14th Mass., Capt. J.W.B. Wright

**2nd Division, Brig. Gen. Robert B. Potter**

*First Brigade,* **Col. Zenas R. Bliss**
36th Mass., Maj. William F. Draper
58th Mass., Lt. Col. John C. Whiton
51st N.Y., Col. Charles W. Le Gendre
45th Pa., Col John I. Curtin
48th Pa., Lt. Col. Henry Pleasants
7th R.I., Capt. Theodore Winn

*2nd Brigade,* **Col. Simon G. Griffin**
31st Me., Lt. Col. Thomas Hight
32nd Me., Maj. Arthur Deering
6th N.H., Lt. Col. Henry H. Pearson
9th N.H., Lt. Col. John W. Babbitt
11th N.H., Col. Walter Harriman

*17th Vt.*, Lt. Col. Charles Cummings

*Artillery:*
*11th Mass.*, Capt Edward J. Jones
*19th N.Y.*, Capt. Edward W. Rogers

## 3rd Division, Brig. Gen. Orlando B. Willcox
### 1st Brigade, Col. John F. Hartranft
*2nd Mich.*, Col. William Humphreys
*8th Mich.*, Col. Frank Graves
*17th Mich.*, Col. Constant Luce
*27th Mich. (1st and 2nd Cos. Mich. Sharpshooters* attached), Maj. Samuel Moody
*109th N.Y.*, Col. Benjamin F. Tracy
*51st Pa.*, Lt. Col. Edwin Schall

### 2nd Brigade, Col. Benjamin C. Christ
*1st Mich. Sharpshooters*, Col. Charles V. De Land
*20th Mich.*, Lt. Col. Byron M. Cutcheon
*79th N.Y.*, Col. David Morrison
*60th Ohio (9th and 10th Cos. Ohio Sharpshooters* attached), Lt. Col. James N. McElroy
*50th Pa.*, Lt. Col. Edward Overton, Jr.

*Artillery:*
*7th Me.*, Capt. Adelbert B. Twitchell
*34th N.Y.*, Capt. Jacob Roemer

## 4th Division, Brig. Gen. Edward Ferrero
### 1st Brigade, Col. Joshua K. Sigfried
*27th U.S.C.T*, Lt. Col. Charles J. Wright
*30th U.S.C.T.*, Col. Delavan Bates

*39th U.S.C.T.*, Col. Ozora P. Stearns
*43rd U.S.C.T.*, Lt. Col. H. Seymour Hall

### 2nd Brigade, Col. Henry G. Thomas
*30th Conn.* (detachment), Capt. Charles Robinson
*19th U.S.C.T.*, Lt. Col. Joseph G. Perkins
*23rd U.S.C.T.*, Lt. Col. Cleaveland J. Campbell

*Artillery:*
*Pa Bat.*, George W. Durell
*3rd Vt.*, Capt Romeo H. Start

*Cavalry:*
*3rd N.J.*, Col Andrew J. Morrison
*22nd N.Y.*, Col. Samuel J. Crooks
*2nd Ohio*, Lt. Col. George A. Purington
*13th Pa.*, Maj. Michael Kerwin

## Reserve Artillery, Capt. John Edwards
*27 N.Y.*, Capt. John B. Eaton
*1st R.I., Bat. D*, Capt. William W. Buckley
*1st R.I., Bat. H*, Captain Crawford Allen, Jr.
*2nd U.S., Bat. E*, 2nd U.S., Lt. James S. Dudley
*3rd U.S., Bat. G*, Lt. Edmund Pendleton
*3rd U.S., Bat. L and M*, Lt. Erskine Gittings

## Provisional Brigade, Col. Elisha G. Marshall
*24th N.Y. Cav.* (dismounted), Col. William C. Raulston
*14th N.Y., Heavy Artillery*, Lt. Col. Clarence H. Corning
*2nd Pa., Provisional Heavy Artillery*, Col. Thomas Wilhelm

# Cavalry Corps, Maj. Gen. Philip H. Sheridan

*Escort*: 6th U.S., Capt. Ira W. Claflin

## 1st Division, Brig. Gen. A.T.A. Torbert

**1st Brigade, Brig. Gen., George A. Custer**
1st Mich., Lt. Col. Peter Stagg
5th Mich., Col. Russell A. Alger
6th Mich., Maj. James H. Kidd
7th Mich., Maj. Henry W. Granger

**2nd Brigade, Col. Thomas C. Devin**
4th N.Y., Lt. Col. William R. Parnell
6th N.Y., Lt. Col. William H. Crocker
9th N.Y., Col. William Sackett
17th Pa., Lt. Col. James Q. Anderson

**Reserve Brigade, Brig. Gen. Wesley Merritt**
19th N.Y. (1st Dragoons), Col. Alfred Gibbs
6th Pa., Maj. James Starr
1st U.S., Capt., Nelson B. Sweitzer
2nd U.S., Capt. T.F. Rodenbough
5th U.S., Capt. Abraham K. Arnold

## 2nd Division, Brig. Gen. David McM. Gregg

**1st Brigade, Brig. Gen. Henry E. Davies, Jr.**
1st Mass., Maj. Lucius M. Sargent

1st N.J., Lt. Col. John W. Kester
6th Ohio, Col. William Stedman
1st Pa., Col. John P. Taylor

**2nd Brigade, Col. J. Irvin Gregg**
1st Me., Col. Charles H. Smith
10th N.Y., Maj. M. Henry Avery
2nd Pa., Lt. Col. Joseph P. Brinton
4th Pa., Lt. Col. George H. Covode
8th Pa., Lt. Col. Samuel Wilson
16th Pa., Lt. Col. John K. Robinson

## 3rd Division, Brig. Gen. James H. Wilson

*Escort*, 8th Ill. (detachment), Lt. William W. Long

**1st Brigade, Col. Timothy M. Bryan, Jr., Col. John B. McIntosh**
1st Conn., Maj. Erastus Blakeslee
2nd N.Y., Col. Otto Harhaus
5th N.Y., Lt. Col. John Hammond
18th Pa., Lt. Col. William P. Brinton

**2nd Brigade, Col. George H. Chapman**
3rd Indiana, Maj. William Patton
8th N.Y., Lt. Col. William H. Benjamin
1st Vt., Lt. Col. Addison W. Preston

# Artillery, Brig. Gen. Henry J. Hunt

**Artillery Reserve, Col. Henry S. Burton**

**1st Brigade, Col. J. Howard Kitching**
6th N.Y. Heavy, Lt. Col. Edmund R. Travis
15th N.Y. Heavy, Col. Louis Schirmer

**2nd Brigade, Maj. John A. Tompkins**
5th Me., Capt. Greenleaf T. Stevens
1st N.J., Capt. William Hexamer
2nd N.J., Capt., A. Judson Clark
5th N.Y., Capt. Elijah D. Taft

*12th N.Y.*, Capt. George F. McKnight

*1st N.Y., Bat. B,* Capt. Albert S. Sheldon

### 3rd *Brigade,* Maj. Robert H. Fitzhugh

*9th Mass.,* Capt. John Bigelow

*15th N.Y.,* Capt Patrick Hart

*1st N.Y., Bat. C,* Lt. William H. Phillips

*11th N.Y.,* Capt. John E. Burton

*1st Ohio, Bat. H,* Lt. William A. Ewing

*5th U.S., Bat. E,* Lt. John R. Brinckle

## *Horse Artillery*

### 1st *Brigade,* Capt James M. Robertson

*6th N.Y.,* Capt. Joseph W. Martin

*2nd U.S., Bats. B* and *L,* Lt. Edward Heaton

*2nd U.S., Bat. D,* Edward B. Williston

*2nd U.S., Bat. M,* Lt. A.C.M. Pennington

*4th U.S., Bat. A,* Lt. Rufus King, Jr.

*4th U.S., Bats. C* and *E,* Lt. Charles Fitzhugh

### 2nd *Brigade,* Capt. Dunbar R. Ransom

*1st U.S., Bats. E* and *G, 1st U.S.,* Lt. Frank S. French

*Bats. H* and *I,* Capt. Alanson M. Randol

*1st U.S., Bat. K,* Lt. John Egan

*2nd U.S., Bat. A,* Lt. Robert Clark

*2nd U.S., Bat. G,* Lt. William N. Dennison

*3rd U.S., Bats. C, F, K,* Lt. James R. Kelly

# Army of Northern Virginia

General Robert E. Lee,
commanding

## First Army Corps, Lt. Gen. James Longstreet

### Kershaw's Division, Brig. Gen. Joseph B. Kershaw

**Kershaw's Brigade, Col. John W. Henagan**
2nd S.C., Lt. Col. F. Gaillard
3rd S.C., Col. James D. Nance
7th S.C., Capt. James Mitchell
8th S.C., Lt. Col. E.T. Stackhouse
15th S.C., John B. Davis
3rd S.C. Battalion, Capt., B.M. Whitener

**Humphreys' Brigade, Brig. Gen. Benjamin Humphreys**
13th Miss, Maj. G.L. Donald
17th Miss.
18th Miss., Capt. W.H. Lewis
21st Miss., Col. D.N. Moody

**Wofford's Brigade, Brig. Gen. William T. Wofford**
16th Ga.
18th Ga.
24th, Ga.
Cobb's Ga. Legion
Phillips Ga. Legion
3rd Ga. Battalion of Sharpshooters

**Bryan's Brigade, Brig. Gen. Goode Bryan**
10th Ga., Col. Willis C. Holt
50th Ga., Col. P. McGlashan
51st Ga., Col. E. Ball
53rd Ga., Col. James P. Simms

### Field's Division, Maj. Gen. Charles Field

**Jenkins' Brigade, Brig. Gen. Micah Jenkins**
1st S.C., Col. James R. Hagood
2nd S.C. (Rifles), Col. R.E. Bowen
5th S.C., Col. A. Coward
6th S.C., Col. John Bratton
Palmetto (S.C.) Sharpshooters, Col. Joseph Walker

**Anderson's Brigade, Brig. Gen. George T. Anderson**
7th Ga.
8th Ga.
9th Ga.
11th Ga.
59th Ga., Lt. Col. B.H. Gee

**Law's Brigade, Brig. Gen., E. McIver Law**
4th Ala., Col. P.D. Bowles
15th Ala.
44th Ala., Col. W.F. Perry
47th Ala.
48th Ala, Lt. Col. W.M. Hardwick

**Gregg's Brigade, Brig. Gen. John Gregg**
3rd Ark., Col. Van H. Manning
1st Tex.
4th Tex., Col. J.P. Bane
5th Tex., Lt. Col. K. Bryan

**Benning's Brigade, Brig. Gen. Henry L. Benning**
2nd Ga.,15th Ga., Col. D.M. DuBose
17th Ga.
20th Ga.

### Artillery, Brig. Gen. E. Porter Alexander

Huger's Battalion, Lt. Col. Frank Huger
Fickling's (Va.) Bat.
Moody's (La.) Bat.
Parker's (Va.) Bat.
J.D. Smith's (Va.) Bat.
Taylor's (Va.) Bat.

Woolfolk's (Va.) Bat.
Haskell's Bat., Maj. John C.
Haskell
Flanner's (N.C.) Bat.
Garden's (S.C.) Bat.
Lamkin's (Va.) Bat.
Ramsay's (N.C.) Bat.

Cabell's Battalion, Col. Henry C.
Cabell
Callaway's (Ga.) Bat.
Carlton's (Ga.) Bat.
McCarthy's (VA.) Bat.
Manly's (N.C.) Bat.

# Second Army Corps, Lt. Gen. Richard S. Ewell

## Early's Division, Maj. Gen. Jubal Early

### Hay's Brigade, Brig. Gen. Harry T. Hays
5th La., Lt. Col. Bruce Menger
6th La., Maj. William H. Manning
7th. La., Maj. J.M. Wilson
8th. La.
9th La.

### Pegram's Brigade, Brig. Gen. John Pegram
13th Va., Col. James B. Terrill
31st Va., Col. John S. Hoffman
49th Va., Col. J.C. Gibson
52nd Va.
58th Va.

### Gordon's Brigade, Brig. Gen. John B. Gordon
13th Ga.
26th Ga., Col. E.N. Atkinson
31st Ga., Col. C.A. Evans
38th Ga.
60th Ga., Lt. Col. Thomas J. Berry
61st Ga.

## Johnson's Division, Maj. Gen. Edward Johnson

### Stonewall Brigade, Brig. Gen James A. Walker
2nd Va., Capt. C.H. Stewart
4th Va., Col. William Terry
5th Va.
27th Va., Lt. Col. Charles L. Haynes
33rd Va.

### Steuart's Brigade, Brig. Gen. George H. Steuart
1st N.C., Col. H.A. Brown
3rd N.C., Col. S.D. Thruston
10th Va.
23rd Va.
37th Va.

### Jones' Brigade, Brig. Gen. John M. Jones
21st Va.
25th Va., Col J.C. Higginbotham
42nd Va
44th Va.
48th Va.
50th Va.

### Stafford's Brigade, Brig. Gen. Leroy A. Stafford
1st La.
2nd La., Col J.M. Williams
10th La.
14th La.
15th La.

## Rodes' Division, Maj. Gen. Robert E. Rodes

### Daniel's Brigade, Brig. Gen. Junius Daniel
32nd N.C.
43rd N.C.
45th N.C.
53rd N.C.
2nd S.C. Bat.

### Ramseur's Brigade, Brig. Gen. Stephen D. Ramseur
2nd N.C., Col. W.R. Cox
4th N.C., Col Bryan Grimes
14th N.C., Co. R.T. Bennett

233

30th N.C., Col. F.M. Parker

**Doles' Brigade, Brig. Gen.**
**George Doles**
4th Ga.
12th Ga., Col. Edward Willis
44th Ga., Col. W.H. Peebles

**Battle's Brigade, Brig. Gen.**
**Cullen A. Battle**
3rd Ala., Col. Charles Forsyth
5th Ala.
6th Ala.
12th Ala.
26th Ala.
26th Ala.

**Johnston's Brigade, Brig. Gen.**
**Robert D. Johnston**
5th N.C., Col. T.M. Garrett
12th N.C., Col. H.E. Collman
20th N.C., Col. Thomas F. Toon
23rd N.C.

**Artillery, Brig. Gen.**
**Armistead L. Long**
**Hardaway's Battalion, Lt. Col.**
**R.A. Hardaway**
Dance's (Va.) Bat.
Graham's (Va. Bat.
C.B. Griffin's (Va.) Bat.
Jones' (Va.) Bat.
B.H. Smith's Bat.

**Nelson's Battalion, Maj. W.E.**
**Cutshaw**
Carrington's (Va.) Bat.
A.W. Garber's (Va.) Bat.
Tanner's (Va.) Bat.

**Page's Battalion, Maj. R.C.M.**
**Page**
W.P. Carter's (Va.) Bat.
Fry's (Va.) Bat.
Page's (Va.) Bat.
Reese's (Ala.) Bat.

# Third Army Corps, Lt. Gen. Ambrose P. Hill

**Anderson's Division, Maj.**
**Gen. Richard H.**
**Anderson**
**Perrin's Brigade, Brig. Gen.**
**Abner Perrin**
8th Ala.
9th Ala.
10th Ala.
11th Ala.
14th Ala.

**Mahone's Brigade, Brig. Gen.**
**William Mahone**
6th Va., Lt. Col. H.W. Williamson
12th Va., Col. D.A. Weisiger
16th Va., Lt. Col. R.O. Whitehead
41st Va.
61st Va., Col V.D. Groner

**Harris' Brigade, Brig. Gen.**
**Nathaniel H. Harris**
12 Miss.
16th Miss., Col S.E. Baker
19th Miss., Col. T.J. Hardin
48th Miss.

**Wright's Brigade, Brig. Gen.**
**Ambrose R. Wright**
3rd Ga.
22nd Ga.
48th Ga.
2nd Ga. Battalion, Maj. C.J. Moffet

**Perry's Brigade, Brig. Gen.**
**E.A. Perry**
2nd Fla.
5th Fla.
8th Fla.

**Heth's Division, Maj. Henry**
**Heth**
**Davis' Brigade, Brig. Gen.**
**Joseph R. Davis**
2nd Miss.
11th Miss.
42nd Miss.
55th N.C.

**Cooke's Brigade, Brig. Gen.**
**John R. Cooke**
15th N.C.

27th N.C.
46th N.C.
48th N.C.

### Kirkland's Brigade, Brigadier General William W. Kirkland

11th N.C.
26th N.C.
44th N.C.
47th N.C.
52nd N.C.

### Walker's Brigade, Brig. Gen. Henry H. Walker

40th Va.
47th Va., Col R.M. Mayo
55th Va., Col W.S. Christian
22nd Va. Bn.

### Archer's Brigade, Brig. Gen. James J. Archer

13th Ala.
1st Tenn. (Prov. Army), Maj. F.G. Buchanan
7th Tenn., Lt. Col. S.G. Shepard
14th Tenn.,Col. William McComb

## Wilcox's Division, Maj. Gen. Cadmus M. Wilcox

### Lane's Brigade, Brig. Gen. James H. Lane

7th N.C., Lt. Col. W. Lee Davidson
18th N.C., Col. John D. Barry
28th N.C.
33rd N.C., Lt. Col., R.V. Cowan
37th N.C., Col. J.H. Hyman
16th N.C., Col. W.A. Stowe
22nd N.C.
34th N.C., Col W.L. Lowrance
38th N.C., Lt. Col. John Ashford

### McGowan's Brigade, Brig. Gen. Samuel McGowan

1st S.C. (Prov. Army), Lt. Col. W.P. Shooter

12th S.C. Col. John L. Miller
13th S.C., Col. B.T. Brockman
14th S.C., Col. Joseph N. Brown
1st S.C. (Orr's) Rifles, Lt. Col. G. McDonald Miller

### Thomas' Brigade, Brig. Gen., Edward L. Thomas

14th Ga.
35th Ga.
45th Ga.
49th Ga., Lt. Col. J.T. Jordan

## Artillery, Col. R. Lindsay Walker

### Poague's Battalion, Lt. Col. William T. Poague

Richards' (Miss) Bat.
Utterback's (Va.) Bat.
Williams' (N.C.) Bat.
Wyatt's (Va.) Bat.

### McIntosh's Battalion, Lt. Col. D.G. McIntosh

Clutter's (Va.) Bat.
Donald's (Va.) Bat.
Hurt's (Ala.) Bat.

### Pegram's Battalion, Lt. Col. W.J. Pegram

Brander's (Va.) Bat.
Cayce's (Va.) Bat.
Ellet's (Va.) Bat.
Marye's (Va.) Bat.
Zimmerman's (S.C.) Bat.

### Cutt's Battalion, Col. A.S. Cutts

Patterson's (Ga.) Bat.
Ross' (Ga.) Bat.
Wingfield's (Ga.) Bat.

### Richardson's Battalion, Lt. Col. Charles Richardson

Grandy's (Va.) Bat.
Landry's (La.) Bat.
Penick's (Va.) Bat.

# Cavalry Corps, Maj. Gen. James E.B. Stuart

**Hampton's Division, Maj. Gen. Wade Hampton**

**Young's Brigade, Brig. Gen. P.M.B. Young**
7th Ga., Col. W.P. White
Cobb's (Ga.) Legion, Col. G.J. Wright
Phillips (Ga.) Legion
20th Ga. Battalion, Lt. Col. John M. Millen
Jeff Davis (Miss) Legion

**Rosser's Brigade, Brig. Gen. Thomas L. Rosser**
7th Va., Col. R.H. Dulany
11th Va.
12th Va., Lt. Col. Thomas B. Massie
35th Va. Battalion

**Butler's Brigade, Brig. Gen. M.C. Butler**
4th S.C. Col. B.H. Rutledge
5th S.C., Col. John Dunovant
6th S.C. Col. Hugh K. Aiken

**Fitz Lee's Division, Maj. Gen. Fitzhugh Lee**

**Lomax's Brigade, Brig. Gen. Lunsford L. Lomax**
5th Va., Col. Henry C. Pate
6th Va.

15th Va.

**Wickham's Brigade, Brig Gen. Williams C. Wickham**
1st Va.
2nd Va., Col Thomas T. Munford
3rd Va., Col. Thomas H. Owen
4th Va.

**W.H.F. Lee's Division, Maj. Gen. W.H.F. Lee**

**Chambliss' Brigade, Brig. Gen. John R. Chambliss, Jr.**
9th Va.
10th Va.
13th Va.

**Gordon's Brigade, Brig. Gen James B. Gordon**
1st N.C.
2nd N.C., Col. C.M. Andrews
5th N.C., Col. S.B. Evans

**Horse Artillery, Maj. R.P. Chew**
Breathed's Battalion, Maj. James Breathed
Hart's (S.C.) Bat.
Johnston's (Va.) Bat.
McGregor's (Va.) Bat.
Shoemaker's (Va.) Bat.
Thompson's (Va.) Bat.

Confederate records for the Wilderness campaing are incomplete. It is therefore impossible to assess the casualty figures for the Army of Northern Virginia during the campaign with any precision.

# Index